CONFEDERATE MILITARY HISTORY

Volume

VIII

CONFEDERATE MILITARY HISTORY

A LIBRARY OF CONFEDERATE STATES HISTORY, IN THIRTEEN VOLUMES, WRITTEN BY DISTINGUISHED MEN OF THE SOUTH, AND EDITED BY GEN. CLEMENT A. EVANS OF GEORGIA....

VOL. VIII.

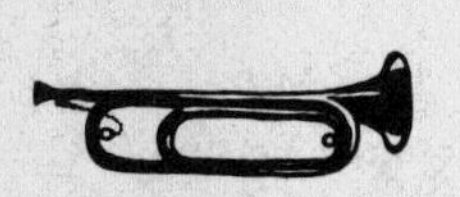

The
Blue & Grey
Press

Printed in the United States of America

TABLE OF CONTENTS.

PAGE.

CONTENTS.

LIST OF ILLUSTRATIONS.

TENNESSEE

BY

JAMES D. PORTER.

JAMES D. PORTER

CHAPTER I.

FORMAL SECESSION FROM THE UNITED STATES—UNION WITH THE CONFEDERATE STATES—PREPARATION FOR WAR—ORGANIZATION OF TROOPS—GENERAL POLK IN COMMAND—OCCUPATION OF COLUMBUS—BATTLE OF BELMONT.

IN June, 1796, the Congress of the United States passed an act, approved by President George Washington, providing that, "The State of Tennessee is hereby declared to be one of the sixteen United States of America." The framers of the constitution under which admission to the Federal Union was secured, were such men as Andrew Jackson, James Robertson, William Blount, Archibald Roane, John Tipton and their associate delegates, men who were conspicuous for their love of liberty and who had attested their devotion to it at King Mountain. John Sevier, one of the heroes of that famous battle, was the first governor of the new State.

Under the political leadership of these men and their successors, the love of religious and political freedom, and patriotic devotion to the State and to the Federal Union, characterized the people of Tennessee, without regard to party alliance. This devotion found practical illustration in the war of 1812, in the Indian wars, and in the war with Mexico. The people of Tennessee were descended from North Carolina and Virginia families, many of their own descendants had become citizens of Arkansas, Mississippi and Texas, and their kith and kin were in large numbers in all the States of the Union. Their love for the fatherland, for their own children and kindred, grew apace, and in time this became their paramount faith. But aggression followed aggression upon their rights of property; agitation growing in volume and respectability brought a sense of insecurity to all, until devotion to the Union of the States was weakened, and a determination was made to share the fortunes of the States of the South.

In January, 1861, Gov. Isham G. Harris by proclamation convened the legislature of Tennessee in extraordinary session to consider the condition of the country, and especially to determine whether a constitutional convention should be called. The State of South Carolina had already seceded from the Federal Union, and other States were about to consummate that act. After a month of debate and discussion the question was submitted to a vote of the people of the State, and the proposition was voted down by a large majority.

The people of Tennessee wished to avoid a war between the States and were anxious for a settlement of the questions of difference. Their old love for the Union of the States animated them, and they believed that the conservative sentiment of all the States could devise an adjustment that would prevent a resort to arms. They opposed a convention because of the belief that it meant secession, and that, in their judgment, must only follow after the failure of all plans of settlement. Before adjournment the legislature elected twelve commissioners, eminent and influential citizens of the State, to attend a peace conference called to assemble at the city of Washington. This conference was intended to represent all the States, and it was hoped that war could be averted, and that through the agency of the peace congress a settlement of all perplexing questions could be made. The conference met, ex-President John Tyler presided over its deliberations; many wise and patriotic gentlemen from all of the walks of life were present as delegates from the several States; but no acceptable settlement could be derived, and the action of the conference was without result.

The general assembly, while considering every suggestion that would avoid the withdrawal of any of the States from the Federal Union, was not forgetful of the rights of Tennessee, or of its duty to the other States of the South. Before adjournment it adopted with substantial unanimity a resolution pledging coöperation with the States of the South in case the Federal government should resort to force. This declaration represented the dominant sentiment of the people of Tennessee, and was responsive to the message of the governor, in which he declared that "whatever line of policy may be adopted by the people of Tennessee with regard to the present Federal relations of the State, I am sure that the swords of her brave and gallant sons will never be drawn for the purpose of coercing, subjugating, or holding as a conquered province any one of her sister States whose people may declare their independence of the Federal government."

In less than two months thereafter, the proclamation of Abraham Lincoln calling for 75,000 troops was issued; the people of Tennessee accepted it as a declaration of war, and with decency and dignity began preparation to meet it.

On the 25th of April, 1861, the governor again convened the general assembly in extraordinary session for the purpose, as stated in his message, of taking "such action as will most likely contribute to the defense of our rights, the preservation of our liberties, the sovereignty of the State, and the safety of our people." He informed the legislature that President Lincoln had called upon the State of Tennessee to furnish 2,000 troops to aid in "suppressing the rebellion," and that he had declined to honor the call.

On the 1st of May, 1861, the general assembly provided for the appointment of commissioners "to enter into a military league with the authorities of the Confederate States, and with the authorities of the other slave-holding States as may wish to enter into it, having in view the protection and defense of the entire South against the war that is now being carried on against it." On the 7th of the same month, Henry W. Hilliard, commissioner for the Confederate States, and Gustavus A. Henry, A. O. Totten and Washington Barrow, commissioners on the part of Tennessee, entered into a "temporary convention agreement and military league" for the purpose of protecting the interests and safety of the contracting parties. On the same day the general assembly ratified and confirmed this agreement, and pledged "the faith and honor of the State of Tennessee" to its observance.

On the 6th of May, 1861, the legislature submitted an ordinance to the people of the State which embraced the question of "separation" from the Federal government, and of union with the Confederate States, to be voted upon on the 8th day of June following. On the 24th of the same month the governor issued his proclamation declaring that "it appears from the official returns that the people of the State of Tennessee have, in their sovereign capacity, by an overwhelming majority, cast their votes for separation, dissolving all political connection with the United States, and adopted the provisional government of the Confederate States of America."

The political union thus established was followed by the election of delegates to the Provisional Congress, and in a few months by the adoption of the permanent government and constitution, the election of Jefferson Davis as President by the people, and the election of senators and representatives to the Congress of the Confederate States.

The legislature provided for the organization of an army of 50,000 men, appropriated $5,000,000 toward its equipment, and provided for a complete general staff to be appointed by the governor, and for the pay of officers and men. Authority was also given for the appointment of a military and financial board. On the 9th of May, 1861, the governor appointed, by and with the advice and consent of the general assembly, to be major-generals, Gideon J. Pillow and Samuel R. Anderson; brigadier-generals, Felix K. Zollicoffer, B. F. Cheatham, Robert C. Foster 3rd, John L. T. Sneed and William R. Caswell; adjutant-general, Daniel S. Donelson; inspector-general, William H. Carroll; surgeon-general, B. W. Avent; chief of artillery, John P. McCown; assistant adjutant-generals, W. C. Whitthorn, James D. Porter, Hiram S. Bradford and D. M. Key, with assistants for all departments; and on the 28th of June following he appointed Bushrod R. Johnson, colonel and chief of engineers, and made Moses H. Wright captain and chief of ordnance. For military and financial board, Neill S. Brown, James E. Bailey and William G. Harding were selected. V. K. Stevenson was made colonel and chief quartermaster, with a full complement of assistants. Maj. George W. Cunningham was placed in charge of the depot at Nashville for the accumulation of supplies, and there, and subsequently at Atlanta, Ga., he exhibited extraordinary skill and energy in the discharge of his duty. The military and financial board rendered great assistance to the chiefs of the several departments of the army. The services of the members of the board were recognized as of the first importance; their functions ceased with the transfer of the troops to the Confederate States.

John Heriges, keeper of public arms, reported in January, 1861, that the State arsenal contained 8,761 muskets and rifles, 350 carbines, 4 pieces of artillery, and a small lot of pistols and sabers, with 1,815 muskets and rifles, 228 pistols and 220 sabers in the hands of volunteer companies. Of the muskets in the arsenal, 280 were percussion, the balance were flint-lock, and over 4,300 of them were badly damaged; the carbines were flint-lock and unserviceable, and two of the four pieces of artillery were in the same condition. The governor reported in his message, dated April 2, 1861, that since the date of the report of the keeper of public arms, he had "ordered and received at the arsenal 1,400 rifle muskets." This constituted the armament of the State of Tennessee.

The chief of ordnance, Capt. M. H. Wright, thoroughly educated to the duties of his place, soon organized a force for the repair of arms, the manufacture and preparation of ammunition and the equipments of the soldiers, and for the conversion of the flint-lock muskets to percussion; and aided by patriotic citizens like Samuel D. Morgan, established a plant for the manufacture of percussion caps. Thus he was able to supply the troops of Tennessee as they took the field. Shipments of caps were made to the authorities at Richmond, who used them very largely at the first battle of Manassas. About 3,000 pounds of powder were being manufactured daily. Foundries for the manufacture of field guns were constructed at Nashville and Memphis, and by November, guns of good pattern were turned out at both points at the rate of six a week. Capt. W. R. Hunt, of the ordnance department, was the efficient head at Memphis.

Nashville soon became a great depot of supplies for the Confederate States. The manufacture of powder was stimulated, fixed ammunition was made in large quantities, large supplies of leather and material for clothing and blankets were gathered in, and factories for the manufacture of shoes and hats on a large scale were established. Great stores of bacon and flour and everything required by an army were provided. From these stores supplies were sent to Virginia and all points in the Southwest, and Nashville attained a degree of importance it never before enjoyed and perhaps will not soon again enjoy.

Major-General Pillow established his headquarters at Memphis and very soon organized the Provisional Army of Tennessee. Before the close of the month of May, twenty-one regiments of infantry were armed and equipped and in the field, and ten artillery companies and one regiment of cavalry were organized and mustered into the service of the State, besides three regiments of infantry then in Virginia already mustered into the service of the Confederate States. More than double that number of troops had tendered their services to the State, as the governor stated in his message of June 18th, "without even a call being made;" but their services were declined until the necessities of the State required a larger force and until arms could be provided. Before the close of the year 1861, the official records of the office of the Secretary of State show, seventy-one regiments of infantry and twenty-two batteries of artillery were mustered into the service of the State, and twenty-one regiments of cavalry, nine battalions, and enough independent companies and partisan rangers to have constituted eight full regiments were organized.

In the summer of 1861 all the troops were transferred to the service of the Confederate States, and the following-named general officers of Tennessee were commissioned brigadier-generals by President Davis: Gideon J. Pillow, Samuel R. Anderson, Felix K. Zollicoffer and B. F. Cheatham. These were soon followed by the appointment of John P. McCown, Bushrod R. Johnson, Alexander P. Stewart and William H. Carroll to the same rank.

On the 13th of January, 1861, Gen. Leonidas Polk, recently commissioned major-general in the Confederate States army, established his headquarters at Memphis as commander of Department No. 1. On the 31st of July the Army of Tennessee was transferred to the Confederate States.

General Polk's first campaign was organized for the relief of the State of Missouri. General Pillow, who was ordered to the command of the expedition, embracing 6,000 troops of all arms, took possession of New Madrid on the 28th of July with the advance of his forces, and was joined in a few days by Gen. Frank Cheatham, who marched through the country from Union City, Tenn., with a brigade of about 3,000 infantry, composed of the Fifth Tennessee, Col. William H. Stephens; the Ninth Tennessee, Col. H. L. Douglass; Blythe's Mississippi regiment, Col. A. K. Blythe; Miller's Mississippi battalion of cavalry, Lieut.-Col. J. H. Miller, and Capt. Melancthon Smith's Mississippi battery of six field pieces. By the 21st of August General Pillow's command had increased to 10,000 men of all arms, 2,000 of whom were Missourians, the balance Tennesseeans, with the exceptions named. The movement contemplated the occupation of Ironton and St. Louis, but was largely dependent upon the coöperation of Brigadier-General Hardee, then stationed at Greenville, Mo., near the border of Arkansas, with a command of about 5,000 Arkansas troops. This command was so deficient in arms, clothing and transportation that a forward movement was impossible. General Hardee therefore retired to Pitman's Ferry, on the Arkansas river, and the campaign for the redemption of Missouri was abandoned.

On the 3d of September the troops were transferred to Hickman and Columbus, Ky., the occupation of which points brought forth a vigorous protest from Governor Harris, of Tennessee, who had undertaken to have observed the legislative neutrality of the State of Kentucky. President Davis was solicitous on this point. He, too, wished to observe "Kentucky neutrality," but in a dispatch to General Polk, dated the 4th of September, after the occupation of Columbus, he said, "The necessity justifies the action." Reinforcements were sent to General Polk, mainly from Tennessee; strong lines of earthworks were provided, siege guns of the largest caliber were placed in a fort commanding the river front, and very soon Columbus became strongly fortified. At this time Brig.-Gen. U. S. Grant, U. S. V., commanded the district of Cairo, Ill., with Brig.-Gen. C. F. Smith in charge of the troops stationed at Paducah, Ky.

General Polk had under his command, in November, twenty-one regiments of infantry, eight field batteries, one battery of siege guns, two battalions, and six unattached companies of cavalry, all divided into three divisions, commanded, respectively, by General Pillow, General Cheatham and Col. John S. Bowen. The latter was at Camp Beauregard, fifteen miles distant. The Thirteenth Arkansas, Col. J. C. Tappan, Beltzhoover's Louisiana battery of six guns, and two troops of cavalry belonging to the Mississippi battalion commanded by Col. J. H. Miller, were stationed at Belmont, Mo., on the Mississippi river, opposite Columbus.

On the morning of the 7th of November, 1861, General Grant, with two brigades of infantry, consisting of five regiments and two troops of cavalry, in all 3,114 men, under cover of two gunboats, debarked from transports on the Missouri shore, above Belmont, at a point just out of range of Polk's batteries, and moved in line of battle in the direction of the camp of Colonel Tappan. General Polk, advised of the landing of the forces under Grant, ordered Brigadier-General Pillow to cross the river with the Twelfth Tennessee, Col. R. M. Russell; the Thirteenth Tennessee, Col. John V. Wright; the Twenty-first Tennessee, Col. Ed. Pickett, Jr., and the Twenty-second Tennessee, Col. T. J. Freeman. Very soon the Second Tennessee, Col. J. Knox Walker, and the Fifteenth Tennessee, Lieut.-Col. R. C. Tyler commanding, joined General Pillow, and with Tappan's regiment and Beltzhoover's battery, and the two companies of cavalry commanded by Capt. A. J. Bowles and Lieut. L. Jones, made General Pillow's strength slightly in excess of the Federal troops. Making his dispositions to receive Grant's attack, skirmishers were hotly engaged immediately afterward and were soon forced back on the main line.

General Grant's first battle was on; it was fierce and well fought, and according to General Pillow's official report, continued for four hours. In General Grant's order of the following day, thanking his troops for their good conduct at Belmont, he stated that it had been his fortune to be present in all the battles fought in Mexico by Generals Scott and Taylor, save Buena Vista, and he never saw one more hotly contested. The Federal line slowly but steadily advanced until the Confederate forces were driven to the river bank; Beltzhoover's battery was captured and the guns turned upon the Confederate transports; Tappan's camp was captured and his tents and stores destroyed. Of this movement General Pillow, in his report of the battle, states: "When the enemy's lines reached the bank of the river he was met by the fire of Smith's battery, of Cheatham's division, from the opposite side of the river, which, being well directed, together with the heavy guns from the works above Columbus, made him recoil from the point." The siege guns were directed by Maj. A. P. Stewart.

Just as the Federal forces began to retire, the Eleventh Louisiana regiment, Col. S. F. Marks, of McCown's division, reported to General Pillow and was ordered to move up the river, "and by a flank movement take the enemy in the rear." Marks moved to a point "where the fire of the enemy seemed to be the hottest," and in conjunction with Colonel Russell, of the Twelfth Tennessee, inflicted very serious punishment upon the enemy. His own regiment sustained a loss of 54 killed and wounded.

At the same hour, General Cheatham, who had been sent across the river, a part of his command to follow, reformed the Second Tennessee, Colonel Walker; the Thirteenth Tennessee, Lieutenant-Colonel Vaughn commanding, Colonel Wright having been disabled in the previous engagement; the Thirteenth Arkansas, Colonel Tappan, and a detachment of the Twenty-second Tennessee under Maj. F. M. Stewart; and with this command fell upon the rear of Grant's troops, routed them, recaptured two pieces of artillery, took 40 prisoners, and killed and disabled a considerable number, with trifling loss to his command. Now, also, Col. Preston Smith, commanding the First brigade of Cheatham's division, composed of the One Hundred and Fifty-fourth senior regiment of Tennessee, Lieut.-Col. M. J. Wright, and Blythe's Mississippi regiment, arrived on the field and joined in the pursuit of the enemy, now disorganized and in flight. It was a race with this command and the troops of Grant for the transports. Smith succeeded only in reaching musket range of the retreating enemy, and opening fire punished him severely, capturing a dozen prisoners. His own command sustained a loss of 1 killed and 12 wounded from the fire of the Federal gunboats.

General Grant reported his entire loss at 85 killed, 301 wounded and 99 missing. General Polk reported his loss at 105 killed, 419 wounded, 107 missing. Brig.-Gen. C. F. Smith, under Grant's order, made a demonstration in force in the direction of Columbus in aid of his own attack. This menace was successful in inducing the belief on the part of General Polk that Columbus was to be attacked from the land front, and to this misapprehension General Grant owes his escape from Belmont.

On the 6th of December following, the Congress of the Confederate States adopted resolutions of thanks to Generals Polk, Pillow and Cheatham, and the officers and men of their commands, "for the glorious victory achieved at Belmont, . . . whereby the reduction of Columbus was prevented, and the contemplated descent of the enemy down the Mississippi river effectually stayed." The gallant gentlemen who bore the burden of that battle have never claimed that this was a fitting commendation.

General Polk, in his official report, makes honorable mention of Generals Pillow and McCown; Col. John V. Wright, Thirteenth Tennessee; Maj. A. P. Stewart, afterward distinguished as commander of a brigade, division and army corps; Capt. M. Smith and the officers of his staff; and referring to another famous Tennesseean, said,

"I am indebted also to General Cheatham who, at a later hour, by his promptitude and gallantry, rallied the broken fragments of our column and directed them with such resistless energy against the enemy's flank."

CHAPTER II.

LOSS OF THE LINE OF THE CUMBERLAND—BATTLE OF FISHING CREEK—DEATH OF GENERAL ZOLLICOFFER — FALL OF FORT HENRY — BATTLE OF DOVER AND CAPITULATION OF FORT DONELSON—NEW MADRID AND ISLAND No. 10—EVACUATION OF NASHVILLE.

GEN. GEORGE B. CRITTENDEN, commanding the Confederate forces in east Tennessee, under date of January 18, 1862, advised Gen. A. S. Johnston from his camp at Beech Grove, Ky., on the north side of the Cumberland river, that he was threatened "by a superior force of the enemy in front, and finding it impossible to cross the river, I will have to make the fight on the ground I now occupy." He had under his command 4,000 effective men in two brigades: The First, commanded by Brig.-Gen. Felix K. Zollicoffer, was composed of the Fifteenth Mississippi, Lieut.-Col. E. C. Walthall; Nineteenth Tennessee, Col. D. H. Cummings; Twentieth Tennessee, Col. Joel A. Battle; Twenty-fifth Tennessee, Col. S. S. Stanton; Rutledge's battery of four guns, Capt. A. M. Rutledge, and two companies of cavalry commanded by Captains Saunders and Bledsoe. The Second brigade, commanded by Brig.-Gen. William H. Carroll, was composed of the Seventeenth Tennessee, Lieutenant-Colonel Miller; Twenty-eighth Tennessee, Col. John P. Murray; Twenty-ninth Tennessee, Col. Samuel Powell; two guns of McClung's battery, Captain McClung; Sixteenth Alabama, Col. W. B. Wood, and the cavalry battalions of Lieutenant-Colonel Brauner and Lieut.-Col. George McClellan. The movement to the north of the Cumberland was made by General Zollicoffer without the approval of General Johnston. In a dispatch to the latter, dated December 10, 1861, Zollicoffer said: "I infer from yours that I should not have crossed the river, but it is now too late. My means of recrossing is so limited, I could hardly accomplish it in the face of the enemy."

General Crittenden united his two brigades, and after consulting with their commanders, decided to attack the enemy. Soon after daylight on the 19th of January, the advance was made, and after a march of nine miles, Zollicoffer in front formed his command and made the attack with the Nineteenth Tennessee. This gallant regiment charged into the woods, driving the Tenth Indiana regiment, when General Zollicoffer, under a fatal misapprehension, rode up and ordered Colonel Cummings to cease firing, believing that the attack was upon one of his own regiments. He then advanced as if to give an order, and was killed just as he discovered his mistake. This caused the Nineteenth to break its line and fall back. The Twenty-fifth Tennessee had also engaged the enemy, and Colonel Stanton was wounded and disabled at the head of the regiment which now, impressed with the same idea which had proved fatal to the brigade commander, that it was firing on friends, broke its line and fell back. Colonel Cummings, senior colonel, assumed command of the brigade; the Fifteenth Mississippi and Twentieth Tennessee were moved into action, and Carroll's brigade coming up, a general advance was made. General Crittenden in his report of the battle says: "Very soon the enemy began to gain ground on our left," when General Carroll, who was at that point, ordered "the Nineteenth Tennessee, now commanded by Lieut.-Col. Frank Walker, to meet this movement of the enemy, and moved the Seventeenth Tennessee to its support. The Twenty-eighth, Twenty-fifth and Nineteenth Tennessee were driven back by the enemy, and while reforming in the rear of the Seventeenth Tennessee, that well-disciplined regiment met and held in check the entire right wing of the Northern army. For an hour now the Fifteenth Mississippi and Twentieth Tennessee had been struggling with the superior forces of the enemy." Their valor was heroic. These regiments only abandoned their position when the forces on the left retired and exposed them to a destructive flank fire; the Twenty-ninth Tennessee came to their rescue and checked the flank movement for a time with a raking fire at thirty paces. It was here that Colonel Powell was badly wounded. Valuable service was rendered at this critical moment by the Sixteenth Alabama, but the battle was lost after three hours of fighting. Owing to the formation of the field the Confederates were unable to use artillery; the rain which was falling rendered useless the flint-lock muskets, with which more than half of them were armed; and the death of General Zollicoffer and the peculiar circumstances attending it were very demoralizing to the troops. General Crittenden retreated without molestation from the enemy to his original camp, and during the night fell back to the south side of the Cumberland river, abandoning from necessity his artillery, ammunition, wagons, horses and stores of every description. General Thomas had in action, or in striking distance, the Ninth, Fourteenth, Seventeenth, Thirty-first and Thirty-eighth Ohio regiments; the Second Minnesota, Tenth Indiana, Carter's Tennessee brigade, Tenth and Twelfth Kentucky regiments, Wolford's cavalry, and Kenny's, Wetmore's and Standarts' batteries. General Crittenden reported his loss at 125 killed, 309 wounded, 99 missing. Of this loss the Twentieth Tennessee had 33 killed, 59 wounded; Fifteenth Mississippi, 44 killed, 153 wounded; Nineteenth Tennessee, 10 killed, 22 wounded; Twenty-fifth Tennessee, 10 killed, 28 wounded; Seventeenth Tennessee, 11 killed, 25 wounded; Twenty-eighth Tennessee, 3 killed, 4 wounded; Twenty-ninth Tennessee, 5 killed, 12 wounded; Sixteenth Alabama, 9 killed, 5 wounded. General Thomas reported his loss at 39 killed, 207 wounded.

The State of Tennessee echoed the words of General Crittenden when he reported the death of General Zollicoffer: "In counsel he has always shown wisdom, and in battle braved dangers, while coolly directing the movements of his troops." He was a statesman and soldier, and all lamented his death, as well as that of his accomplished aide-de-camp, Henry R. M. Fogg, Lieut. Bailie Peyton, of the Twentieth Tennessee, and others whose names were not reported.

Soon following this disaster, on the right of the Confederate line established by Gen. Albert Sidney Johnston, occurred the loss of the forts which commanded the lower Tennessee and Cumberland rivers.

The engagement at Fort Henry lasted two hours and ten minutes. Brig.-Gen. Lloyd Tilghman was in command of the Confederate forces, consisting of 2,610 officers and men of all arms. Gen. U. S. Grant, commanding an army of 16,000 men, had landed at Bailey's ferry, four miles below Fort Henry, on the 4th of February, 1862, and proceeded with the investment of the fort, awaiting its reduction by Flag-Officer A. H. Foote. The squadron commanded by the latter, composed of the ironclad gunboats Cincinnati, the flagship Essex, the Carondelet, the St. Louis, the Conestoga, the Tyler and the Lexington, armed with 54 heavy guns, steamed up to within 1,700 yards of the fort, and at thirty minutes past noon of the 6th, the fire was opened and responded to by the eleven guns of the fort. The distance between the fort and fleet was reduced to 1,200 yards and soon to 600. The most available gun in the fort in a short time burst and disabled every man at the piece. Soon the vent of the only 10-inch columbiad was closed and rendered useless, leaving nothing for defense except the ordinary 32-pounders.

At this juncture General Tilghman ordered Col. A. Heiman, Tenth Tennessee, the next officer in rank, to retire to Fort Donelson with the entire command, leaving with himself only Capt. Jesse Taylor's artillery company of Tennesseeans, who manned the heavy guns. Captain Taylor's company had fifty men present for duty, with Lieutenants West and Miller. The captain, a native of Lexington, Tenn., was an officer of skill and courage, and the result of the battle with the Federal fleet shows how well his guns were served. Thirty-one shots struck and disabled the flagship Cincinnati, killing 1 and wounding 9; the Essex received 22 shots, one of which passed through the ship, opening one of her boilers, disabling 28 of her crew, and taking off the head of the captain's aide; the St. Louis was struck seven times, and the Carondelet six times. Flag-Officer Foote, in his report of the attack on Fort Henry, states that it "was defended with most determined gallantry," and that it was surrendered after seven of the eleven guns had been disabled. During the fight General Tilghman himself served one of the guns, and his gallant bearing was an inspiration to Captain Taylor's company. In his official report he makes honorable mention of the officers and men of the company, and states that "Lieutenant Watts is the coolest officer under fire I ever saw." Taylor's casualties amounted to 16 killed and wounded.

The location of Fort Henry was unfortunate, and at the date of the attack the high water in the Tennessee river had surrounded and separated it from the outside line of works. The forces were entirely inadequate for its defense, and General Tilghman made the best defense possible. He maintained it long enough to enable Colonel Heiman to escape with the forces, and sacrificed himself and Captain Taylor's company of Tennesseeans.

General Grant invested Fort Donelson on the 12th of February, 1862, with 15,000 troops, reinforced that evening by six regiments of infantry and Flag-Officer Foote's fleet of four ironclad and two wooden gunboats—the St. Louis, Carondelet, Louisville, Pittsburg, Tyler and

Conestoga. Reinforcements continued to arrive. Wallace's division was brought over from Fort Henry, 10,000 men were sent by General Buell, and the Confederate lines were enveloped by 24,000 troops. General Buckner states, in his report, that at the close of the attack Grant's forces exceeded 50,000. Brig.-Gen. John B. Floyd, of Virginia, commanded the Confederate forces, amounting to 12,000 men. General Pillow commanded the left, General Buckner the right.

The Tennesseeans present were, the Third Tennessee, Col. John C. Brown; Eighteenth, Col. Jos. B. Palmer; Twenty-sixth, Col. John M. Lillard; Thirty-second, Col. Ed. C. Cook; Forty-first, Col. Robert Farquharson; Tenth, Col. A. Heiman; Forty-second, Col. W. A. Quarles; Thirtieth, Col. John W. Head; Forty-ninth, Col. James E. Bailey; Forty-eighth, Col. W. M. Voorhees; Tennessee battalion, Colonel Browder; Fiftieth, Colonel Sugg; five companies of infantry, Col. S. H. Colms; Fifty-third, Col. Alfred H. Abernathy; Forrest's regiment of cavalry, Col. N. B. Forrest; Ninth battalion of cavalry, Lieut.-Col. George Gantt; Maney's light battery of four guns, Capt. Grant Maney; Green's battery, Captain Green; Porter's battery, six guns, Capt. Thomas Kennedy Porter. The heavy guns were commanded by Capt. J. H. Dixon; one battery of 32-pounders, one rifle gun, one 10-inch columbiad and two howitzers were commanded by Capt. R. R. Ross; Capt. B. G. Bidwell, Thirtieth Tennessee infantry, was assigned to a battery of four 32-pounders; Capt. T. W. Beaumont, Company A, Fiftieth Tennessee infantry, had charge of a battery of four 32-pounders, and a battery of eight 32-pounders was commanded by Capt. Jacob Culbertson. Brig.-Gen. Gideon J. Pillow, Brig.-Gen. Simon B. Buckner and Brig.-Gen. Bushrod R. Johnson commanded the troops, General Floyd in chief command. The Tennessee brigade commanders were Col. A. Heiman, Col. John C. Brown and Col. James E. Bailey, the latter commanding the garrison of the fort; Col. N. B. Forrest commanded the cavalry.

The investment of Fort Donelson and the works occupied by the Confederate forces was complete by the afternoon of the 12th of February, and on the 13th an unsuccessful assault was made on Bushrod Johnson's left wing. It was met gallantly and repulsed by the Tenth Tennessee, Lieut.-Col. R. W. MacGavock; the Fifty-third Tennessee, Lieut.-Col. Thomas F. Winston; the Forty-eighth Tennessee, Col. W. M. Voorhees; the Forty-second Tennessee, Col. W. A. Quarles, and Maney's battery. General Johnson and Colonel Heiman both commended in high terms the conduct of the men who met this attack. After a second and third assault, the enemy retired, leaving his dead and wounded on the field. He had met three bloody repulses. The principal sufferer on the part of Heiman's brigade was Maney's battery; it was fought without protection and with skill and courage, but his loss, chiefly from sharpshooters, was such that he was afterward unable to man two of his four guns. Colonel Brown, commanding brigade, reports that pending this engagement of two hours' duration, "the enemy planted one section of a battery (of field guns) almost in front of Captain Graves, commanding a Kentucky battery, and opened an enfilading fire upon the left of my line, and at the same time a cross-fire upon Colonel Heiman. Captain Graves, handling his favorite rifle piece with the same fearless courage that characterized his conduct during the entire week, in less than ten minutes knocked one of the enemy's guns from its carriage, and almost at the same moment the gallant Porter (commanding battery) disabled and silenced the other, while the supporting infantry retreated precipitately before the storm of grape and canister poured into their ranks from both batteries." Two hours before this assault on Heiman's brigade, General Buckner reports, "the enemy made a vigorous attack on Hanson's position (the Second Kentucky, Col. Roger W. Hanson), but was repulsed with heavy loss. The attack was subsequently renewed by three heavy regiments, but was again repulsed by the Second Kentucky, aided by a part of the Eighteenth Tennessee (Colonel Palmer). In both of these affairs, also in a third repulse of the enemy from the same position, Porter's battery played a conspicuous part." Col. Roger Hanson, in his report of this action, states that "in resisting these attacks I was greatly assisted by Porter's battery upon the left. It always fired at the right time and to the right place."

General Grant had so far failed to accomplish anything with his army. On the 14th the main attack was made with the enemy's gunboats. Flag-Officer A. H. Foote, United States navy, reported that the action continued one hour and a half, and that "in the latter part of the action his fleet was less than 400 yards from the fort." "The wheel of this vessel [the flagship], by a shot through her pilot-house, was carried away, and the tiller-ropes of the Louisville also disabled by a shot, which rendered the two boats wholly unmanageable. They then drifted down the river. The two remaining boats, the Pittsburg and Carondelet, were also greatly damaged between wind and water, and soon followed us, the enemy rapidly renewing the fire as we drifted helplessly down the river. This vessel, the St. Louis, alone received 59 shots, four between wind and water, and one in the pilot-house, mortally wounding the pilot and others. There were 54 killed and wounded" on the several vessels.

Capt. Joseph H. Dixon, an officer of great intelligence and courage, was killed on the evening of the 13th when a few shots were exchanged between the fleet and fort. One shot came through the embrasure, striking the left cheek of one of the gun-carriages out of which a screw bolt was driven, striking him in the forehead, killing him instantly. This was the only casualty sustained by the batteries. Colonel Bailey's brigade constituted the garrison of the fort and rendered great assistance to the gunners.

No battle or combat of the war was more decided than that between the heavy batteries and the Federal fleet, and there were no higher intelligence and gallantry displayed on any field of service than that exhibited by Captains Dixon, Culbertson, Ross, Beaumont, Bidwell and Graham. Lieutenants Stankiewitz, Fitzgerald, Sparkman, Bedford, George Martin and W. C. Allen were honorably mentioned. Captain Culberson reported that "our success is mainly attributed" to Lieut. H. S. Bedford, who directed the 10-inch gun. Captain Bidwell, referring to Private John G. Frequa (or Fuqua) in his report, stated that "at the highest gun in my battery he stood perfectly upright, calm, cool and collected. I heard him say, 'Now, boys, see me take a chimney.' The chimney [of the vessel] and the flag both fell. Very soon he sent a ball through a porthole and the boat fell back." Captain Beaumont makes honorable mention of Major Robertson, who volunteered to serve one of his guns; also of Sergt. J. S. Martin, Corps. W. H. Proctor and Dan C. Lyle, and of Privates Elisha Downs, Poston Couts, Nelson Davis, Isaac Christie, Wm. Trotter, Thomas Pearce and R. M. Crumpler. But no duty was omitted by officers or men, and Tennessee will always hold in grateful memory the prowess of her sons who manned the heavy guns in the defense of Fort Donelson.

On the 15th of February a combined attack was made by the two divisions commanded by Generals Pillow and Buckner. General Pillow led the left to the attack, soon followed by the right. Pillow's division constituted two-thirds of the army. The battle raged from daylight to 1 o'clock and to that hour was a great success. It was won by the troops of all of the States. Virginia, Kentucky, Mississippi, Tennessee, Texas, Alabama, all shared alike in the glory of the achievement. The object of this attack is stated in the report of General Floyd to have been, as the result of a consultation with the officers of divisions and brigades, "to dislodge the enemy from the position on our left, and thus to pass our people into the open country."

Col. John G. Brown reported that when his brigade moved out on Saturday morning it "was provided with three days' cooked rations and marched with knapsacks, the purpose being to turn the enemy's right wing and march out on the Wynn's Ferry road to fall back on Nashville." After several fierce combats in coöperation with the left division he reports that he "led the Third, Eighteenth and Thirty-second Tennessee across an open field on the right of Wynn's Ferry road under the fire of a battery posted on that road." The infantry support retreated, leaving one section of the battery in his hands. He pursued the retreating forces. After this another fierce combat ensued, but after the firing of a few volleys of musketry the enemy abandoned the field, leaving 800 killed and wounded. In this last combat Colonel Brown was reinforced by the Fourteenth Mississippi regiment and Graves' battery. The brigade lost 50 in killed and wounded, among them Col. Thomas M. Gordon of the Third, wounded, and the accomplished Lieut.-Col. W. P. Moore, mortally wounded.

General Pillow, leaving Heiman's brigade in the trenches, with the balance of the left division, assisted by Forrest's cavalry, engaged the enemy hotly for two hours and succeeded in driving him back on Buckner's division. Forrest's cavalry charged the infantry support of and captured a battery composed of four field pieces and two 24-pounders. Gen. Bushrod Johnson, of Tennessee, always reliable and strong in battle, contributed largely to the success of the movement. His command became united with the forces of General Buckner as the enemy retired, as General Pillow reports, "and engaged the enemy in a hot contest of nearly one hour, with large forces of fresh troops that had now met us. This position of the enemy being carried by our joint forces, I called off further pursuit after seven hours of continuous and bloody conflict, in which our loss was severe, and leaving not less than 1,000 of the enemy dead on the field." The object of this battle seemed to be accomplished, but our council of war was divided, and the troops were ordered to their original position in the intrenchments.

As Buckner returned he found the Federal forces of Gen. C. F. Smith advancing rapidly to take possession of his portion of our works, bravely opposed by Maj. James J. Turner of the Thirtieth Tennessee. He had a stubborn conflict lasting one hour and a half, resulting in the seizure of our extreme right. This position was in rear of the Confederate river batteries and field-work for their protection, and was the key to the Confederate situation. It took Buckner in reverse and necessitated the ultimate surrender of our forces. The position seized by the Federal forces had been occupied by the Second Kentucky. In the struggle to regain it, this gallant regiment was reinforced by the Eighteenth, the Third and Thirty-second Tennessee, and subsequently by the regiments of Colonels Quarles, Sugg and Bailey. General Buckner reported that "the enemy made repeated attempts to storm my line on the right, but the well-directed fire of Porter's and Graves' artillery, and the musketry fire of the infantry, repelled the attempts and forced him to shelter. Porter's battery, from its exposed position, lost more than half its gunners, and the intrepid commander was severely wounded late in the afternoon of Saturday, being succeeded in command by the gallant Lieutenant Morton."

The artillery of Tennessee was especially conspicuous. Colonel Heiman reported that in the battle of the 13th, referring to Maney's battery. "First Lieutenant Burns was one of the first who fell. Second Lieutenant Massie was also mortally wounded. but the gallant Maney, with the balance of his men, stood by their guns like true heroes." Generals Pillow and Bushrod Johnson warmly commended Captains Maney and Green; and General Floyd, commander-in-chief, in his report of the battle of the 13th, said: "Too high praise cannot be bestowed upon the battery of Captain Porter for their participation in the rout of the enemy in this assault. My position was immediately in front of the point of attack, and I was thus enabled to witness the incidents of it." Col. John C. Brown reported that Captains Porter and Graves "excited the admiration of the whole command by an exhibition of coolness and bravery, under a heavy fire from which they had no protection, which could not be excelled. Captain Porter fell dangerously wounded by a minie ball through his thigh while working one of his guns, his gunners being nearly all of them disabled or killed. The command then devolved upon Lieutenant Morton, a beardless youth, who stepped forward like an old veteran, and nobly did he emulate the example of his brave captain." Lieutenant Morton subsequently became distinguished as captain of Morton's battery of Forrest's cavalry.

Gen. N. B. Forrest, then colonel of Forrest's Tennessee cavalry, disputed the advance of General Grant on Fort Donelson with commendable enterprise and skill, no other obstacle being offered to the march from Fort Henry, and pending the engagement he was actively employed on the flanks of our army. Besides his own regiment, three mounted companies from Kentucky, commanded by Captains Williams, Wilcox and Henry, were assigned to his command, and gallantly assisted him. He also had assigned to him Gantt's Tennessee battalion. Forrest reported that he "charged two batteries of artillery, taking nine pieces of artillery with 4,000 stand of arms." He lost between 300 and 400 men, killed, wounded and missing, a greater loss than was sustained by any other regiment of the army. Among his killed was

Capt. Charles May, who fell leading his company to a charge on the enemy. Fort Donelson was the opening of a career to Forrest that carried his name and fame to the civilized world and yet excites the admiration of all who read of his personal prowess and heroic actions. He retired from Fort Donelson before its final surrender. General Floyd with his brigade, and General Pillow with his staff, left on a transport pending negotiations.

The Confederate forces amounted to 12,000 to 14,500 men. General Badeau, in his life of Grant, Vol. I, page 36, says, on the last day of the fight Grant had 27,000 men, and other reinforcements arrived after the surrender; but General Buckner believed that this was far below the number, and General Buell stated in 1865 that Grant had 30,000 to 35,000 exclusive of the naval contingent.

The Federal loss amounted to 2,500 killed, wounded and missing. The Confederate loss was about 1,420. On Thursday there was a rainfall, followed by snow on Friday, with freezing weather, and by the evening of Saturday, the 15th, the men who had spent a week in the trenches without sleep and without fire to warm them, were worn out to such an extent that General Buckner decided he could not longer maintain himself, and surrendered the troops on the morning of the 16th. This was a great disappointment to Gen. Albert Sidney Johnston, commander of the department. On the 14th he telegraphed General Floyd: "If you lose the fort, bring your troops to Nashville, if possible." Roger Hanson in his report said that "up to the time (1 o'clock p. m. of the 15th) when we were ordered back to the trenches, our success was complete and our escape secure," but "our success" was misleading and defeated the wishes of General Johnston.

Columbus, Ky., was still held by the Confederate troops, as well as New Madrid and Island No. 10. Maj. John P. McCown was detached from Columbus, on the

26th of February, 1862, and ordered to New Madrid, Mo., and placed in command. General Beauregard dispatched General Polk on the same day that the place "must be watched and held at all cost."

Three days earlier Major-General Pope, of the Federal army, had assumed command of the army of the Mississippi, then concentrated at Commerce, Mo. This was made Pope's base of operations against New Madrid. In a week he was in motion, and on the 3d of March he was in front of New Madrid. At once he drove in the Confederate outposts and invested the place. General Pope reported his strength at 22,808 present for duty. His division commanders were Brig.-Gens. D. S. Stanley, Schuyler Hamilton, John M. Palmer, E. A. Paine, J. B. Plummer and Gordon Granger. Eleven batteries of artillery, and the Second and Third Michigan regiments of cavalry, over 2,000 strong, constituted a part of his army, to which was attached a flotilla brigade, under Col. N. B. Buford, 2,251 strong. Equipments, arms and ammunition were perfect.

To meet this well-appointed army, General McCown had 5,000 infantry and three companies of artillery. Brig.-Gen. A. P. Stewart, of Tennessee, was assigned to the command of the forces. Commodore Hollins, Confederate States navy, with five small wooden gunboats, was present under McCown's orders. New Madrid was defended by a small earthwork called Fort Thompson, in honor of Brig.-Gen. M. Jeff. Thompson, of the Missouri State Guard. The work was garrisoned by the Eleventh and Twelfth Arkansas regiments of infantry, Stewart's Louisiana battery and Upton's Tennessee battery, commanded by Col. E. W. Gantt, Twelfth Arkansas regiment. Another work at the mouth of Bayou St. John was garrisoned by the Fifth and Fortieth Tennessee, two Arkansas regiments under Col. L. M. Walker, the First Alabama, Mississippi and Tennessee regiments, and Bankhead's Tennessee battery.

On the 4th of March the enemy made a demonstration in force on McCown's lines and was driven back by Hollins' fleet and our land batteries. On the 6th, Pope occupied Point Pleasant, twelve miles below, with infantry and artillery, fortified the place, and established a blockade of the river against transports. General McCown reported, under date of March 31st, that on the same day the enemy with "a white flag induced Capt. J. W. Dunnington (of Tennessee), commanding the gunboat Ponchartrain, to near the shore, when she was fired into by musketry, killing and wounding several." Skirmishing continued from day to day until the 13th, the enemy having made gradual approaches and planted batteries of heavy guns commanding Fort Thompson and the river. When convinced that the gunboats could not maintain a contest with land batteries, General McCown ordered the evacuation of New Madrid. A heavy rainstorm continued during the night and made the evacuation disorderly, and caused the abandonment of the heavy guns and a considerable quantity of quartermaster and commissary stores.

General Beauregard made demand for an explanation of the causes leading to the evacuation, and when the reports were submitted they were referred to Major Brent for examination, who reported on the 15th of April: "1, that the works at New Madrid could have held out longer, the enemy up to the date of the evacuation having been several times signally repulsed; 2, that disorder and confusion prevailed at Fort Thompson on the night of the 13th, the men were disinclined to obey orders, and orders were given apparently without authority; that sufficient means for transportation were not furnished; that part of the abandoned guns could have been saved." But nothing came of the investigation except to demonstrate the unfitness of the commander at Fort Thompson. The force under McCown was inadequate for the defense of New Madrid; and though General Beauregard considered its maintenance and defense important, on the 15th of March he approved the projected evacuation. General McCown, in reporting the result to him, said: "The principal object I had in holding New Madrid was to possess a landing for reinforcements to fight the enemy should I receive them."

Dr. W. S. Ball, medical director, Captain West, provost marshal, Lieutenant Robinson of Upton's battery, and one man were killed; Capt. William D. Hallum, of the Fifth Tennessee, and eight men were wounded. Hallum received a fearful wound, the ball passing through his neck, and was reported by McCown as killed, but he recovered in a short time, served throughout the war, and made an honorable record.

McCown, with his troops, transports, and Hollins' fleet, fell back to Tiptonville, on the Tennessee side of the river. General Stewart with his brigade was forwarded to Corinth and participated conspicuously in the battle of Shiloh.

Meanwhile, on the 17th of March, the Federal gunboats had made a vigorous attack without effect at Island No. 10, the fire being principally directed at the battery commanded by Captain Rucker, who returned it, the action continuing during the day. McCown, pursuant to orders, turned the command over to Brig.-Gen. L. M. Walker, just promoted. On the 19th he was ordered to return to Madrid Bend. On the 31st he relinquished command, under orders, to Brig.-Gen. W. W. Mackall. General Mackall found himself in command of 2,273 infantry, rank and file, with 58 heavy guns, ten 8-inch columbiads, the balance 32-pounders. Five batteries were upon the mainland and three upon Island No. 10. The infantry force consisted of the Fifty-fifth Tennessee, Col. A. J. Brown, with 50 unarmed men; the Eleventh Arkansas, Colonel Smith, armed with every variety of sporting guns; the Forty-sixth Tennessee, Col. John M. Clark, with 160 armed men out of a total of 400 present for duty; the Fourth Arkansas battalion, Major McKay, poorly armed, and two companies of cavalry. Hollins' fleet was well armed, but the boats were worthless. General Walker and Colonel Steadman, next in rank, were absent, sick. One battery on the island was under water. The line occupied was about 25 miles in length, with about 1,000 available infantry for its defense, confronted by Pope's army and a powerful fleet of gunboats. Success, or the delay of the enemy, was impossible. Subsequently General Beauregard informed Mackall in writing, that "when I sent you there, I considered matters in a desperate condition, and that you were going on a forlorn hope." Brig.-Gen. J. Trudeau was chief of artillery. The battery commanders, Capts. E. W. Rucker, Robert Sterling, Hoadley, Andrew Jackson, Jr., Jones, J. B. Caruthers, W. Y. C. Humes, Dismukes, Fisher, Johnston, were Tennesseeans. The artillerymen were in good discipline, and although the approaches to the island batteries were under water, and the batteries ultimately were submerged, the men were in good form and full of confidence.

The only losses sustained by the Confederates in the attack of the 17th of March was Lieut. William M. Clark, of Rucker's battery, killed, and Sergt. I. T. Postlethwaite and six men slightly wounded. Four shots struck Foote's fleet without effect. The exchange of shots continued at intervals until the 6th of April, when Captain Jackson, senior officer, under orders, spiked the guns and withdrew across Reelfoot lake with the entire artillery force. Flag-Officer Foote's experience at Forts Henry and Donelson caused him to keep without the range of Confederate guns. With his tactics the forts would never have been reduced. It was only when Pope's army crossed to the Tennessee shore, and capture was imminent, that Island No. 10 was abandoned. General Mackall being cut off from the forts and heavy batteries, on the night of the same day undertook to save the infantry and light battery by a retreat through Tiptonville, the only way open. His occupation of that place was anticipated by the Federal army, and on the morning of the 7th he wisely surrendered the forces under his command, consisting, as reported by him, of Stewart's field artillery company of 5 guns, and 2,900 infantry, of whom 400 were unarmed. There were 58 heavy guns abandoned, including 10 guns of the floating battery which were sunk in desperation in the Mississippi river. But General Pope reported to General Halleck "that 273 field and company officers, 6,700 privates, 123 pieces of heavy artillery, 35 pieces of field artillery, all of the very best character and latest patterns, 7,000 stand of small-arms, tents for 12,000 men, several wharfboats," and hundreds of horses and mules, with immense stores of ammunition, were surrendered to him. Col. W. G. Cumming, Fifty-first Illinois, commanding brigade, in an official report, dated the 10th of April, said: "Soon after the surrender I was ordered by Major-General Pope to take charge of the prisoners, who were about 3,000 in number." On the 8th of April, when the affair was fresh in his memory, General Pope telegraphed the department commander that "2,000 prisoners, including General Mackall," had surrendered and were prisoners of war.

Nashville had been defended at Fort Donelson. The surrender of one made it necessary to abandon the other. General Johnston determined to concentrate his own troops with those at Columbus, Ky., and at Pensacola, at Corinth, Miss., the junction of the Mobile & Ohio and the Memphis & Charleston railroads. General Grant was moving on the same point, and Gen. Don Carlos Buell, of the Federal army, who had been in front of Bowling Green with an army of 40,000 men, occupied Nashville as soon as it was abandoned by the Confederate forces, and began the movement of his troops that enabled him to form a junction with Grant in time to save the army of the latter from annihilation.

CHAPTER III.

THE BATTLE OF SHILOH — ORGANIZATION OF THE CONFEDERATE ARMY — ASSIGNMENT OF TENNESSEE REGIMENTS — THEIR PROMINENCE IN THE ARMY — GALLANT SERVICE IN THE TWO DAYS' BATTLE — TENNESSEE ARTILLERY — LOCKRIDGE MILL FIGHT.

WHEN Gen. Albert Sidney Johnston had united his forces from Nashville with those collected under General Beauregard at Corinth—the latter including the reinforcements from Pensacola and Mobile under General Bragg, and Polk's command from Columbus, which was evacuated—he organized his army with Gen. G. T. Beauregard second in command, and Maj.-Gen. Braxton Bragg chief of staff and in immediate charge of the Second corps. Maj.-Gen. Leonidas Polk commanded the First corps, Maj.-Gen. W. J. Hardee the Third, and Maj.-Gen. John C. Breckinridge the Reserve corps.

The Tennesseeans were assigned as follows: In Polk's corps, First division, Brig.-Gen. Charles Clark commanding—the Twelfth, Thirteenth and Twenty-second regiments, and Bankhead's battery, to the First brigade, Col. R. M. Russell; the Fourth and Fifth regiments to the Second brigade, Brig.-Gen. A. P. Stewart. Second division, Maj.-Gen. B. F. Cheatham commanding—the Second (Knox Walker's), Fifteenth, One Hundred and Fifty-fourth (senior), and Polk's battery, to the First brigade, Brig.-Cen. Bushrod R. Johnson; the First, Sixth and Ninth to the Second brigade, Col. W. H. Stephens.

In Bragg's corps, the Thirty-eighth regiment was assigned to Col. Preston Pond's brigade of Ruggles' division; the Fifty-first and Fifty-second to Brigadier-General Chalmers' brigade of Withers' division. In Hardee's corps, Brigadier-General Cleburne's brigade included the Thirty-fifth, Twenty-third and Twenty-fourth regiments, and Brig.-Gen. S. A. M. Wood's brigade, the Twenty-seventh, Forty-fourth and Fifty-fifth. The Reserve corps had the Nineteenth, Twentieth, Twenty-eighth and Forty-fifth regiments, and Rutledge's battery, in the brigade of Col. W. S. Statham, and Crew's battalion, in Col. R. P. Trabue's brigade. Forrest's cavalry was under the immediate orders of the general commanding.

At 11 a. m. of the battle of the 6th, when Gen. Bushrod Johnson was disabled by a painful wound, the command of the brigade devolved upon Col. Preston Smith, of the One Hundred and Fifty-fourth Tennessee, and the command of that gallant regiment upon Lieut.-Col. Marcus J. Wright. At 2:30 p. m. of the same day, Col. George Maney, senior officer of Stephens' brigade, assumed the command of it; and Maj. Hume R. Feild, next in rank present, took command of the First Tennessee.

Polk's corps, with the exception of Blythe's Mississippi, the Eleventh Louisiana and the Thirteenth Arkansas, was composed entirely of Tennesseeans. Colonel Lindsay's Mississippi regiment of cavalry reported to General Polk. This splendid regiment had been known up to this date as Miller's battalion, Lieut.-Col. J. H. Miller commanding.

On the 3d day of April General Johnston issued an address to the troops, in which he announced, "I have put you in motion to offer battle to the invaders of your country." Hon. Jacob Thompson, of Mississippi, aide to General Beauregard, in his report of April 9th states that this advance was made "in consequence of the information brought from General Cheatham," who occupied Bethel Station and the town of Purdy with his division.

In the attack about to be made on General Grant, General Johnston expected to beat him back to his transports and there capture him and his forces, then cross the Tennessee river and give battle to Buell, known to be advancing to Grant's assistance. General Johnston rapidly concentrated his troops and delivered battle in the early morning of the 6th of April. That peerless soldier was in immediate and active command of the troops, General Beauregard being at his quarters in very feeble health, and his presence inspired unbounded enthusiasm. The disasters at Fishing creek and Forts Henry and Donelson had subjected him to the criticism of politicians, but the army and intelligent people of all classes gave him support and confidence. No fault can be named in his plan of attack, and it was successful at all points.

Grant's troops made a stout resistance, but retired slowly from the moment of the firing of the first gun by Hardee until the fall of Johnston at 2 o'clock p. m., when the battle of Shiloh was already won and the Federal hosts were driven back in confusion from the field. Gen. James R. Chalmers, who occupied the advance of the Confederate army at the close of the day, in a published letter, said: "One more resolute movement forward would have captured Grant and his whole army." That movement was not made. The troops were withdrawn to receive an attack from the combined forces of Grant and Buell on the following day. Another battle of Shiloh was fought, with varying success, until our forces began to yield about noon, and at 2 p. m. received orders from General Beauregard to retire.

Tennessee was represented on all parts of the field and in all commands. Her sons sustained and promoted the character and reputation of the State, and elevated the standard of courage, fidelity and patriotism. Their death-roll shows that they were in the fore-front of the battle, and with a single exception there was no failure of duty. That exception was the Fifty-second regiment of infantry,

Chalmers' brigade, which was unfortunate in its field officers. General Chalmers, in his official report, stated that the Fifty-second Tennessee, except two companies under Capts. J. A. Russell and A. N. Wilson, who fought with the Fifth Mississippi, behaved badly.

The sons of Tennessee, of every rank, were conspicuous for dash and steadiness in action, and for the maintenance of regimental and company organizations under all conditions. General Beauregard, in his report, made honorable mention of Generals Cheatham and Bushrod Johnson; and General Polk, referring to the brigades of Johnson and Russell and their charge on Sherman's division, and to the valor of friend and foe, mentions the dangerous wounds received by Generals Clark and Johnson, the death of the noble Col. A. K. Blythe of Mississippi (a son of Tennessee); the wounding of gallant Capt. Marsh T. Polk, who lost a leg; and the final dislodgment of the enemy and the capture of two batteries, one by the One Hundred and Fifty-fourth Senior Tennessee, Col. Preston Smith, the other by the Thirteenth Tennessee, Col. A. J. Vaughan, Jr.

Polk also called attention to the "brilliant courage" of the Fifth Tennessee, Col. C. D. Venable, and the Thirty-third Tennessee, Col. Alex. W. Campbell, and to the gallantry of Lieut.-Col. O. F. Strahl, who, in reply to the inquiry of his intrepid brigade commander, General Stewart, "Can you take that battery?" said, "We will try," and at the order, Forward, moved at a double-quick to within thirty paces of the enemy's guns, halted, delivered one round, and with a yell charged the battery, capturing several prisoners and the guns; but the valorous Fourth lost Maj. John F. Henry and Capt. John Sutherland, with 31 men killed and 150 wounded. The battery captured was composed of heavy guns, supported by several regiments of infantry.

Of another famous incident of the battle, General Polk reported that about 5 p. m. of the 6th, his line attacked the enemy's troops (the last that were left upon the field) in an encampment on his right. The attack was made in front and flank. The resistance was sharp but short, when the enemy, perceiving he was flanked and his position completely turned, hoisted his white flag and surrendered with his command, 2,200 strong. The Federal commander's sword being delivered to Col. R. M. Russell, commanding First brigade, it was found the forces captured were those of Brig.-Gen. B. M. Prentiss, Sixth division of Grant's army.

At 8 a. m. of the 7th General Polk ordered Cheatham's division, reinforced by the Thirty-third and Twenty-seventh Tennessee, and Gibson's Louisiana brigade, to move "past Shiloh church to form on left of our line." "They engaged the enemy so soon as they were formed and fought him, for four hours, one of the most desperately-contested conflicts of the battle. The enemy was driven gradually from his position." General Cheatham declared that this conflict was "the most hotly contested I ever witnessed." He had met fresh troops under McCook. General Polk made honorable mention of Generals Cheatham, Clark, Stewart and Johnson, and Colonels Russell, Maney, Stephens and Preston Smith. Of General Cheatham he said: "In the operations of this morning (the 7th), as well as the day before, those of my troops under the immediate orders of Major-General Cheatham bore themselves with conspicuous gallantry. One charge particularly was made under the eye of the commander-in-chief and his staff, and drew forth expressions of the most unqualified applause."

Cheatham carried into battle 3,801 officers and men. He lost 1,213 killed and wounded, nearly one-third of the command. Among the killed was noble young John Campbell, acting aide; Colonel Wickliffe and Major Welborn, Seventh Kentucky; Capts. J. B. Freeman and G. G. Persons, and Lieut. Isaac M. Jackson, Sixth Tennessee; Adjt. Robert Thomas, Ninth Tennessee; Capt.

E. M. Cheairs, One Hundred and Fifty-fourth regiment, and others not reported. Colonel Pond, commanding brigade, in his report of the battle makes honorable mention of Col. Robert F. Looney, Thirty-eighth Tennessee. Colonel Looney in his own report states that he was ordered by General Polk to charge a battery and camp on the morning of the 6th, and "I ordered the charge, which was promptly and successfully executed as to the camp and battery, and I suppose at least 1,000 prisoners."

Col. D. H. Cummings, Nineteenth Tennessee, Reserve corps, had been on detached service, with the First Tennessee, under orders from General Johnston; at 2:30 p. m. of the 6th, he reported through his adjutant, Melville Doak, to General Cheatham, and was now advanced, with the First and Ninth Tennessee under Colonel Maney, to a final attack on the only position held by the enemy in Cheatham's front. The enemy was routed and fled the field. Lieut.-Col. J. H. Miller, with his battalion of Mississippi cavalry, was ordered by Cheatham to fall upon him in his flight. This resulted in the capture of Ross' Michigan battery of six guns, with officers and men. Colonel Cummings made no report, neither did Colonel Statham, commanding brigade, but it is known that the Nineteenth was an active participant in all of the stirring events of the two days' battle, and bore an honorable part in the movement resulting in the capture of Prentiss' division. It lost 25 per cent.; among the wounded being Colonel Cummings and Major Fulkerson, and in the list of killed, Capts. Z. T. Willett and Thomas H. Walker.

Hardee, who opened the battle of the 6th at dawn of day, stated in his official report that in the first assault made by Cleburne, "Colonel Bate, Second Tennessee, fell severely wounded while bravely leading his regiment." Colonel Bate was afterward brigadier and major-general. At the same time, gallant Maj. W. R.

Doak and Capts. Joseph P. Tyree and Humphrey Bate, and Lieuts. E. R. Cryer, J. A. Akers and G. C. Fugitt, of the same regiment, were killed.

In the attack on the left center of General Hardee's line, "Brigadier-General Wood charged a battery on a gentle acclivity and captured six guns, with the Second (Bate's) and Twenty-seventh Tennessee and Sixteenth Alabama. In this attack Col. Christopher H. Williams of the Twenty-seventh Tennessee was killed. The army and the Confederacy sustained a severe loss in the death of this gallant officer." General Wood, referring in his report to that noble man and to the same charge, says: "Colonel Williams, of the Twenty-seventh Tennessee, a modest, unassuming gentleman and Christian soldier, faithful in every duty, devoted to his country, his native State, and the cause of liberty, fell and died. Lieutenant-Colonel Brown of the same regiment was seriously wounded; Captain Hearn and Lieutenant Henry were killed." Maj. Samuel T. Love of the Twenty-seventh, serving under Cheatham on the 7th, was killed in a charge on the enemy.

General Cleburne made honorable mention of Colonel Bate, and said of his regiment: "Tennessee can never mourn for a nobler band than fell this day in her Second regiment." He refers in terms of praise to Col. Matt Martin, Twenty-third Tennessee, who arrived on the field pending the action, rallied his regiment and remained with it until wounded later in the day; also to the Twenty-fourth Tennessee, which he said "won a character for steady valor, and its commander, Lieutenant-Colonel Peebles, showed that he possessed all the qualifications of a commander in the field." The Thirty-fifth Tennessee, Col. Benjamin J. Hill, was conspicuous in Cleburne's first and final charge on the enemy. General Cleburne, concluding his report, said: "I would like to do justice to the many acts of individual valor and intrepid daring during the fight. . . . Col. Ben Hill,

Fifth Tennessee; Lieutenant-Colonel Peebles, Twenty-fourth Tennessee; Lieut. R. H. Keeble, Captain Ridley and Lieutenant-Colonel Neil of the Twenty-third Tennessee, were among the number."

General Wood reported that "Col. C. A. McDaniel, of the Forty-fourth Tennessee, acted with great bravery and directed his men with good judgment until wounded on Monday." In his own report, Colonel McDaniel said that Lieutenant-Colonel Shied, of his regiment, was badly wounded on the 6th, and that "his officers and men conducted themselves gallantly and chivalrously." The Fifty-fifth Tennessee, Col. William McKoin, was in Wood's brigade, and held the right of Wood's line in the successful attack of the early morning on the enemy's camp. Of Lieut.-Col. J. M. Crews, of Crews' battalion, Colonel Trabue reported that he "behaved well." The battalion lost 55 in killed and wounded.

Forrest's regiment of cavalry added renown to the reputation made at Fort Donelson. He was in advance of Breckinridge as he moved out of Corinth, covered the flank of our army with the greatest intelligence and courage, and participated in the movement which forced from Prentiss all support on his left. On the morning of the 7th he gave notice of the advance of Nelson's division, made a dash at his skirmish line, captured 50 prisoners, and held the enemy in check until ordered by General Hardee to retire. Colonel Forrest was with Breckinridge in covering the Confederate retreat to Corinth, and in a combat with the Federal advance was severely wounded.

After the abandonment of the capital of Tennessee, Gov. Isham G. Harris determined to promote the cause of the South at any sacrifice. No effort was left untried to induce continued enlistments in the army, and every possible encouragement was offered to our people, in the districts outside of the Federal lines, to continue the production of supplies for the army. Hearty responses were made to these calls, and the spirit of resistance was stimulated by the governor's words and personal example. So soon as the army was concentrated at Corinth, he reported for service to General Johnston and was assigned to duty as aide-de-camp. He was with the general on the field of Shiloh, in the active performance of duty, and present when that great chieftain received his death-wound. In General Beauregard's report of the battle it is recorded that "Gov. Isham G. Harris, of Tennessee, went upon the field with General Johnston, was by his side when he was shot, aided him from his horse, and received him in his arms when he died. Subsequently the governor joined my staff and remained with me throughout the next day, except when carrying orders or employed in encouraging the troops of his own State, to whom he gave a conspicuous example of coolness, zeal and intrepidity."

The Forty-seventh Tennessee regiment, Col. M. R. Hill, arrived on the field on the morning of the 7th and reported to General Polk. It was poorly armed with sporting rifles and shotguns, and before going into action was conducted by a staff officer of General Cheatham to the point where Prentiss surrendered, and was at once armed with new Springfield muskets, and supplied with ammunition, from the Federal store. It turned these guns upon the enemy, and made a good record with Cheatham (attached to the brigade commanded by Col. Preston Smith) in his battle with McCook's division of Buell's army. There were three battalions of regulars in Rousseau's brigade of this division, and of Buell's loss of 3,753, the heaviest part was sustained by McCook in his combat with Cheatham.

The Tennessee artillery—Bankhead's battery, Capt. Smith P. Bankhead; Polk's battery, Capt. M. Y. Polk; Rutledge's battery, Capt. A. M. Rutledge—rendered conspicuous and valuable services. General Wood, reporting the battle of the 7th, testified that when "large masses of the enemy were coming up and pressing my right, a battery, which I afterward learned was commanded by Captain Rutledge, came up to this point and held them in check for more than half an hour." Captain Polk was seriously wounded on the 6th; Stanford's Mississippi battery served with Stewart's brigade and rendered good service.

Capt. Melancthon Smith's battery, composed of Mississippians, was attached to Stephens', afterward Maney's, brigade. It entered the service with Cheatham and was mustered into the provisional army of Tennessee. It was with Cheatham on the 6th and in his battle of the 7th with McCook, and was referred to by General Cheatham as having rendered "splendid service," Captain Smith and his officers and men being "distinguished examples of gallantry." Captain Smith was afterward major and colonel of artillery. The battery continued with Cheatham until after the battle of Nashville, under the command of Lieut. W. B. Turner, made captain after Chickamauga. On the field of Shiloh, Captain Smith exchanged his 6-pounder guns for 12-pounders captured from the enemy.

General Cheatham reported the death of Colonel Blythe and Lieutenant-Colonel Herron of Blythe's Mississippi regiment, and the wounding of Gen. Bushrod R. Johnson, Col. R. C. Tyler (afterward brigadier-general) of the Fifteenth Tennessee, and Captain Polk. Maj. R. P. Caldwell, Twelfth Tennessee, conspicuous for his bearing, reports that after the commissioned officers of companies B and G had all been killed or disabled by wounds, Private A. T. Fielder took charge of them "and led these two companies all day in the thickest part of the battle." Lieut.-Col. F. M. Stewart and Capt. W. Dawson, Twenty-second Tennessee, were severely wounded. The Thirteenth lost 137 killed and wounded, among the former, Lieuts. C. H. Whitmore and W. F. Cowan.

Col. A. W. Campbell of the Thirty-third, afterward brigadier-general, reported that Maj. Henry C. McNeill displayed "throughout a cool bravery rarely equaled." The regiment lost 123 killed and wounded. Col. Preston Smith reported that the officers and men of his brigade conducted themselves well and courageously. The One Hundred and Fifty-fourth Tennessee lost 188 in killed and wounded.

The great body of the Tennessee troops never fought better than at Shiloh. Though many of them had little training, they fought in the open field and exhibited remarkable steadiness and readiness to obey orders. While company and regimental organizations were observed, it was next to impossible to maintain brigade and division organizations. The field seemed to be full of roving staff officers begging for a regiment to support a hard-pressed part of the line. In many instances they assumed to be clothed with authority to order a regiment from its own brigade to another. The consequence was that in a few hours after the opening of the battle the efficiency of the troops was seriously affected, and some of them were made the victims of great injustice.

The retirement to Corinth was made in good order. No pursuit was made or attempted. General Beauregard reports the Confederate loss at 10,699. Swinton fixes the loss of Grant and Buell in killed, wounded and captured, at 15,000.

In May, 1862, Colonel Lowe, afterward brigadier-general, commanding the Federal forces at Forts Henry and Heiman, sent out an expedition in the direction of Paris and Dresden, for the capture of medical supplies reported to have been forwarded from Paducah to the Confederate army. The expedition, consisting of three companies of cavalry, was commanded by Maj. Carl Shaeffer de Boernstein. Col. Thomas Claiborne, Sixth Tennessee cavalry, with his own and the Seventh Tennessee, Col. W. H. Jackson, the whole force 1,250 strong, hearing of the Federal expedition, made pursuit from Paris, where he expected to meet it, to Lockridge's mill in Weakley county. Capt. John G. Ballentine, of the Seventh Tennessee, with five companies in advance, surprised the pickets, and with a yell, Ballentine's force, followed by the entire command, charged the Federals and pursued them in a hot chase for fourteen miles. The Federal force was dispersed and scattered in all directions. Six were killed, 16 wounded, and 67 captured.

In his official report Colonel Claiborne stated that Captain Ballentine was most of all conspicuous for his gallant bearing and use of his saber and pistol. He fired at and mortally wounded Maj. Carl Shaeffer de Boernstein. He engaged in a saber hand-to-hand combat with a brave fellow named Hoffman, who several times pierced the captain's coat with his saber, but was forced to yield. Captain Ballentine also received blows inflicted with a carbine, and was severely bruised.

In the autumn of 1861, Captain Ballentine had made a reconnoissance under orders from General Polk on Paducah and other points occupied by the Federal forces, and near Paducah attacked a strong outpost, having a fierce combat, in which James M. Fleming, afterward a prominent citizen of Tennessee, was wounded and permanently disabled. Fleming was the first Tennesseean wounded in the Southwest. A number of Federals were killed and wounded. In this affair Captain, afterward Colonel, Ballentine exhibited the enterprise, dash and splendid courage for which he was so often subsequently distinguished. Colonel Claiborne, of the Sixth Tennessee, after the campaign of 1862 accepted service on the staff of General Buckner, where he served with distinction. He was an officer of the United States army who had resigned as captain of mounted rifles, and offered his sword to his native State of Tennessee. He was a veteran of the war with Mexico, and was brevetted for gallantry at Cerro Gordo. Colonel Jackson was afterward brigadier-general, and a prominent commander of a cavalry division.

CHAPTER IV.

BRAGG AND KIRBY SMITH IN KENTUCKY—VICTORY AT RICHMOND—THE BATTLE OF PERRYVILLE—IMPORTANT SERVICE OF TENNESSEEANS—FRUITS OF THE CAMPAIGN.

ON June 17, 1862, Gen. Braxton Bragg was placed in command of the army, known afterward as the army of Tennessee, General Beauregard commanding the department. The army was concentrated at Tupelo, Miss., and after rest and reorganization was ready for the field. General Bragg had before him the alternatives of idleness at Tupelo, an attack on Halleck at Corinth, an attack on Buell at or about Chattanooga, or an attack on Grant in west Tennessee. The threatened advance of Buell meant the severance of the Confederate States, the East from the West. General Bragg, seeing this danger, determined, he said, "to move to Chattanooga, and drive the enemy from our important country in western Alabama, middle Tennessee and Kentucky."

A small division of troops was sent from Tupelo to the department of East Tennessee, then commanded by Maj.-Gen. E. Kirby Smith, and later, Smith was further reinforced by the brigades of P. R. Cleburne and Preston Smith. On the 16th of August, 1862, the army of Kentucky, commanded by Maj.-Gen. Kirby Smith, crossed the Cumberland mountains into the State of Kentucky; and on the 27th and 28th of August, General Bragg crossed the Tennessee river, after which the army of Tennessee took up its march over Walden's ridge and the Cumberland mountains for middle Tennessee. It was found upon reaching that territory that the main forces of the Federal army had been concentrated at Nashville, which was strongly fortified. A demonstration was made against that point, and Bragg's army was thrown rapidly to Glasgow, Ky., reaching there on the 13th of September.

In the meantime, on the 30th of August, General Smith had met the Federal forces at Richmond, Ky., and won one of the most decisive victories of the war. The Federal troops were commanded by Brig.-Gen. M. D. Manson until 2 p. m., when Maj.-Gen. William Nelson reached the field and took command. According to General Manson, "the Union troops did not exceed 6,500," and General Smith reported his whole force at 5,000 officers and men.

The attack was made and resisted with energy and vigor, so much so that Smith believed that he had encountered 10,000 men, and Manson was confident that he was beaten by an army of veterans 16,000 strong. General Nelson reported, under date of 31st of August, that he "arrived on the field three miles south of Richmond, at 2 p. m., and found the command in a disorganized retreat, or rather a rout. With great exertion I rallied about 2,200 men, moved them to a strong position, where I was confident I could hold them in check until night, and then resume the retreat. The enemy attacked in front and on both flanks simultaneously with vigor. Our troops stood about three rounds when, struck by a panic, they fled in disorder. I was left with my staff almost alone.' General Nelson was wounded in this combat and General Manson captured. The return of casualties in the United States forces shows that 206 officers and men were killed, 844 wounded, and 4,303 captured.

Major-General Smith, in his report of the battle, said that his leading division under General Cleburne found the enemy in a fine position six miles from Richmond. Without waiting for support, Cleburne commenced the action. A brigade under Gen. Thomas J. Churchill was moved up to turn the enemy's right. While he was in motion, the enemy made a bold and well-conducted attempt to turn Cleburne's right. This was admirably foiled by the firmness of Preston Smith's brigade, Cleburne's division, which repulsed the enemy with great slaughter. In this affair, General Cleburne was badly wounded, and the command of the division devolved on Preston Smith, Col. A. J. Vaughan, Jr., taking command of the brigade. The Federal troops fell back and took position two miles to the rear, where Churchill with McCray's brigade, from Texas and Arkansas, assailed their line and completely routed it, just as the cheers of Preston Smith's division announced its presence on the field.

Manson fell back two miles, and then it was that Major-General Nelson assumed command of the Federal forces. He formed his line of defense in front of Richmond. The gallant Churchill again led the advance with McNair's brigade and attacked with great fury. In the meanwhile Preston Smith, bringing up his division at a double-quick, formed with wonderful precision and rapidity in front of the enemy's center and left. Almost without waiting for orders, his men advanced and drove the opposing forces from the field in great confusion. Gen. Kirby Smith issued a congratulatory order to his troops, and said in its concluding paragraph: "To-morrow being Sunday, the General desires that the troops shall assemble and, under their several chaplains, shall return thanks to Almighty God, to whose mercy and goodness these victories are due."

The cavalry, under Col. J. S. Scott, of the First Louisiana, consisted of his own regiment, the Third Tennessee, Col. J. W. Starnes; the First Georgia, Col. J. J. Morrison; and the Buckner Guards, one company, Captain Montgomery; the whole numbering 850 men. This command was active and efficient, and having passed to the rear of the enemy, captured the largest part of the prisoners taken.

The infantry regiments of General Smith's little army

were from Arkansas, Texas and Tennessee. The Tennesseeans were in Cleburne's division—the Second (Walker's), Lieut.-Col. J. A. Butler commanding; Thirty-fifth, Lieutenant-Colonel Smith; and Forty-eighth, Col. Geo. H. Nixon, in the brigade commanded by Col. B. J. Hill, of the Thirty-fifth; and the One Hundred and Fifty-fourth (senior), Col. Edward Fitzgerald; Thirteenth, Col. A. J. Vaughan, Jr.; Twelfth and Forty-seventh, Col. L. P. McMurray, in the brigade commanded by Col. Preston Smith, and later by Colonel Vaughan. The Confederate forces lost 78 killed and 372 wounded. Among the latter were Col. Geo. H. Nixon, Forty-eighth, and Col. L. P. McMurray, Twelfth and Forty-seventh; among the killed, Lieut.-Col. J. A. Butler, Second Tennessee, who fell gallantly leading his regiment in the last charge before Richmond, and Col. Edward Fitzgerald, One Hundred and Fifty-fourth regiment, who fell in the first engagement at the head of his command. Col. Preston Smith characterized the latter as an officer diligent in executing the orders of his superior, and as a leader in battle ever to be found in the foremost ranks. Young, full of military ardor, he died too soon for his country. Colonel Smith also referred in handsome terms to Col. B. J. Hill, Col. A. J. Vaughn, and to Lieut.-Col. C. J. Polignac; Col. B. J. Hill said of the latter that he "seized the colors of the Thirty-fifth Tennessee, bearing the flag triumphantly through the thickest of the fight." Colonel Polignac was afterward made a brigadier-general. He was a descendant of Charles X of France, and after the war between the States was a general of division in the army of his native country. Capt. J. J. Newsom, Second Tennessee, was distinguished in command of sharpshooters, and was seriously wounded. Captain Yancey, of the same regiment, led the skirmish line of Hill's brigade in the final conflict.

The immediate fruits of the victory were 4,303 prisoners, 9 pieces of artillery, 10,000 stand of small-arms and large quantities of supplies. After one day of rest, Major-General Smith pursued his advance, and on the 2d of September occupied Lexington, Ky.

Waiting two days at Glasgow, General Bragg advanced with the intention of forming a junction with Major-General Smith. The advance brigade under Brigadier-General Chalmers (says General Bragg) was thrown forward in the direction of Munfordville to cut the railroad and observe the enemy, but was led forward indiscreetly to attack a superior force strongly fortified. After a desperate fight, General Chalmers was repulsed with a loss of 300 killed and wounded; whereupon General Bragg moved forward with his whole command, surrounded the place, and received its unconditional surrender without firing a gun; 4,267 prisoners, an equal number of small-arms, 10 pieces of artillery, with munitions and supplies, were captured.

The offer of battle was made to the Federal army under General Buell, now advancing on Bragg's rear, with a force nearly double that of the Confederates, but Buell avoided the conflict, and Bragg moved on to Bardstown, where subsistence for the army could be obtained. There, General Polk was left in command, while General Bragg joined Major-General Smith at Lexington. In the meantime Buell had reached Louisville, and began his movement toward Perryville, and on October 7th information was received that Hardee was being pressed by the enemy at that point. At once Cheatham, now at Harrodsburg, was ordered forward.

Our forces near Perryville consisted of three divisions of infantry, 14,500 men, and two small brigades of cavalry, 1,500 strong. To this, the enemy at first opposed Gilbert's corps of 18,000. General Bragg expected our forces to attack at daylight, and General Buell in his report said, "I had somewhat expected an attack early in the morning on Gilbert's corps while it was isolated;" but the action was delayed until noon of the 8th, when a second corps of the enemy, McCook's, 18,000 strong, had reached the field, and at the close of the day Crittenden's corps was in action. It is stated in the official report of General Buell that "the effective force which advanced on Perryville on the 7th and 8th under my command, was about 58,000 infantry, artillery and cavalry."

Of General Polk's right wing of the Confederate army but one division, the Tennessee division, under Maj.-Gen. B. F. Cheatham, was present. General Polk being in immediate command of the army until the arrival of General Bragg, General Cheatham was in command of the right wing, Brig.-Gen. Daniel S. Donelson taking temporary command of his division.

Cheatham's division was almost exclusively Tennesseeans, the First brigade (Donelson's), temporarily commanded by Col. John H. Savage, comprising the Eighth regiment, Col. W. L. Moore; Fifteenth, Col. R. C. Tyler; Sixteenth, Col. John H. Savage; Thirty-eighth, Col. John C. Carter; Fifty-first, Col. John Chester; and Capt. W. W. Carnes' battery. The Second brigade, commanded by A. P. Stewart, included the Fourth Tennessee, Col. O. F. Strahl; Fifth, Col. C. D. Venable; Twenty-fourth, Lieut.-Col. H. L. W. Bratton; Thirty-fourth, Col. E. E. Tansil; Thirty-third, Col. W. P. Jones. The Third brigade, Maney's, had one Georgia regiment in addition to the First Tennessee, Col. H. R. Feild; Sixth, Col. George C. Porter; Ninth, Lieut.-Col. John W. Buford; Twenty-seventh, Lieut.-Col. W. Frierson. The Fourth brigade, Gen. Preston Smith, was detached, but the Thirteenth Tennessee, Colonel Vaughan, appears to have been somewhat engaged.

General Hardee's wing comprised the divisions of Patton Anderson and S. B. Buckner. Tennessee was represented in Col. Samuel Powell's brigade of Anderson's division, by Powell's regiment, the Twenty-ninth; by the Second in Cleburne's brigade of Buckner's division; and in the same division by the Tennessee brigade of Bushrod

R. Johnson, comprising the Fifth Confederate, Col. J. A. Smith; Seventeenth, Col. A. S. Marks; Twenty-third, Lieut.-Col. R. H. Keeble; Twenty-fifth, Col. John M. Hughs; Twenty-seventh, Col. Moses White; Forty-fourth, Col. John S. Fulton. The Fourth cavalry was with Wharton.

Skirmishing began at 10 a. m. of the 8th, and soon Liddell's brigade, of Buckner's division, was hotly engaged, but was withdrawn to our main line. Cheatham was moved from left to right, with Wharton's cavalry on his right, to meet a movement of the enemy. General Bragg now (at 1 o'clock) ordered the advance of his whole command. Wharton charged the left of the enemy with great fury, rushing over stone walls and ravines, and driving the opposing infantry several hundred yards. Wharton was followed by Cheatham, with the brigades of Donelson, Stewart and Maney, who mounted the steep and difficult cliffs of Chaplin river and moved forward without halt. They were met by a storm of shot and shell and heavy masses of infantry, but our brave fellows pushed on, driving the enemy before them and capturing three of his batteries. The enemy was pushed back a mile, and his three lines crowded into one. General Polk declared that this charge of the Tennessee brigades was one of the most heroic and brilliant of the war, and considering the disparity of the troops engaged, the strength of the enemy's position, the steadiness with which they endured the havoc made in their ranks, the firmness with which they moved upon the opposing masses, it would compare favorably with the most brilliant achievements of historic valor. In this charge Gen. J. S. Jackson, commanding a division of the Federal army, was killed among the guns of one of the captured batteries. It appears from the report of General Buell that General McCook, against whose corps Cheatham made his attack, "represented that his corps was very much crippled, the division of General Jackson having, in fact, almost disappeared as a body." McCook stated that "when Terrill's brigade of Jackson's division gave way, seven guns of Parsons' eight-gun battery fell into the hands of the enemy; at 6 p. m., four of the guns of Harris' Nineteenth Indiana also fell into the hands of the enemy." General Terrill was among the killed.

So conspicuous was the part of Cheatham's brigades, that when General Bragg issued his general order authorizing the several commands engaged in the battle at Perryville to inscribe the name of that field on their colors, he said: "The corps of Cheatham's division, which made the gallant and desperate charge resulting in the capture of three of the enemy's batteries, will, in addition to the name, place the cross-cannon inverted." The guns of Carnes' and Turner's batteries were served with coolness and courage, and were important factors in the success of Cheatham's division.

But Cheatham paid dearly for his success. Donelson's brigade sustained a loss of 347 killed and wounded; the Sixteenth under Colonel Savage losing 199, more than half the casualties of the brigade. Among the killed was Capt. J. B. Vance. General Cheatham said of the gallant Savage that "in battle he had an instinctive knowledge of the point of difficulty and danger and went to it." Stewart's brigade lost 428 killed and wounded; Maney's brigade, 687.

The First Tennessee lost 179 killed and wounded. Among its dead was the gallant Lieut.-Col. John Patterson. Colonel Feild, one of the most dashing and reliable soldiers of Tennessee, reported that after deploying the regiment to the extreme right, it advanced to the charge with close, compact ranks, killing all the horses and men of the battery in his front, and driving its support away. Through a misapprehension of orders the regiment fell back, and the enemy returned to the guns, but Feild reformed and led the regiment up the hill without support, under a heavy fire of musketry, and took the guns of the battery a second time. At this point the First lost 40 or 50 officers and men.

The Sixth Tennessee, always conspicuous in battle, sustained a loss of 91. Colonel Porter said that in assaulting McCook's line, Capt. Thomas B. Rains and Lieuts. Ed. Seabrook, C. N. Carter and N. A. Butler were killed. The color-bearer, John Andrews, being badly wounded, the colors were seized by John Ayeres, one of the color squad, who was in a few moments killed A. W. Pegues next caught up the flag, but was very soon shot in three places and disabled. Ed. Quinn, private Company H, then bore them in advance of the regiment across the field, where he too was killed.

The Ninth Tennessee suffered a loss of 154. Among the wounded were the gallant Col. John W. Buford, Capts. J. W. Hubbard, C. B. Simonton, H. C. Irby, J. L. Hall and H. A. Rogers; and among the dead were Capt. J. M. McDonald, Lieuts. P. J. Fitzpatrick, W. T. Sanler, James I. Hall, J. M. Mathews and D. M. Bell. After the fall of Colonel Buford the command of the regiment devolved on Maj. George W. Kelsoe, who led it skillfully and courageously.

The Twenty-seventh was commanded by Lieutenant-Colonel Frierson until disabled, when he was succeeded by Maj. A. C. Allen. The story of the Twenty-seventh is the same as that of all the regiments of this brigade—duty well and gallantly performed by officers and men. Colonel Frierson named with honor his color-bearer, Private John Olive. The regiment had a roll of killed and wounded numbering 108. Capt. John M. Taylor and Lieut. E. E. Pate were reported mortally wounded, but Captain Taylor recovered, after long suffering, and has been deservedly honored by his countrymen in civil life.

The Fourth regiment was superb in discipline and training. It lost nearly one-third of those present for duty. It was noted for the courage and steadiness always displayed; when McCook's line was driven back this regiment stacked arms. It was armed with new Enfield rifles abandoned by the Federal troops, and used them in the advance immediately made. Capt. John B. Turner, Lieut. W. O. Capers and Hugh Banks were among the killed.

The Fifth sustained the credit won at Shiloh. Colonel Venable was seriously injured by a fall from his horse, but never left his post. Lieut.-Col. W. C. Suor had his horse killed, but served gallantly on foot. The gallant Capts. John W. Harris, John T. Irwin and James P. Cooper, Lieuts. George C. Kemp, Sam Kirkpatrick and Coleman Wilson, and Color-Bearer J. B. Jones were seriously wounded. Captain Cooper lost 20 men killed and wounded out of 34 present. And there were many brave men killed and wounded whose names are not reported. Private Haygood of the Fifth, shot through the breast with an iron ramrod, drew it out himself. Another private soldier, Tip Allen, was shot in the neck with a minie ball, which in a few minutes was ejected through his mouth. Both these soldiers marched from the field to Knoxville, Tenn.

The Fifth Confederate lost 45 killed and wounded; the Seventeenth, 24. The Twenty-third suffered a loss of 52 killed and wounded out of a total of 201, among the killed being Capt. W. A. Ott. The Twenty-fifth had a loss of 8; the Thirty-seventh, of 39; and the Forty-fourth lost 43. The Federal forces in front of these regiments (Bushrod Johnson's brigade) were Ohio, Kentucky and Indiana men, commanded by the accomplished Col. Wm. H. Lytle, of Ohio. He was wounded and captured by a soldier of Johnson's brigade. On his recovery and exchange, being made a brigadier-general, he fell at Chickamauga.

The left of the Confederate line, under General Hardee, was held by the brigades of Gen. D. W. Adams and Col. Sam Powell (wounded in action). Bushrod Johnson's brigade gallantly led the advance supported by Cleburne.

The brigades of John C. Brown (wounded in action) and Jones, of Anderson's division, and S. A. M. Wood were on the left of Cheatham. Liddell's brigade was in reserve, until toward the close of the day it went to the support of Cheatham. Forming on his extreme right, Liddell took the enemy in flank, and inflicted great slaughter upon the left of Rousseau's division.

The cavalry commanded by Gens. Joseph Wheeler and John A. Wharton rendered most conspicuous service. The charges led by General Wheeler on the left, and by Wharton on the right, were as gallant and effective as any made during the war.

General Buell's losses were, killed, wounded and missing, 4,241, and the total loss of Bragg's army was 3,212. This loss attests the severity of the battle. General McCook, of the Federal army, referred to it in his report as the "bloodiest battle of modern times, for the number of troops engaged on our side."

General Bragg, ascertaining that Buell was heavily reinforced during the night, retired the next morning to Harrodsburg, where he was joined by Major-General Smith, and thence to Bryantsville, where he remained until the 13th, affording ample time to Buell to attack. Instead of that, the latter occupied himself in destroying mills from which General Bragg had been drawing breadstuffs.

The Confederate army was not strong enough for an offensive campaign, and disappointed in recruiting his strength in Kentucky, General Bragg retired by way of Cumberland Gap to middle Tennessee. The army had on this campaign captured more than 12,000 prisoners (Gen. John Morgan captured 2,000 additional, and General Forrest, operating in Tennessee, over 7,000), 30 pieces of artillery, 17,000 small-arms, with ammunition, wagons, teams, and an immense amount of supplies and clothing for the troops. Cumberland Gap was ours, north Alabama and middle Tennessee had been recovered, and

General Bragg was in front of Nashville, with his army in good form, and stronger than when the campaign began. Gen. Kirby Smith was in undisputed possession of east Tennessee. He had forced the evacuation of Cumberland Gap, had won the victory at Richmond, Ky., and had traversed the State of Kentucky without let or hindrance, in spite of the grand strategy of General Halleck, commander-in-chief of the armies of the United States in the Southwest, who said in a dispatch to Buell, dated Corinth, June 11, 1862: "Smith must abandon east Tennessee or be captured."

On the 23d of October, General Bragg ordered Lieutenant-General Polk to proceed with his command to Murfreesboro, Tenn.

CHAPTER V.

THE BATTLE OF MURFREESBORO—TENNESSEE COMMANDS ENGAGED—OPERATIONS OF THE CAVALRY—McCOWN OPENS THE BATTLE—HEROIC DEEDS OF THE TENNESSEE BRIGADES—SEVERE LOSSES—CHEATHAM AND HIS DIVISION.

ON the 20th of November, 1862, the Confederate army of Tennessee was constituted under Gen. Braxton Bragg, consisting of the army corps of Lieut.-Gen. E. Kirby Smith, Lieut.-Gen. Leonidas Polk and Lieut.-Gen. W. J. Hardee.

At the conclusion of the campaign in Kentucky, Major-General Buell, the Federal commander, was relieved, and Maj.-Gen. W. S. Rosecrans assigned to the command of the army of the Cumberland.

The Federal army occupied Nashville, and after months of preparation General Rosecrans began his advance on the 26th of December. The Confederate center was at Murfreesboro under General Polk, the right wing at Readyville under Maj.-Gen. John P. McCown, the left at Triune and Eagleville under General Hardee. The right and left were withdrawn, and the forces concentrated at Murfreesboro ready to receive the attack made by Rosecrans. Rosecrans' plan of movement was for Major-General McCook with three divisions to advance by Triune, Maj.-Gen. George H. Thomas to advance on his right with two divisions, Major-General Crittenden with three divisions to move directly on Murfreesboro. At 3 o'clock p. m. of the 30th, General Palmer, in advance, sent back a signal message that he "was in sight of Murfreesboro, and that the enemy were running." An order was promptly sent forward to "occupy Murfreesboro."

General Cheatham's division was yet composed of the brigades commanded by Gens. Daniel S. Donelson, Alex. P. Stewart, George P. Maney and Preston Smith. This division, with that of Maj.-Gen. Jones M. Withers, constituted Polk's corps.

The Sixteenth Tennessee, Col. John H. Savage; the Thirty-eighth, Col. John C. Carter; the Eighth, Col. W. L. Moore; the Fifty-first, Col. John Chester; the Eighty-fourth, Col. S. S. Stanton, and Carnes' battery, constituted Donelson's brigade.

The Fourth and Fifth Tennessee consolidated, Col. O. F. Strahl; the Twenty-fourth, Col. H. L. W. Bratton; the Nineteenth, Col. F. M. Walker; the Thirty-first and Thirty-third consolidated, Col. E. E. Tansil, and Stanford's Mississippi battery, constituted Stewart's brigade.

The First and Twenty-seventh Tennessee consolidated, Col. H. R. Feild; the Fourth (Confederate), Col. J. A. McMurray; the Sixth and Ninth consolidated, Col. C. S. Hurt, Capt. Frank Maney's sharpshooters, and Turner's Mississippi battery, constituted Maney's brigade.

The One Hundred and Fifty-fourth (senior) Tennessee regiment, Lieut.-Col. M. Magevney, Jr.; the Thirteenth, Col. A. J. Vaughan; the Twelfth, Maj. J. N. Wyatt; the Forty-seventh, Capt. W. M. Watkins; the Twenty-ninth, Maj. J. B. Johnson; the Ninth Texas, Col. W. H. Young; Allin's Tennessee sharpshooters, Lieut. J. R. J. Creighton, and the Tennessee battery of Capt. W. L. Scott, constituted Smith's brigade, commanded during the battle by Col. A. J. Vaughan, Lieut.-Col. W. E. Morgan commanding the Thirteenth regiment.

Hardee's corps included the divisions of Maj.-Gens. John C. Breckinridge, P. R. Cleburne and J. P. McCown. The Eleventh Tennessee, Col. George W. Gordon, was a part of the command of Brig.-Gen. James E. Rains, McCown's division. Brig.-Gen. Gideon J. Pillow was assigned to the command of Col. J. B. Palmer's Second brigade of Breckinridge's division, on the afternoon of the 2d of January; it was composed of the Eighteenth Tennessee, Col. J. B. Palmer; the Twenty-sixth, Col. John M. Lillard; the Forty-fifth, Col. A. Searcy; the Twenty-eighth, Col. P. D. Cunningham, and Moses' battery. (The Thirty-second Tennessee, Col. Ed. C. Cook, of this brigade, was on detached service.)

The Twentieth Tennessee regiment, Col. T. B. Smith, and the Tennessee battery of Capt. E. E. Wright were in Gen. William Preston's brigade of Breckinridge's division. The Second Tennessee, Col. W. D. Robinson; Thirty-fifth, Col. B. J. Hill; Fifth (Confederate), Col. J. A. Smith, constituted a part of the brigade under Gen. Lucius E. Polk, Cleburne's division. The brigade of Gen. Bushrod R. Johnson, Cleburne's division, included the Thirty-seventh Tennessee, Col. Moses White; Forty-fourth, Col. John S. Fulton; Twenty-fifth, Col. John M. Hughs; Seventeenth, Col. A. S. Marks; Twenty-third, Lieut.-Col. R. H. Keeble.

The First Tennessee cavalry, Col. James E. Carter, and the Tennessee battalions of Maj. DeWitt C. Douglass and Maj. D. W. Holman were part of Wheeler's brigade of the cavalry division commanded by Gen. Joseph Wheeler. The Second cavalry, Col. H. M. Ashby; Fourth, Col. Baxter Smith; Murray's Tennessee cavalry, Maj. W. S. Bledsoe; Wharton's escort company, Capt. Paul F. Anderson, and the battery of Capt. B. F. White, Jr., were the Tennessee commands in the cavalry brigade of Gen. John A. Wharton.

Rosecrans consumed four days in advancing a distance of twenty miles over macadamized roads, his movements being delayed and embarrassed by the watchfulness of the cavalry commanded by Generals Wheeler and Wharton. On the 26th, Wheeler engaged Rosecrans during the entire day, falling back only three miles, and on the 28th and 29th he killed and wounded large numbers, his own command sustaining slight loss. At midnight of the 29th, General Wheeler, reinforced by Col. James E. Carter, First Tennessee cavalry, was ordered to the rear of the enemy. He reported that at daylight he met near Jefferson a brigade train which he took and destroyed, capturing 50 prisoners; at Lavergne attacked and captured 700 prisoners and destroyed immense trains amounting to many hundred thousand dollars in value; at Rock Springs captured and destroyed another large train; at Nolensville captured large trains, stores and arms, and 300 prisoners; after which he proceeded to the left of the Confederate army, thus making a compass of the enemy's rear.

At the dawn of day, December 31st, Major-General McCown (Tennessee) opened the battle of Murfreesboro with his division, composed of Ector's, McNair's and Rains' brigades. A volley was delivered after advancing for several hundred yards under fire, and with fixed bayonets the position and batteries of the enemy were taken, and the officer in command, Brigadier-General Willich, was captured. McCown, continuing his advance, supported by Cleburne's division, reached a point near the Wilkinson road, where, finding the enemy strongly posted, the division was pushed forward and after a fierce struggle again routed the forces opposing. It was at this point that Brig.-Gen. James E. Rains (Tennessee) fell, shot through the heart. General McCown reported that the fall of this gallant officer and accomplished gentleman threw his brigade into confusion. The division, after driving the enemy two miles, was ordered to retire a short distance for reformation; about the same time the gallant Col. G. W. Gordon, Eleventh Tennessee, afterward brigadier-general, fell dangerously wounded.

Cleburne, advancing with his division, composed of L. E. Polk's, Bushrod Johnson's, St. John Liddell's and S. A. M. Wood's brigades, soon found himself in the front line, skirmishing over broken ground filled with limestone boulders and cedar bushes to such an extent that his advance was attended with much difficulty, and Polk's and Johnson's brigades had to move more than once by the flank. At the distance of three-quarters of a mile in advance of his bivouac of the previous night, he encountered the enemy's line of battle, established behind a fence and natural breastworks of limestone. The fight was short and bloody, lasting about twenty-five minutes, when the enemy gave way and fell back on his second line, which was again assaulted. This soon yielded and both lines, pressed into one, left the field, Liddell capturing two rifled cannon, which were immediately turned upon the enemy.

The Seventeenth Tennessee, Col. A. S. Marks, captured a battery of four guns. When the regiment came in sight of it, Colonel Marks said, "Boys, do you see that battery? It is ours, is it not?" The regiment rushed upon it, drove back its support, and took the guns, but the gallant colonel fell, maimed for life. Cleburne mentioned him as "one of the best officers in the division." Others wounded in Johnson's brigade were Maj. H. C. Ewing, Forty-seventh, mortally; Col. Moses White and Lieut.-Col. R. D. Frayser, Thirty-seventh, and Col. J. M. Hughs, Twenty-fifth.

Bushrod Johnson's brigade and Liddell's were already the chief sufferers. The latter, now in advance, was reinforced by Johnson in double-quick time, and taking position behind a fence and ledge of rocks, a battery of four Parrott guns was silenced and captured, and after a conflict of twenty minutes the enemy's force was routed. But, observing the supporting troops on the right falling back without apparent cause, Johnson's brigade retired in confusion without orders. The loss of life in Johnson's front was enormous, many lying side by side in the position assumed to await the approach of the Confederates, while large numbers fell as they turned to retreat. It was in this combat that Capt. M. R. Allen,

Twenty-third, was mortally wounded, and Capt. F. M. Orr, Seventeenth, Lieuts. Simpson Isom, Twenty-fifth, and J. J. Hill, Forty-fourth, were killed, and Maj. J. T. McReynolds, the last field officer on duty, of the Thirty-seventh, was mortally wounded.

Polk's brigade on the right advanced with Johnson's and shared its fortunes. Their gallant commanders could always be trusted for promptness, courage and intelligence on the battlefield. Col. B. J. Hill, Thirty-fifth, on Polk's right, was first engaged when advancing across the Franklin dirt road. The brigade, aided by Calvert's battery, drove the enemy in confusion, pursuing to a point where he had reformed, then again assailing and forcing back the Federals in disorder. A third successful assault was made with the brigades of Wood and Johnson. Yet again going forward with Liddell's and Johnson's brigades, and Preston Smith's, Col. A. J. Vaughan commanding, the enemy was found posted on the railroad near the Nashville turnpike, with several batteries of artillery. In a few moments the new Federal line was broken and forced back to cedar brakes in its rear, the Confederates pursuing. Here Adjt. F. T. Smith, Fifth Confederate, was badly wounded at the moment he was cheering his men with the colors of the regiment in his hand.

This point, thought Brigadier-General Polk, was the key to the Federal position. If Confederate reinforcements had arrived when this last successful assault was made at 2 p. m., the enemy's line of communication would have been cut, and a position in the rear of Rosecrans secured. Capt. C. P. Moore and Lieut. J. L. Gifford, of the Second, were killed. General Polk names with honor Col. W. D. Robinson and Lieut.-Col. W. J. Hale, Second; Maj. R. J. Person, Fifth Confederate; and recommended promotion for Col. J. A. Smith and Col. B. J. Hill, which was in time accorded to both.

Gen. Bushrod Johnson made honorable mention of Col

A. S. Marks and Lieut.-Col. W. W. Floyd, Seventeenth; Lieut.-Col. R. H. Keeble, Twenty-third; Col. John S. Fulton and Lieut.-Col. John L. McEwen, Jr., Forty-fourth; Capt. Putnam Darden, of Darden's battery; Capts. R. B. Snowden, assistant adjutant-general, twice wounded; John Overton, volunteer aide, wounded; Lieut. George H. Smith, wounded; and Capt. Jo. H. Vanleer, volunteer aide, who, after having his horse disabled, fought in the ranks with a rifle.

General Cleburne called particular attention to the gallant conduct of Sergt. William N. Cameron, color-bearer of the Twenty-fifth regiment, who in the last combat advanced in front of his regiment so far that when it fell back he was unable to follow and was captured. He tore the flag from the staff, concealed it upon his person, and made his escape at Bowling Green, Ky., bringing back with him the colors of his regiment.

Colonel Palmer's brigade occupied the left center in Breckinridge's line of battle. On Wednesday morning, Palmer, learning that there were Federal troops in his front, ordered his skirmishers under Capt. G. H. Love to advance, assigning Capt. David H. C. Spence of his staff to direct their operations. Uniting with a detachment of Pegram's cavalry, Captain Spence captured 18 wagons and 170 prisoners without sustaining loss. At noon of the same day, this brigade, with Preston's, under orders from General Breckinridge, moved across Stone's river to the left wing of the army, then hotly engaged, and assailed at once the enemy's position just west of the Cowan house, which was carried after a stout resistance. The brigade charged across an open field for a distance of 400 yards, under a heavy musketry and artillery fire. It was during this advance that the Twentieth Tennessee, Preston's brigade, passing to the right of the Cowan house, engaged the enemy with vigor, captured 25 prisoners and cleared the woods in front. The regiment sustained serious losses, and Col. Thomas B. Smith, referred to by General Preston as "a brave and skillful officer," was severely wounded.

With Polk's corps, the battle of Murfreesboro opened at sunset on the 30th of December. Robertson's Florida battery was placed in the Triune road, supported by the One Hundred and Fifty-fourth Tennessee and two Alabama regiments of Loomis' brigade, Withers' division. Soon after going into position the battery was assailed by three Federal regiments, which were repulsed, the battery and its supports sustaining serious losses. Darkness suspended hostilities.

At daylight on the 31st the attack made by McCown on the extreme left was taken up by Loomis' brigade, acting under orders of General Cheatham; it having been agreed on account of the character of the country and the formation of the corps that the brigades of Manigault and Loomis should receive orders from General Cheatham, and the brigades of Donelson and Stewart should be under the control of General Withers.

The enemy was 300 yards in front of Loomis as he advanced to the attack, which was vigorously made; but on reaching the cedar woods, he found superior numbers and was forced to retire to his original position. The supporting brigade (Preston Smith's), under Col. A. J. Vaughan, repeated the attack over the same ground, driving the enemy from his battery, so fatal to Loomis, and capturing two of his guns; but, receiving an enfilading fire of artillery and musketry from his right, Vaughn was content to hold what he had so bravely won. He was in good order and was again sent forward by Cheatham. In the attack by Colonel Loomis he was badly wounded, the command of his brigade devolving upon Col. J. G. Coltart; and in the desperate charge made by Colonel Vaughan, Lieut.-Col. W. E. Morgan and Maj. Peter H. Cole (Thirteenth) were mortally wounded.

Manigault, advancing simultaneously with Loomis, was compelled to fall back by the latter's retirement, and then reforming, gallantly advanced the second time, but was forced back to his original position. Then forming on the right of Maney's brigade, the two advanced, led by Cheatham, toward the Wilkinson road, near the Harding place, and were opened upon by two of the enemy's batteries, one on Manigault's right on the west side of the road, the other on the east side. Turner's battery, placed in position by General Maney near a brick kiln, opened on the battery on the east and soon silenced it. Uniting with Colonel Vaughn, commanding Smith's brigade, the Wilkinson road was crossed, the enemy's battery on the right was silenced, its support driven away and the guns abandoned.

At this point the advancing line found the brigade of Gen. Alex. P. Stewart in a hot fight, the result of which was the capture of three guns of the First Missouri battery. In the assault, Col. H. L. W. Bratton, the gallant commander of the Twenty-fourth, was killed.

Vaughan was now ordered by General Cheatham to advance with Cleburne's division, and the enemy was driven from two of his guns and fell back to the Nashville road, where he was heavily reinforced. Vaughan's brigade, flushed with victory and rushing forward with great spirit, outstripped the force on the right, when suddenly it was subjected to a heavy enfilading fire. He retired in order, a short distance, to the Wilkinson road, where, unmolested by the enemy, he bivouacked for the night, before doing so having driven the enemy from another battery, which he was unable to bring off. Vaughan led his brigade with skill and judgment and with characteristic gallantry, was ably supported by his regimental officers, and his veteran soldiers were always reliable. He reported that "when Color-Bearer Quinn, a gallant soldier of the One Hundred and Fifty-fourth Tennessee, was killed, Maj. J. W. Dawson snatched the broken staff and carried it with the colors at the head of the regiment during the fight." Likewise Colonel

Young, of the Ninth Texas, seized the flag of his regiment and carried it through one of the most desperate charges made by the brigade. The brigade lost 705 officers and men out of a total present of 1,813. Among the killed were Lieuts. J. S. Fielder and J. H. Patterson, Twelfth Tennessee; Capt. J. H. Sinclair, Forty-seventh; Lieut.-Col. C. S. Hall, One Hundred and Fifty-fourth; Lieuts. A. M. Burch and J. R. J. Creighton, Allin's sharpshooters. The gallant Capt. John R. Duncan, Twelfth, was mortally wounded.

After the capture of the guns of the First Missouri battery, General Stewart drove the enemy steadily before him. While moving through the cedar forest the brigade of Gen. John K. Jackson came up, and the Fifth Georgia on his right, uniting with the Fourth and Fifth Tennessee, advanced beyond the general line and delivered a heavy and well-sustained fire upon the retreating ranks of the enemy, doing great execution. Referring to the assault made on the Federal line, Maj.-Gen. Withers says that at the critical moment, "Brig.-Gen. A. P. Stewart was ordered forward to the support. In splendid order and with a cheer this fine brigade moved forward under its gallant and accomplished commander, attacked and drove back the enemy, and completed the rout of his first line and the capture of his batteries." At this point the reserve artillery, consisting of three or four batteries of the enemy, opened on Stewart and exposed his brigade to a terrific fire of shell and canister, and without artillery himself, he could make no further advance.

In Stewart's last assault, Lieut.-Col. W. B. Ross, formerly of the Second (Walker's) Tennessee, acting aide to General Stewart, was mortally wounded; Lieut. J. P. Ferguson, Fourth and Fifth; Capt. S. J. Frazier and Lieut. S. G. Abernathy, Nineteenth; Capt. Jesse Irwin and Lieuts. J. B. Arnold and J. S. Hardison, Twenty-fourth; Lieut. W. P. Hutcheson, Thirty-first and Thirty-third, and Lieut. A. A. Hardin, Stanford's battery, were killed; and Lieut.-Col. J. A. Wilson and Adjt. H. W. Mott, Twenty-fourth; Maj. R. A. Jarnigan, Nineteenth, and Capt. T. H. Francis, Fourth, were wounded. Lieut.-Col. Andrew J. Keller, of the Fourth, was very sick, but in spite of his disability was at his post. Stewart lost one-fourth of his brigade; the Nineteenth, under gallant Frank Walker, suffered more heavily than any other regiment. Colonel Walker reported the brave conduct of Orderly-Sergt. Joseph Thompson, Company I, who, after the brigade had halted, advanced far into the field and captured two prisoners.

Donelson's brigade, advanced as a support to Chalmers of Withers' division, was under fire of shot and shell until nightfall, and sustained losses in killed and wounded in every part of the field of battle early in the action. When General Chalmers was wounded, causing his brigade to fall back in confusion, Donelson moved up, under heavy fire, to its place in the front line. Reaching the Cowan house, the brigade separated, the Sixteenth and three companies of the Fifty-first being forced to the right because of the picket fencing. This detachment, under the gallant Col. John H. Savage, advanced upon the enemy until checked by three batteries with heavy infantry supports, and then unable to advance and determined not to retire, the veteran Savage deployed his command as skirmishers, and held his ground against great odds for three hours, and until reinforced by Adams' brigade. Adams made a spirited attack but did not move the enemy; subsequently, this position was assaulted by Preston's brigade with the same result; the two bivouacked for the night close upon the Federal position. If the attack had been a combined one, the result might have been disastrous to the enemy. In this combat the Sixteenth lost Lieut.-Col. L. N. Savage, mortally wounded, Capt. D. C. Spurlock, killed, and Major Womack was badly wounded. Colonel Savage carried 400 men into action and had 208 killed, wounded and missing, of which 36 were killed on the line. After the fall of Captain Spurlock, no officer of his company surviving him, Private Hackett was placed in command, who exhibited courage and good conduct. After Color-bearer Sergeant Marberry was wounded, the flag was taken by Private Womack. He, too, was wounded, the colors were shot into fragments, and the flagstaff severed by a rifle ball.

The Eighth, Thirty-eighth, and seven companies of the Fifty-first advanced to the left of the Cowan house, charged and broke the enemy, and inflicted great losses. In this charge, Col. W. L. Moore of the Eighth, after his horse was shot and fell upon him, disengaged himself, went forward on foot with his regiment, and died with the shout of victory in his ears. A noble gentleman, a soldier and a patriot, his loss was a severe blow to the service. The gallant Lieut.-Col. J. H. Anderson succeeded to the command of the regiment. General Donelson reported the capture of 11 pieces of artillery and 1,000 prisoners, and the successful holding of the position the brigade had won.

The conduct of Donelson's brigade won high commendation from Cheatham, the division commander. The fruit of the bravery of the men was great, but the loss was severe—out of 1,400 men, 691 killed, wounded and missing, the 19 missing being prisoners of war. The Eighth Tennessee showed a long list of killed and wounded; in Company D, Capt. M. C. Shook was killed, and out of 12 officers and 62 men engaged, but 1 corporal and 20 men escaped unhurt. Capt. William Sadler, and Lieuts. Thomas O. Blacknall and N. Martin Kerby were killed. Capt. B. H. Holland, of the Thirty-eighth, was killed with the colors of the regiment in his hands. Color-Sergt. J. M. Rice, being shot down, clung to the flag, and crawling on his knees, carried it a short distance, when he was killed by a second bullet. Adjt.

R. L. Caruthers, of the Thirty-eighth, was severely wounded; Capt. T. C. Campbell, of the Fifty-first, was killed, and Capts. J. A. Russell and James F. Franklin and Lieuts. G. C. Howard and R. A. Burford were severely wounded.

Maney's brigade was in support of Manigault, but soon advanced under Cheatham's orders to the front line, at "the brick kiln," where they encountered fierce opposition. Colonel Feild, of the First Tennessee, said this was the only place where "we actually engaged the enemy." The latter was driven from his guns, pursued across the Wilkinson road, driven from another battery of four guns in reserve and the guns captured, and the brigade then bivouacked on the line from which the enemy was driven, and held it until our forces retired to Shelbyville and Tullahoma, three days after the conflict.

The First Tennessee lost Lieut. R. F. James, killed (an officer trusted by Colonel Feild with the performance of duties demanding tact and courage), and 80 men killed and wounded; the Fourth lost Capt. D. P. Skelton, mortally wounded, and Capt. C. Brown, Lieut. John Shane and 40 men wounded. Conspicuous in a regiment famous for its courage was Sergeant Oakley, color-bearer, who found no place too perilous for the display of the regimental flag. The Sixth and Ninth lost Lieuts. W. D. Irby, A. J. Bucey and F. J. Gilliam, killed, and Capt. E. B. McClanahan, wounded, and 40 men killed and wounded. The aggregate loss of the brigade was 196.

The officers and men of Carnes' battery, Capt. W. W. Carnes; Smith's battery, Lieut. W. B. Turner; Stanford's battery, Capt. E. J. Stanford, and Scott's battery, Capt. W. L. Scott, were conspicuous for steadiness, skill and courage in action.

When General Wheeler had returned from his successful raid of the 30th he found the battle on, and his cavalry joined in the attack and drove the enemy for two miles, engaging him until dark. Then Wharton's cavalry was ordered to the rear of the enemy, but, he says, so vigorous was the attack of our left (made by McCown's division) that he had to proceed first at a trot and then at a gallop two and a half miles before he could execute his orders. Reaching a point near the Wilkinson pike, with the enemy in his front, Capt. B. F. White (Tennessee) was ordered to open with his battery. The First Confederate regiment, Col. John T. Cox, charged and captured the Seventy-fifth Illinois infantry. Four companies of the Eighth Texas, under Capt. S. P. Christian, charged and captured a four-gun battery complete.

Wharton sent his 1,500 prisoners to the rear, and moved across the country a short distance near the Nashville road, until he found a large body of Federal cavalry facing him. White's battery again opened the ball, and the Second Tennessee, Col. H. M. Ashby, and McCown's escort company, Capt. L. T. Hardy, with the Eighth Texas on the right, were ordered to charge. They were met by a countercharge, supposed to be by the Fourth regulars, but the enemy was routed, and retreated in wild confusion, abandoning several hundred wagons. One thousand infantrymen were captured.

Wharton's forces too zealously followed the retreating enemy. Soon another Federal force of about 300 cavalry, seeing White's battery unprotected, moved down rapidly, and when within 400 yards General Wharton opportunely returned from the pursuit. Col. Baxter Smith, Fourth Tennessee, promptly formed about 20 men, the guns were unlimbered, several shells were exploded in the enemy's ranks, and they retired in disorder. The same Federal command subsequently attacked the guard of the captured wagon train and recovered a portion of them and several of the prisoners, but a large number of wagons, 5 or 6 pieces of artillery, 400 prisoners, 327 beef cattle, and a large number of mules were secured. Col. Baxter Smith, said General Wharton, "behaved with the utmost gallantry and judgment," and he named

Captain White, "whose gallantry upon this and every other field was most conspicuous." The entire strength of the brigade was 2,000. The loss was 108 killed and wounded, 107 captured.

After placing the captured property within our lines and arming his command with improved arms captured from the enemy, General Wharton returned to the rear of the enemy and engaged him until nightfall. Then he placed his command upon the left of the Confederate army and picketed for its protection.

On Friday afternoon, January 2d, Major-General Breckinridge was ordered by the commanding general, in person, to take the crest of the hill in his front on the east side of Stone's river. Capt. E. Eldridge Wright's battery, which had been detached, was ordered to rejoin Preston's brigade. Brigadier-General Pillow, who had reported for duty, was assigned by General Bragg to Colonel Palmer's brigade, and "that fine officer resumed command of his regiment," the Eighteenth. The division advanced, Pillow with the Tennesseeans on the right, supported by Preston; Hanson on the left with the Second, Fourth, Sixth and Ninth Kentucky and Forty-first Alabama, supported by Adams' brigade, Col. R. L. Gibson, Sixteenth Louisiana, commanding. As soon as the field was entered, the battle opened, and the enemy was driven over the crest of the hill. Wright's battery was advanced, and the Twentieth Tennessee, on the right of Preston, soon in the front line, suffered severely; but it dashed forward and drove the enemy down the hill, capturing 200 prisoners. The division moved to the charge in perfect order, and in a few minutes the Federal division in its front was routed and driven from the crest, but the ground so gallantly won by Breckinridge was commanded by the enemy's batteries within easy range. The Federal guns swept the front, right, and left, and large numbers of fresh troops were rapidly concentrated, forcing Breckinridge back to his original line.

"Wright's battery was bravely fought," said General Preston, "but lost its gallant commander, who was killed at his guns." At his fall, Lieut. J. W. Mebane, himself wounded, succeeded in withdrawing all of the battery except two pieces. According to General Breckinridge, "one was lost because there was but one boy left (Private Wright) to limber the piece, and his strength was unequal to it." The "boy" named by General Breckinridge was Luke E. Wright, younger brother of the gallant captain, and afterward junior-lieutenant of the battery. The experience of that fateful day made him a veteran and a conspicuous soldier; he survived the war and attained civil prominence as one of the leaders of the bar of Tennessee. Before the fragment of the company was hardly out of the battery, in obedience to orders to retire, the Federal flag was flying on one of their lost guns. Lieutenants Grant and Phillips, with the guns saved, stood fast and covered the retreat of the attacking division, which fell back in the face of overwhelming numbers, and with the conviction that somebody had blundered. General Hardee, the corps commander, said in his official report, "this movement was made without my knowledge."

On the 20th of April, 1863, Lieutenant-General Hardee, under instructions, furnished the following names of officers of his corps who fell at Murfreesboro, who were conspicuous for their valor, to be inscribed on the guns of one of the reserve batteries: Maj. Henry C. Erwin, Forty-fourth; Maj. James T. McReynolds, Thirty-seventh; Capt. E. Eldridge Wright, Wright's battery, and Capt. Edwin Allen, Company C, Twenty-sixth. General Preston recommended for promotion Sergt. Frank Battle for conspicuous gallantry. "After four color-bearers of the Twentieth had been shot down and the regiment was in confusion, he seized the colors and bravely rallied the men under my eye."

It was stated by Maj.-Gen. George H. Thomas, Federal, in his official report of the battle, referring to the assault made by Breckinridge: "I sent orders to Negley to advance to the support of Crittenden's troops. This order was obeyed in most gallant style and resulted in the complete annihilation of the Twenty-sixth Tennessee regiment." But, in fact, the Twenty-sixth, Colonel Lillard, with Palmer's brigade in this attack, left the field over 300 strong, in perfect order, in obedience to command. It had 1 officer and 8 men killed, 71 wounded, and 17 captured, during the engagements of the 31st of December and 2d of January, and was distinguished in the subsequent battles of the war.

Col. Joseph B. Palmer, Sixteenth, afterward brigadier-general, a soldier of judgment and undaunted courage, three times wounded in this attack, said in his official report that "the entire force on the right bank of the river was completely routed and driven by our division either across or down the stream; but they had massed a force of many thousands on the opposite bank, where they had a large force of artillery, so located and arranged that both their small-arms and batteries could be brought to bear upon and rake all the western portion of the field over which their troops had been driven. It therefore became proper for our forces to withdraw, although they had not been repulsed."

General Rosecrans reported that Breckinridge's attack was upon Van Cleve's division, supported by a brigade of Gen. John M. Palmer's division. "Breckinridge advanced steadily," says Rosecrans, "to within 100 yards of the front of Van Cleve, when a short and fierce contest ensued. Van Cleve's division giving way, retired in considerable confusion across the river, followed closely by the enemy." The strength of the force assailed by Breckinridge, according to the Federal return, was 5,221. After Van Cleve's rout, according to Rosecrans, the onset of the Confederates was met by "two brigades of Negley's division and the Pioneer brigade;" which, by the return published at that time, were 5,520 strong.

Breckinridge made the assault with a force of 4,500, of all arms, and lost 1,700 killed, wounded and missing. Among the dead Tennesseeans were the gallant Col. P. D. Cunningham, Thirty-second regiment; Capt. John Dick and Lieut. Samuel M. Smith, Eighteenth; Capt. Edward Allen, Twenty-sixth; Lieuts. J. L. Proffitt and J. M. Saylors, Twenty-eighth; Capt. J. W. Watkins and Lieut. F. B. Crosthwait, Twentieth. Seven of the ten captains of the Eighteenth; Lieut.-Col. J. L. Bottles and Maj. R. M. Saffell, Twenty-sixth; Adjt. John M. Douglass and Sergt.-Maj. Fletcher R. Burns, Eighteenth, were wounded. Colonel Palmer stated that after five color-bearers of the Eighteenth had been shot down, "Logan H. Nelson, a private soldier of Company C, gallantly sprang forward, raised the flag from the side of dying comrades and carried it triumphantly throughout the combat." Maj. F. Claybrooke, Twentieth, reported that four of his "color-bearers were shot, and the flag-staff twice shot in two and the colors riddled by balls."

On the 1st of January, General Wheeler, with his own and Wharton's cavalry, returned to the rear of the Federal army. He dispersed the guards of a large train near Lavergne, destroyed a number of wagons and stores and captured one piece of artillery. At 9 o'clock of the evening of the same day he again went to the rear of the enemy, capturing trains of wagons, horses and prisoners, and regained his position at 2 o'clock of the next morning on the left flank of the army, where he remained all day, engaging the enemy at every opportunity. At 9 o'clock that evening he made his fourth sortie to the rear of the enemy, and next morning, the 3d, captured prisoners, wagons and horses. On regaining his position on the left flank on the morning of the 4th, he learned that General Bragg had fallen back. At 3 o'clock p. m. of the 4th, Rosecrans advanced to the river and commenced a skirmish. After dark he retired a short distance. The cavalry pickets were not molested during the night. At daylight on the 5th, General Wheeler retired three miles from Murfreesboro; at 3 p. m. the Federals advanced a brigade of infantry, with artillery and cavalry, but were driven back. In his report General Wheeler included Capt. Richard McCann of Tennessee, commanding a detachment, among those of whom he said, "during the many engagements incident to the battle of Murfreesboro, I take pleasure in commending their gallantry and good soldierly conduct."

General Rosecrans, commanding the Federal army at Murfreesboro, reported his strength at 46,940 officers and men of all arms; killed and wounded, 8,778; lost by capture, 2,800; but the revised statement accompanying his report shows that he lost 3,673 captured by the Confederates, a total of 12,451; and a loss of 28 pieces of artillery, 3 battery wagons and 5 forges was admitted. General Rosecrans reported a reserve of 7,495 at Nashville, 3,550 at Gallatin, and nearly 4,000 at Bowling Green and Clarksville. Maj. W. K. Beard, inspector-general on the staff of General Bragg, made an official report in which he accounted for 6,273 prisoners captured at Murfreesboro.

Colonel Brent, adjutant-general on the staff of General Bragg, reported that we had present and in the battle 37,712 officers and men of all arms, including 4,237 cavalry. Bragg's loss amounted to 10,266, of which 9,000 were killed and wounded, and 1,200 of the badly wounded, left in the hospitals at Murfreesboro, constituted the largest part of Rosecrans' captures.

Nearly one-third of the army of Tennessee were Tennesseeans; many of them fought and fell almost in call of their own wives and children; there were no holiday soldiers among them and no desertions, and they fell back from their homes with a loss of 3,500 killed and wounded, nearly half of the entire loss. The greatest loss of the army was in Cheatham's division of Tennesseeans, 36 per cent killed and wounded. Johnson's Tennessee brigade, of Cleburne's division, lost 29½ per cent, Palmer's Tennessee brigade the same, and the Tennessee troops in other commands sustained about the same loss.

They fought heroically and were led superbly, took the enemy's positions, his artillery and small-arms and many prisoners, and met the perils of the battlefield, and death, with the high-born courage that springs from a sense of duty. Yet the commanding general in his official report had no word of commendation for them, or for the men who led them with so much skill and courage.

Cheatham, the ranking officer of Tennessee, with a division of the troops of the State, seemed inspired by the fierceness of the battle. He was like Marshal Massena, as described by the Emperor Napoleon: "His conversation gave few indications of genius, but at the first cannon shot his mental energy redoubled, and when surrounded by danger his thoughts were clear and forcible. In the midst of the dying and the dead, the balls sweeping away those who encircled him, he was himself, and gave his orders with the greatest coolness and precision."

The striking feature of this battle is that Rosecrans, who led the attacking army, was on the defensive every hour of the battle, never pursued an advantage if it was won, in the actual fighting was beaten at all points and driven from the battlefield with enormous losses. He permitted three days to pass, after the battle of the 31st of December, without firing a shot, except on the skirmish line and to defend himself from the assault of Breckinridge on the afternoon of the 2d of January.

Bragg retired at 2 o'clock a. m. on the morning of the 4th, and two hours later the cavalry under General Wheeler occupied his position, and continued in it until the break of day on the 5th of January. At 4:30 of that morning, General Rosecrans telegraphed the secretary of war, "God has crowned our arms with victory."

CHAPTER VI.

TENNESSEEANS IN MISSISSIPPI—AT CHICKASAW BAYOU —GREGG'S BRIGADE AT RAYMOND—ONE TENNESSEE BRIGADE COMBATS AN ARMY CORPS—THE BRIGADES OF REYNOLDS AND VAUGHN AT VICKSBURG—THE FIRST REGIMENT HEAVY ARTILLERY —THE STATE'S REPRESENTATION AT PORT HUDSON, LA.

ON the 8th of December, 1862, Major-General Grant, from his headquarters at Oxford, Miss., ordered Maj.-Gen. W. T. Sherman, then at Memphis, to proceed with his forces "down the river to the vicinity of Vicksburg, and with the coöperation of the gunboat fleet, under command of Flag-Officer Porter, *proceed to the reduction* of that place." Accordingly, on Christmas, Sherman's forces, 32,000 strong, with the whole Federal naval squadron of the Mississippi, ironclads and wooden boats, were at the mouth of the Yazoo. On the 26th the land and naval forces proceeded up the river twelve miles to the point selected for debarkation. On landing, Sherman moved his army out in four columns and ordered working parties to unload from his transports "all things necessary for five days' operations," this being considered ample time to enable him to execute General Grant's order. Sherman's plan was by a prompt and concentrated movement to break the Confederate center near Chickasaw bayou.

On the 29th of December the assault was made with the division commanded by Gen. George W. Morgan, together with the brigades of Blair and Thayer of Steele's division; but, according to Sherman's report, his forces "met so withering a fire from the rifle-pits, and cross-fire of grape and canister, that the column faltered and finally fell back, leaving many dead, wounded and prisoners in the hands of the enemy." General Morgan reported a loss of 1,652 killed, wounded and missing in the assaulting column. "When the night of the 29th closed in," said Sherman, "we had suffered a repulse;" and realizing his complete failure, with some pathos he added, "but it is for other minds to devise the way" to take Vicksburg and Dromgoole's Bluff on the Yazoo. Following his repulse and defeat, his troops were embarked on board the transports and retired to Milliken's bend.

The Tennessee regiments which participated in this decisive victory were the Third, Col. Calvin J. Clack; Thirtieth, Col. James J. Turner; Sixty-second (Eightieth), Col. J. A. Rowan; Sixtieth, Col. John H. Crawford, and Eighty-first. The last three regiments constituted the brigade of Gen. John C. Vaughn, who reported a loss of 9 killed and 9 wounded, and declared that officers and men held their position "with steadiness and nerve." Lieut.-Gen. J. C. Pemberton, commanding the Confederate forces, reported that on the left, commanded by Brig.-Gen. John C. Vaughn, the heavy abatis prevented the approach of the enemy except with sharpshooters, who advanced continuously, but were met firmly by his East Tennesseeans; and referring to the assault made by the brigade of F. P. Blair, he said: "The Third, Thirtieth and Sixtieth Tennessee regiments occupied the rifle-pits in front and behaved with distinguished coolness and courage." It was here that the gallant Maj. F. M. Tucker and Lieut. James P. Bass, Third Tennessee, were killed. Major Tucker stood on top of the earthworks, and fell cheering his men to victory.

General Pemberton called the attention of the war department to the Third, Thirtieth and Sixtieth Tennessee, "as entitled to the highest distinction," and in an order, dated May 12, 1863, he conferred it upon them by ordering that "Vicksburg" be inscribed upon their banners.

Brig.-Gen. Stephen D. Lee, who ably commanded the troops that received the assault made by Sherman's forces, said in his official report: "Besides the regiments already mentioned for gallantry, I would mention the Third, Thirtieth and Sixty-second Tennessee regiments, occupying the pits where the enemy made their most formidable attack. They displayed coolness and gallantry, and their fire was terrific." Colonel Turner of the Thirtieth and Colonel Clack of the Third, the first as major and the other as captain, had received the baptism of fire at Fort Donelson. The distinction then won had its sequel at Chickasaw Bayou.

Later in the campaign against Vicksburg, when Grant, after various failures, had landed south of Vicksburg, and advanced to the railroad between Jackson and Vicksburg, a Tennessee brigade, under Brig.-Gen. John Gregg, which had been on duty at Port Hudson, and was ordered thence to Jackson, made a memorable fight against great odds.

Gregg's brigade consisted of the Third Tennessee, Col. C. H. Walker; Tenth and Thirtieth Tennessee (consolidated), Col. Randall W. MacGavock; Forty-first, Col. R. Farquharson; Fiftieth, Lieut.-Col. T. W. Beaumont; First battalion, Maj. S. H. Colms; and the Seventh Texas, Col. H. B. Granbury.

Under the order of Lieutenant-General Pemberton, this brigade left its camp near Jackson, on the evening of the 11th of May, 1863, and camped that night at Raymond. Without definite information or adequate means of obtaining it, no course was left to General Gregg but to await the movements of the enemy. General Pemberton had "intimated" that the main movement of the enemy was towards Edwards depot, but at 10 o'clock a. m. of the next day a Federal force moved up rapidly and opened with artillery upon Gregg's pickets.

General Gregg, misled by the information received from General Pemberton, made his dispositions to capture a brigade of the enemy; but instead of a brigade, encountered Logan's division. He was attacked by three brigades commanded by Brig.-Gens. John E. Smith, E. S. Dennis and John D. Stevenson, with three batteries, and a considerable force of cavalry. Besides all these, General Crocker's Seventh division was hurried into position to support Logan, and finally the whole Seventh army corps, 23,749 strong, commanded by Maj.-Gen. John B. McPherson, was disposed for battle. This great array was met by General Gregg with an aggregate present of 2,500 officers and men, including Bledsoe's Missouri battery of three guns, one of which burst during the action.

General McPherson reported that after "a sharp and severe contest of three hours' duration" the Confederates were driven back. General Logan referred to the battle as a "terrible conflict" that "raged with great fury for at least two hours." The marvel is that Gregg, fighting almost ten times his number of veteran troops, under the ablest leadership in the Federal army, could have held his position for thirty minutes. He was absolutely isolated, no reinforcements expected; but he maintained himself for three hours against great odds. The discipline of his troops was almost perfect, their courage was equal to the great trial to which they were subjected, their regimental commanders were officers of great intelligence and gallantry, and Gregg's generalship was inimitable. No wonder that McPherson reported that he had fought 6,000 troops. Lieutenant-Colonel Davis, commanding the Twenty-third Indiana, declared that he was attacked upon his right and front by the enemy in column, consisting of four lines, and added that the Confederates "opened fire from each line in succession" and continued to advance on him "until they were within bayonet reach. Not having time to fix our bayonets, we attempted to beat them back with our muskets, but being overpowered by numbers we were obliged to fall back" across a creek, where he succeeded in holding his position for an hour and a half, and until the Confederates retired.

The activity and courage of the Confederates caused officers of yet higher rank to overestimate their strength. Brig.-Gen. John D. Stevenson, explaining the disaster to the Third Missouri, reported that "the regiment, being at the base of a hill held by the enemy (the Confederates), resolutely advanced to take possession of it, and whilst under a most terrific fire, was ordered by the commanding officer to retreat, and retired in great disorder and with heavy loss, the enemy in front consisting of three regiments." These "three regiments" were the Tenth and Thirtieth Tennessee (consolidated), not over 300 strong, commanded by Lieut.-Col. James J. Turner. In the latter's report he stated that he "ordered the whole command to cheer and yell and charge the enemy at a double-quick. At them they went, yelling like savages. The enemy stood still and delivered one volley and then broke in utter confusion, and attempted but once to rally on their colors, when we came up within thirty steps, killed their color-bearer, and the rout was complete." Turner pushed on 600 yards, and then observing troops in reserve, retired to the crest of the hill from which the Third Missouri had vainly attempted to drive him.

The Third Tennessee and Seventh Texas were, said General Gregg, "in the most trying part of the engagement," receiving assault after assault for more than two hours from superior numbers, and finally retired from a flanking fire and a threatened movement in their rear to their original position. The Forty-first Tennessee went to their relief, and rendered the two regiments a great service in protecting their retreat. Colm's battalion was engaged on the right and prevented the enemy from throwing a force between Gregg and the town of Raymond. Later, the Forty-first was sent to support the Tenth, Thirtieth and Fiftieth Tennessee, hotly engaged on Gregg's left, but receiving a dispatch from Colonel Adams, of the cavalry, that the enemy had a large supporting force advancing, the brigade was ordered to withdraw. This, General Gregg said, was effected in admirable order. No pursuit was made, and the command was camped for the night five miles from the battlefield.

The Federal forces lost 322 officers and men killed, wounded and captured; the Confederates, 231 officers and men killed and wounded, and 186 captured. Among the killed were Capt. R. T. Cooper and Lieut. W. W. Rutledge, Third Tennessee; Col. Randall W. MacGavock, and Lieut. John Ames, Tenth Tennessee; Capt. Abner S. Boone, Forty-first Tennessee. Lieutenant-Colonel Beaumont, Fiftieth Tennessee, was wounded in the head by a rifle ball and for a time disabled during the action, but his wound was dressed and he returned to his regiment. Colonel MacGavock, who was killed while gallantly urging his command to the conflict, and was succeeded by Lieutenant-Colonel Turner, was referred to as a brave and meritorious officer and an educated and talented gentleman. Gen. Joseph E. Johnston, commanding the department, mentioned his loss with much regret. Gregg's brigade continued with the forces under General Johnston during the siege of Vicksburg and participated in the operations for the relief of that city, and the defense of Jackson.

Two other Tennessee brigades in Mississippi were attached to the forces under the immediate command of General Pemberton. One, under Col. A. W. Reynolds, consisted of the Forty-third Tennessee, Col. J. W. Gillespie; Thirty-first, Col. W. M. Bradford; Third (provisional army), Col. N. J. Lillard, and Fifty-ninth, Col. W. L. Eakin. They left Edwards depot, on the Jackson railroad, on the night of May 15, 1863, as the rear guard of Pemberton's army then marching in the direction of Raymond, Miss. On the following morning the brigade, after a sharp skirmish with the enemy, was relieved by S. D. Lee's brigade, and went forward by Gen. C. L. Stevenson's order to guard his trains to Vicksburg, halting and skirmishing occasionally with the enemy. The brigade reached its destination on the 17th, and went into position on the lines.

On the 18th of May the brigade was assigned position on the left of Barton's brigade, which held the Confederate right, the left resting on the Hall's ferry road, the right of Cumming's brigade. The Thirty-first, Fifty-ninth and five companies of the Third were assigned to the ditches; and the Forty-third and the remainder of the Third were held in reserve. Here for forty-seven days these brave sons of Tennessee endured the rain and heat of summer, living on half rations, half clad, daily under fire, without a murmur, says the brigade commander, and bore themselves with constancy and courage.

On the 29th of May the enemy drove in the picket line; but after nightfall the Tennesseeans drove them back and the line was re-established. On the 1st of June the enemy established a battery 800 yards in front of the brigade. This was soon silenced by Capt. F. D. Claiborne's battery of field pieces, but on the night of June 4th the enemy established a battery of four guns of heavy caliber in front of the Tennesseeans. The fire from these guns was constant from the 5th of June until the surrender on the 4th of July. On the 9th of June another battery of 20-pounder Parrott guns was mounted in front of the Tennesseeans, within 400 yards of their line, our pickets having been gradually withdrawn. The enemy advanced to a point 75 yards distant, and there constructed works stronger than those occupied by our troops, these intrenchments being continuous along the brigade front. The enemy's sharpshooters maintained a constant fire, and the exposure of the person was fatal. Frequent successful sorties were made at night, but the force of the enemy was so superior in numbers that it was impossible to hold a position after it was won.

On the 22d of May, says the same authority, the Forty-third Tennessee reinforced the line held by Gen. Stephen D. Lee, and gallantly assisted in the repulse of the enemy. In this action Capt. Sterling Turner was killed; Asst. Surgeon W. B. Johnson, while attending the wounded, received a mortal wound; Lieut.-Col. David M. Key was seriously wounded, and before his recovery was stricken with malarial fever, but he recovered after a long and doubtful illness. Now in the evening of his days, he enjoys the greatest consideration from his friends and the public, after bearing with honorable distinction the highest civic honors. Colonel Key had drilled and disciplined the regiment under the direction of the noble Gillespie, and made it one of the best in the service.

On the night of June 21st, Capt. A. J. Canood of the Forty-third, with 59 men, part of his own company and a detachment from Captain Wiseman's company, was ordered to assault an intrenched outpost in front of Barkuloo's Georgia regiment. He captured it but could not hold it. Twenty-three of his force were killed and wounded, the gallant Canood received a mortal wound, Lieutenant Cruikshank was killed, and Captain Wiseman severely wounded. On the following night, Capt. W. H. McKamy of the Forty-third, with 47 men, assaulted and carried the same work, but he lost 27 of his command in killed and wounded, and the courageous captain was severely wounded and disabled for life.

The Forty-third was 900 strong when it entered Vicksburg, but forty-seven days of exposure to the burning sun, drenching rains, thick fogs, heavy dews, and the enemy's guns, reduced it to less than half. Its beautiful banner, presented by the ladies of Mt. Sterling, Ky., could show 972 bullet-holes when it was lowered on the 4th of July.

The Third (provisional army), Thirty-ninth and Fifty-ninth were conspicuous for their valor and endurance. The men of the Thirty-ninth were naval heroes as well as soldiers. In February, 1863, three companies were detached and ordered down the Mississippi on a steam ferryboat armed with two field pieces, to watch the movements of the gunboat Queen of the West, which had passed our batteries. They proceeded up Red river and captured the gunboat. Then an expedition was fitted out under Maj. J. L. Brent, and the men of the Thirty-ninth assisted in manning the Queen of the West and steamer Webb. Ascending the river, they met and captured, after a desperate conflict, the ironclad Indianola, with her stores and 112 prisoners. Major Brent, commanding the expedition, made honorable mention of Captain Carnes and Lieuts. H. A. Rice and Henry Miller, of the Thirty-ninth. During the siege this regiment lost 20 men killed and wounded.

Brig.-Gen. John C. Vaughn, of Tennessee, commanded a brigade consisting of the Sixtieth Tennessee, Capt. J. W. Bachman; Sixty-first, Lieut.-Col. James G. Rose, and Sixty-second, Col. John A. Rowan. On May 16th, while the disastrous battle of Baker's Creek was pending, Vaughn's brigade was ordered to protect the railroad bridge over Big Black river in rear of Pemberton's line. The entire command in retreat crossed the bridge, yet Vaughn, in momentary expectation of orders to follow, continued to defend a crossing no longer useful.

After daylight next day, Osterhaus' division of the Federal army assaulted the faithful guard of Tennesseeans. Colonel Rose counted seventeen regimental flags passing to his front. After a fierce struggle the enemy gained an open space enfilading Vaughn's entire line, and the position being no longer tenable, a retreat was ordered. The assault of Osterhaus was almost exclusively on the Sixty-first, which met it bravely and with the free use of buckshot and ball, so that the Federals faltered, halted and only advanced under the pressure of the columns in the rear. The brave Sixty-first was almost annihilated; out of 400 who answered to roll-call in the early morning, Colonel Rose led but 112 back to Vicksburg that evening. The Ninth and Fourteenth divisions of the Thirteenth army corps, which assailed the Sixty-first, lost 279 killed, wounded and missing.

During the siege of Vicksburg, General Vaughn made daily reports of his operations, one day recording one wounded in the Sixtieth; the next day one in the Sixtieth, two in the Sixty-second; the next and the next, one killed in the Sixtieth, one in the Sixty-second, one in the Sixty-first—repeating this pathetic story from day to day until the surrender on the 4th of July.

Another gallant command was the First Tennessee regiment of heavy artillery, Col. Andrew Jackson, Jr., Lieut.-Col. Robert Sterling, Maj. F. W. Hoadley. The regiment was composed of the companies of Captains Dismukes, Weyland, Norman, Parks, J. B. Caruthers, T. N. Johnston and J. P. Lynch. The upper batteries from Fort Hill to the upper bayou were worked by the Tennessee artillery. After the investment of the city, May 18th, unsuccessful attacks on the batteries were daily made for the next week. Col. Edward Higgins, chief of artillery, reports that on the morning of the 27th of May the enemy's ironclad gunboat Cincinnati, mounting 14 guns, was observed approaching our upper batteries, while four ironclads approached the lower batteries. In the engagement, which resulted in the complete repulse of the enemy and the sinking of the Cincinnati, great credit was accorded to Capts. J. P. Lynch and T. N. Johnston, of the First. Daily for the next month these batteries were subjected to a constant fire, and our loss was severe. Among the killed was Maj. F. W. Hoadley, First Tennessee, commanding the upper water battery, of whom Colonel Higgins said: "This battery was exposed constantly to an unceasing fire of mortars, Parrott guns and sharpshooters. The gallant major was always at his post and fell with his face to the foe, struck in the breast by the fragment of a shell." Among the officers who most distinguished themselves by their gallantry and unceasing vigilance during the siege was, according to the same authority, "Colonel Jackson, First Tennessee artillery, who with his gallant regiment bore the brunt of the labors and dangers of the siege, and was always ready, day or night, for any duty to which he might be called." In this high commendation he included Lieutenant-Colonel Sterling and Captains Lynch and Johnston of the same regiment.

On the 25th of May, Maj.-Gen. N. P. Banks, with an army of 20,000 men, invested Port Hudson, La., where Maj.-Gen. Franklin Gardner was in command of the Confederate forces, and after thorough preparation this fortified post was assailed by Banks' army and the fleet commanded by Admiral Farragut. General Banks anticipated the easy capture of the garrison, but he met a determined resistance and was signally defeated, with a loss of 293 killed and 1,549 wounded. On the 10th and 14th of June, assaults were again made without success; and after the last attack, becoming convinced that he could not carry the works by assault, Banks set about the slower operations of a siege, making approaches and skirmishing from day to day, aided actively by the fleet. Farragut maintained the fire from his mortar guns during the whole of every night, the only injury inflicted on the Confederates being banished sleep and the forcing of our artillery officers and men to constant watchfulness without relief. During the day the besieging army kept up an active artillery fire.

This continued from the 25th of May to the 8th of July, when General Gardner surrendered his command as prisoners of war. General Gardner, in commending his men for their gallantry and constant labors in the defense, stated that his surrender was not on account of the fall of Vicksburg or the want of provisions or ammunition, but from the exhaustion of his men, who had been without rest for more than six weeks.

The First Tennessee heavy artillery, Company G, Capt. James A. Fisher; the First light artillery, Company B, Lieut. Oswald Tilghman; the improvised Tennessee battalion, Capt. S. A. Whiteside, composed of details from the Forty-first, Forty-second, Forty-eighth, Forty-ninth, Fifty-third and Fifty-fifth Tennessee regiments, were all constantly engaged, and rendered services of great value. At all hours under the fire of Farragut's fleet, they lost only 4 killed and 6 wounded. Among the killed was Lieut. Thomas B. Cooke, of the heavy artillery.

The only published report of the siege by a Confederate officer was made by Capt. C. M. Jackson, of the staff of General Gardner. He informed General Johnston, on the 9th of July, that provisions were exhausted, and that it was impossible to cut a way out on account of the proximity of the enemy's works. Our casualties during the siege were 200 killed, and between 300 and 400 wounded. At the time of surrender there were only 2,500 men for duty. Banks reported to General Halleck that he had "not more than 14,000 effective men." He lost 706 killed, 3,145 wounded and 307 captured.

CHAPTER VII.

CAMPAIGN IN MIDDLE TENNESSEE—BRAGG RETIRES TO CHATTANOOGA—BATTLE OF CHICKAMAUGA—PART OF TENNESSEEANS IN THE GREAT VICTORY—OPPRESSION OF THE PEOPLE.

AFTER a delay of six months, General Rosecrans placed his army in motion in June, 1863. His equipments and appointments were as thorough and complete as the unlimited resources of his government could make them; his force was ample, his supplies abundant; but his experience at Murfreesboro had made him and his corps commanders timid and hesitating in their advance.

General Bragg determined to offer battle in front of Shelbyville, and ordered Lieutenant-General Polk to move his army corps to Guy's gap on the Murfreesboro road, and assail the enemy before Liberty gap; but learning that the left of Major-General Stewart's division, stationed between Fairfield and Hoover's gap, had been turned, he decided to withdraw the army of Tennessee to Tullahoma.

This flank attack was made by the Federal corps commanded by Maj.-Gen. George H. Thomas, and was met by Bushrod Johnson's, Clayton's and Bate's brigades, of Stewart's division, and Liddell's and Wood's brigades, of Cleburne's division, Hardee's corps. General Bragg, under date of July 3d, referred to these engagements as "a series of skirmishes," but they were continuous from the 24th to the 27th of June, and Johnson's brigade sustained a loss of 36, and Bate's a loss of 145, killed and wounded, out of 650 engaged. Among the killed was the gallant Maj. Fred Claybrooke, Twentieth

Tennessee, greatly distinguished at Murfreesboro. Among the wounded reported were Capt. J. A. Pettigrew and Adjt. James W. Thomas, of the Twentieth, and Maj. Thomas Kennedy Porter, acting chief of artillery on the staff of Major-General Stewart.

On the morning of the 27th the troops named retired under orders to Tullahoma, where General Bragg concentrated the army of Tennessee, taking position and determining to risk a battle; but the enemy pressed back his troops on the Manchester and Hillsboro road, and his communications with his base were temporarily destroyed. His health was very poor, and his corps commanders believing, as stated by General Hardee in a published letter, that he was not able "to take command in the field," advised him to retire. Acting upon this advice, the army abandoned Tullahoma, and on the 30th of June began the retreat, reaching Chattanooga on the 7th of July. Not a gun, or stores of any kind, was lost, and Polk's corps, largely composed of Middle and West Tennessee troops, was 400 stronger than when it retired from Shelbyville.

After resting at Chattanooga during the months of July and August, General Bragg, having received reinforcements of two small divisions from Mississippi, increasing the strength of the army, exclusive of cavalry, to 35,000, determined to attack the advancing enemy whenever an opportunity was offered. Without ability to garrison Chattanooga, the place was abandoned on the 7th and 8th of September, and the army took position from Lee & Gordon's mills to Lafayette in Georgia. Rosecrans immediately occupied the town and pushed forward in pursuit of Bragg, assuming that he was in retreat on Rome, but on the 10th discovered that the Confederate army was being concentrated about Lafayette. The Federal army was then at Gordon's mill, Bailey's cross-roads, at the foot of Stevens' gap, and at Alpine, a distance of 40 miles from flank to flank. General Bragg, who had so far conducted his campaign with great skill, made prompt dispositions to crush McCook's corps, and failing in that, to assail Crittenden's corps; but disappointed in his reasonable expectations, he began a concentration of his army that culminated in the great battle of Chickamauga.

For this greatest battle of the West, more Tennessee organizations were united on the field than ever before. The flower of the State were there, resolved upon victory and the redemption of their homes.

General Cheatham's division was now composed of his four Tennessee brigades, commanded by Brig.-Gens. Preston Smith, George Maney, Marcus J. Wright and Otho F. Strahl, the Georgia and Mississippi brigade of John K. Jackson, and the artillery battalion of Maj. Melancthon Smith.

Smith's brigade included the Eleventh regiment, Col. George W. Gordon; Twelfth and Forty-seventh, Col. William M. Watkins; Thirteenth and One Hundred and Fifty-fourth, Col. A. J. Vaughan; Twenty-ninth, Col. Horace Rice, and Maj. J. W. Dawson's battalion of sharpshooters.

In Maney's brigade were the First and Twenty-seventh, Col. Hume R. Feild; Fourth (Confederate), Col. James A. McMurry; Sixth and Ninth, Col. George C. Porter, battalion of sharpshooters, Maj. Frank Maney.

General Strahl had the old brigade of A. P. Stewart, the Fourth and Fifth regiments, Col. Jonathan J. Lamb; Nineteenth, Col. Francis M. Walker; Twenty-fourth, Col. John A. Wilson; Thirty-first, Col. Egbert E. Tansil; Thirty-third, Col. Warner P. Jones.

The brigade of General Wright, formerly Donelson's, comprised the Eighth regiment, Col. John H. Anderson; Sixteenth, Col. D. M. Donnell; Twenty-eighth, Col. Sidney S. Stanton; Thirty-eighth and Maj. T. B. Murray's battalion, Col. John C. Carter; Fifty-first and Fifty-second, Lieut.-Col. John G. Hall.

Maj. Melancthon Smith's battalion was composed of Capt. W. W. Carnes' Tennessee battery, Scogins' Georgia battery, Capt. W. L. Scott's Tennessee battery, and Smith's and Stanford's Mississippi batteries.

The divisions of Breckinridge and Cleburne were under the corps command of Lieut.-Gen. D. H. Hill, and with Cleburne, in Gen. Lucius E. Polk's brigade, were the Third and Fifth (Confederate) Tennessee, Col. J. A. Smith; Second, Col. William D. Robison; Thirty-fifth, Col. B. J. Hill; Forty-eighth, Col. George H. Nixon, constituting four-fifths of the brigade. Capt. John W. Mebane's battery was a part of Graves' battalion, Breckinridge's division.

A. P. Stewart, promoted to major-general, commanded a division of Buckner's corps that was mainly composed of Tennesseeans. The Seventeenth, Lieut.-Col. Watt W. Floyd; Twenty-third, Col. R. H. Keeble; Twenty-fifth, Lieut.-Col. R. B. Snowden, and Forty-fourth, Lieut.-Col. John L. McEwen, Jr., constituted Bushrod R. Johnson's brigade of this division, under Col. John S. Fulton. The Fifteenth and Thirty-seventh, Col. R. C. Tyler, and Twentieth, Col. Thomas B. Smith, made up half of the brigade of Gen. William B. Bate. The Eighteenth, Col. Joseph B. Palmer; Twenty-sixth, Col. John M. Lillard; Thirty-second, Col. Edmund C. Cook; Forty-fifth, Col. Anderson Searcy, and Twenty-third battalion, Maj. Tazewell W. Newman, formed Gen. John C. Brown's brigade. Capt. J. W. Clark's cavalry company was escort to General Buckner.

William Preston's division of the same corps (Buckner's) included the Sixty-third regiment, Lieut.-Col. Abraham Fulkerson, in Gracie's brigade and the battery of Capt. Edmund D. Baxter was in the battalion of reserve artillery commanded by Maj. Samuel C. Williams.

Brig.-Gen. Bushrod Johnson commanded a provisional division, to which was assigned Gen. John Gregg's brigade, the Third regiment, Col. Calvin H. Walker; Tenth, Col. William Grace; Thirtieth, Lieut.-Col. James J. Turner; Forty-first, Lieut.-Col. James D. Tillman; Fiftieth, Col. Cyrus A. Sugg; First battalion, Maj. Stephen H. Colms, and the Seventh Texas. General Johnson acted under orders from Lieut.-Gen. James Longstreet.

Brig.-Gen. Nathan B. Forrest was in command of a cavalry corps of two divisions, under Gens. Frank C. Armstrong and John Pegram.

In Armstrong's division were his brigade, under Col. James T. Wheeler, including the Eighteenth Tennessee battalion, Maj. Charles McDonald; and Forrest's brigade, under Col. George G. Dibrell, made up of the Fourth Tennessee regiment, Col. William S. McLemore; Eighth, Capt. Hamilton McGinnis; Ninth, Col. Jacob B. Biffle; Tenth, Col. Nicholas N. Cox; Eleventh, Col. Daniel W. Holman; Shaw's and O. P. Hamilton's battalions and R. D. Allison's squadron, consolidated, under Maj. Joseph Shaw, and the batteries of Capt. A. L. Huggins and John W. Morton, Jr.

In Pegram's division the Tennessee organizations were Col. E. W. Rucker's Tennessee legion and Capt. Gustave A. Huwald's battery, of Gen. H. B. Davidson's brigade; and the Second regiment, Col. H. M. Ashby, and Fifth, Col. G. W. McKenzie, of Col. John S. Scott's brigade.

Capt. J. C. Jackson's company was escort to General Forrest.

The Fourth cavalry, Lieut.-Col. Paul F. Anderson, and the battery of Capt. B. F. White, Jr., were with Harrison's brigade, Wharton's division, Wheeler's cavalry.

General Bragg assigned the right wing of the army to Lieutenant-General Polk, and the left wing to Lieut.-Gen. James Longstreet, who had arrived from Virginia with a part of his army corps On the night of September 17, 1863, the commanding general issued orders to his forces to cross the Chickamauga river, the movement to begin at 6 o'clock on the following morning, by the extreme right, at Reed's bridge. The resistance offered by the enemy's cavalry, and the narrow country roads, delayed the advance until late in the afternoon. The movement forward was resumed at daylight on the 19th, and Buckner's corps and Cheatham's division crossed and formed. The division of Gen. W. H. T. Walker had crossed at Byram's ford after night on the 18th.

A sharp engagement was opened on the 19th with Forrest's cavalry on the extreme right. Wilson's brigade of Walker's division reinforced Forrest, and soon thereafter Walker's entire division, with Liddell's, was ordered to attack the enemy. Forrest, judging the enemy too strong for Pegram's small division and Wilson's brigade, was reinforced by Ector's brigade, when the enemy was driven back and a second battery captured; but a largely superior force compelled Forrest to retire. Dibrell's brigade participated in the second advance, dismounted, and moved up in line with the veterans of Ector and Wilson.

Rosecrans concluded that his left, held by Thomas' corps, was the chief point of attack, and that Bragg was seeking to turn it and gain possession of the Lafayette road between him and Chattanooga. Johnson's division of McCook's corps was sent to the assistance of Thomas, whom Crittenden in the meantime had reinforced with Palmer's division.

Walker attacked this force with his own division and Liddell's, with extraordinary vigor, but was forced back for reformation. Cheatham with five brigades was ordered to support Walker, but on coming up in supporting distance, found that he had nothing in his front to support. Communicating the condition of the field to the commanding general, he was ordered to advance and attack the enemy. In his report it appears that his brigade commanders were notified that he had no support on his right or left. Moving forward he met the enemy advancing on Walker's retiring troops. Jackson at once encountered the enemy, and soon the entire line was hotly engaged, with the result that the enemy was driven back three-quarters of a mile with heavy loss. Then taking shelter behind his breastworks, assisted by heavy reinforcements, he checked Cheatham's advance.

After an engagement of two hours' duration, the brigades of Jackson and Smith were withdrawn. These two brigades had driven the enemy "furiously," says Gen. A. J. Vaughan, 600 or 800 yards before them. General Smith reported to the division commander that his ammunition was nearly exhausted, but that he could hold the position until his wants were supplied, or until Strahl could relieve him. No grander spectacle was ever witnessed than the withdrawal of Smith's and Jackson's brigades and the substitution of Maney and Strahl, and no more dangerous experiment was ever made within musket range of an enemy and under a concentrated fire of artillery and small-arms. The advancing and retiring brigades both moved with unbroken lines and with such precision and promptness that the enemy was not, seemingly, sensible of the change. Scogin's Georgia and Scott's Tennessee batteries were in the advance with Jackson and Smith, and were especially distinguished. Lieut. John H. Marsh, commanding Scott's battery, was dangerously wounded in the active performance of his duty.

Thomas' official report shows that he had present for duty 21,448 men of all arms, reinforced by two divisions stronger than Cheatham's. Soon Maney and Strahl were enveloped by overwhelming numbers in front and on both flanks, and after a struggle of unparalleled heroism were forced to fall back to their original position on the right and left of Turner's battery.

The enemy, flushed with his triumph, rushed upon Cheatham's line, coming within short range of the battery. Turner then opened upon the advancing lines with grape, canister and shell. Cheatham and the officers of his staff were with Turner in what seemed the most critical moment of a soldier's life. The Federals, in numbers that made them look almost irresistible, were about to crush him, advancing with shouts of victory, when the division general said, "Now, Lieutenant," and the guns opened. The enemy hesitated, halted, doubled one regiment upon another, and then fled in wild disorder, leaving the field, as far as eye could reach, covered with dead and dying. The grass and dry leaves in front of the battery were soon in flames, and many of the Federal wounded were subjected to the torture of being roasted to death.

Turner had long commanded the battery as first lieutenant, and though deficient in expert knowledge, knew how to fight his guns. He passed over examining boards and was made captain for gallant conduct on the field of Chickamauga. Three pieces of Scogin's Georgia battery were engaged at the same time and rendered excellent service. But for this repulse, says General Cheatham, the enemy would have seized the crossing of the Chickamauga at Alexander's bridge and Hunt's ford, and rendered necessary new combinations and new dispositions for the battle of the next day.

During this engagement, Jackson's brigade took from the enemy three pieces of artillery and sent them to the rear. Wright's brigade occupied the left of the division line, made a brave fight for two hours and was constantly exposed to a flanking fire, which, growing in volume, finally forced it to retire. Carnes' artillery company, of this brigade, lost half its strength; the gallant Lieutenant Van Vleck was killed and most of the battery horses. The guns being abandoned on the field, the enemy undertook to remove them, but was driven off by Cheatham's division, and the guns remained between the contending lines until the subsequent advance of Stewart's division, when they were recovered by Captain Carnes.

About 2 p. m. General Stewart advanced with three brigades—Brown's, Bate's and Clayton's. After an engagement of an hour, Clayton withdrew for ammunition, and his position was occupied by Brown with his veteran brigade of Tennesseeans, who advanced rapidly, driving the enemy for several hundred yards, routing his first line and forcing his second position; but Brown's right was threatened by a heavy force and he was ordered to retire. This brigade captured five pieces of artillery after killing the gunners and horses. General Stewart reported that they were sent to the rear, and that Brown's left regiment, the Twenty-sixth Tennessee, drove the enemy from another battery, but was unable to bring off the guns.

Brown s brigade was relieved by Bate's, who assailed the enemy with great impetuosity. forced him from one position after another, losing and recapturing one piece of artillery. Clayton's brigade coming to his support, the two drove the enemy for half a mile beyond the Chattanooga road, but observing threatening movements on their right and left, they were ordered by General Stewart to fall back leisurely to the east side of the road. In these charges the Fifteenth and Thirty-seventh captured four pieces of artillery, and the Fifty-eighth Alabama, of Bate's brigade, participated with Clayton's brigade in the capture of three others. In the assault on the second line of the enemy, Col. J. B. Palmer, Lieutenant-Colonel Butler, Major Joiner and Maj. T. W. Newman were wounded, and Col. John M. Lillard mortally wounded. General Brown said he felt deeply the loss of Colonel Palmer's services on the field, "for with him on the right, the gallant Cook in the center, and the brave Lillard on the left, I felt the utmost confidence in the unwavering steadiness of my line." In the death of Colonel Lillard, he said, the country lost one of her best men and bravest soldiers.

Bushrod Johnson's division, just organized, consisting

of his own Tennessee brigade under Col. John S. Fulton, Forty-fourth Tennessee, Gregg's Tennessee brigade, McNair's brigade, and Bledsoe's Missouri battery, was first to cross the Chickamauga at 3 p. m. of the 18th, and no other troops, says General Johnson, crossed at any point until he "had swept the west bank in front of their respective places of crossing." He was not seriously engaged until 2 p. m. of the 19th, when, his line being formed about 1,000 yards west of the road to Chattanooga from Lee & Gordon's mills, his skirmishers were driven in. Bledsoe's and Everett's batteries opened fire, and Culpeper's battery of three guns was brought into action on Gregg's left. The enemy advanced on Johnson's and Gregg's brigades, and were easily repulsed, except on Gregg's left. The Fiftieth here lost 12 killed and 45 wounded before it moved from its position. Johnson pushed his command forward with orders to attack whenever opportunity permitted. Robertson's brigade of Hood's division advanced on the right of the Fiftieth, and the enemy was driven back with loss.

About this time General Gregg ventured out too far in front of his brigade to reconnoiter the enemy's position, and endeavoring to return was shot through the neck and fell from his horse. While the enemy was taking his spurs, sword and other valuables from his person, Robertson's Texans dashed forward and gained possession of the general and his horse, and inflicted serious punishment on the enemy. General Johnson, referring to the incident, declared that General Gregg was an able officer in command of a good brigade.

Johnson's brigade, under Colonel Fulton, after advancing 600 yards received a deadly fire of artillery and musketry for an hour, but forced the Federals to retire beyond the Chattanooga road, where they took cover in the woods to the left of a clearing, in which they posted their battery. The gallant Lieut.-Col. Robert B. Snowden, with the Twenty-fifth and part of the Twenty-third, watching his opportunity, wheeled to the right, gained the cover of the fence north of the clearing, fired two or three volleys at the battery, and then charged and captured it complete.

The Seventeenth, Third and Forty-first Tennessee, slightly in advance of the main line, encountered a force of the enemy moving by the flank toward the right of the Confederate army, which penetrated the left of the line of Johnson, filed off to the left and fired a volley into its rear, which caused Fulton to fall back, leaving 71 officers and men (including Major Davis of the Seventeenth) and the captured battery in the hands of the enemy. The enemy's column was then charged by the Third and Forty-first Tennessee and repulsed.

General Johnson reformed his division and bivouacked in line for the next day's battle. His loss was heavy. Among the killed was Lieut.-Col. Thomas W. Beaumont, Fiftieth Tennessee, a soldier of experience and eminence, beloved in Tennessee, a man of intellect and culture and practiced in all the graces of life. He died gloriously at the head of his regiment. The tribute of Colonel Napier, the historian of the Peninsular war, to the brave Colonel Ridge of the British army, who fell at the siege of Badajos can be extended to Colonel Beaumont: "No man died that day with more glory, yet many died, and there was much glory."

Soon after sunset of the 19th, Cleburne's division, supported by Jackson's and Smith's brigades of Cheatham's division, was ordered to attack the enemy, and if possible drive back his left wing. The Federals were posted behind hastily-constructed breastworks, and received the attacking force with a heavy fire of artillery and small-arms. Brigadier-General Polk on the right pressed forward, pushing his artillery within 60 yards of the enemy's line, when the latter ceased firing and disappeared from Cleburne's front. The darkness was so intense that no attempt was made to advance, and the lines were readjusted and the command bivouacked for the night with skirmishers a quarter of a mile in advance.

In this attack a part of Deshler's brigade fell back in some confusion on Smith's brigade, and when General Smith urged them forward, says Gen. A. J. Vaughan in his report, instead of going to the front they obliqued to the left. In the darkness it was not observed that Smith's two right regiments were uncovered, and at a halt in his immediate front, General Smith rode forward for an explanation of the delay, accosting a line in front, which proved to be that of the enemy. He was fired upon, and with his aide, Capt. Thomas H. King, was killed. At the same time Gen. A. J. Vaughan, then colonel of the Thirteenth, was fired upon under similar circumstances, and the shot intended for him killed the gallant Capt. John Donelson, acting assistant adjutant-general. Colonel Vaughn ordered the Thirteenth to fire, and the slayer of Donelson paid the penalty with his own life. In his official report, General Cheatham said: "In this night attack Brig.-Gen. Preston Smith, of Tennessee, received a mortal wound, from which he died in fifty minutes. At the head of his noble brigade, of which he had been the commander as colonel and brigadier-general for two years and a half, he fell in the performance of what he himself with his expiring breath said was his duty. Active, energetic and brave, with a rare fitness for command, full of honorable ambition in harmony with the most elevated patriotism, the State of Tennessee will mourn his fall and do honor to his memory."

Colonel Vaughan, commanding the brigade after Smith's fall, reported the capture of 300 prisoners and the colors of the Seventy-seventh Pennsylvania regiment, sent back to the division commander by Capt. I. B. Carthel, Forty-seventh Tennessee. Under a misapprehension General Cleburne reported the capture of the colors by his own command.

During the battle of the day and night Cheatham lost

1,900 men in killed and wounded, out of a total of 6,578. Among the killed was Col. J. A. McMurry of the Fourth Confederate. General Maney referred to him as "a gentleman of the noblest qualities and an officer of fine abilities and great gallantry." Lieut.-Col. Robert N. Lewis and Maj. Oliver A. Bradshaw, of the same regiment, both officers of great merit, were in quick succession severely wounded, when the command devolved upon Capt. Joseph Bostick. In Turner's battery, Lieutenant Smith was severely wounded and Lieutenant Ingram killed. Both shared with Turner the glory won here and at Perryville and Murfreesboro.

The First and Twenty-seventh, on the right of Maney, held their position for two hours, as Colonel Feild reported, "battling with as many of the enemy as could be brought to bear upon us. We occupied the position after our ammunition was completely exhausted, and then did not retire until the left wing of the brigade had been driven from the field by a movement of the enemy upon its left flank. We brought from the field a gun of one of our batteries (supposed to be Forrest's) that had been abandoned by all but two of its men." The First and Twenty-seventh lost 89 killed and wounded, and the Fourth lost 54. Among the dead was Lieut. Thomas B. Fitzwilliams, named by Captain Bostick as "the modest gentleman, gallant officer, and true soldier."

The Twenty-fourth battalion of sharpshooters, Maj. Frank Maney, already reduced to a skeleton by the casualties of war, went into action on the left of the Fourth Confederate with 39 guns, and only 17 could answer the next roll-call.

Col. George C. Porter, Sixth and Ninth, occupied the left of Maney, a position General Maney said was "most exposed, and the chances of the day demanded of this veteran command a bloody sacrifice." Porter was ordered by the division general, through an officer of his staff, to hold his position at all hazards; that help would surely come to his left. He did not care for odds against his front, but the enfilading attack on his left caused him soon to lose 180 men killed and wounded, out of a total present of 335. Help never came, and this broken and brave command withdrew in order to avoid capture. Lieut. T. F. Ragland was mortally hurt, Maj. J. A. Wilder, Capt. P. N. Conner, Capts. E. C. Harbert, J. L. Hall, Lieuts. J. B. Boyd, William M. Ingram, J. M. Withers, J. B. Stanley, N. McMullen, R. J. Dew and H. W. Head were wounded, many of them severely.

Vaughn's brigade sustained heavy losses. Maj. J. W. Dawson, One Hundred and Fifty-fourth, was seriously wounded while on duty with the skirmish line; Captain Kaneke of the same regiment was killed; Captain Cummings, Twelfth, was seriously injured.

In the list of killed in Wright's brigade were Captain Parks, Sixteenth; Lieutenants Harvey, Murray's battalion, Wade and Color-bearer Bland, Fifty-first and Fifty-second regiments, and Captain Whaley and Lieutenant Craig, Twenty-eighth. Among the wounded were Cols. John H. Anderson, Eighth; D. M. Donnell, Sixteenth; Maj. Thomas G. Randle, Captains Puryear, Cullum and Pond, and Lieutenants Cunningham, Leonard, Flynt and Shaw, Eighth; Lieutenants Potter, Owen, Fisher and Worthington, Sixteenth; Captain McDonald and Lieutenants Apple, Danley and Taylor, Twenty-eighth; Adjutant Caruthers, Lieutenants Banks and Ridout, Thirty-eighth; and Captain Burton, Lieutenants Billings, Chester, White, Haynie, Tilman, Fifty-first and Fifty-second.

During the battle of the 19th the Twenty-sixth Tennessee wavered for a moment (as reported by General Cheatham), and seemed to be in the act of falling back, when the intrepid Col. S. S. Stanton seized the colors of his regiment and, rushing to the front, called his men to follow him. Inspired by this heroic example, the regiment reformed on the colors and at once recovered the lost ground. While the flag was in the hands of Colonel Stanton it was pierced thirty times by the enemy's balls.

Strahl's brigade under its accomplished commander could always be trusted to perform the measure of its duty. It was hardly engaged before the horses of all the field officers of the three right regiments were killed, and Maj. C. W. Heiskell, of the Nineteenth, a very gallant officer, was severely wounded. Stanford's battery advanced with this brigade and was actively engaged. The Fourth and Fifth had Lieut. W. H. Neffer killed. Capt. W. W. Lackay, of the Nineteenth, referred to by Colonel Walker as "a gallant officer, brave soldier, a generous and courteous gentleman," was killed; Captain Frazier and Sergeant Thompson were desperately wounded.

General Bragg issued orders to attack the enemy at day dawn on the 20th, General Polk to assail on the right, and the attack to be taken up in succession rapidly to the left. Orders were sent at 11:30 on the night of the 19th by General Polk to Lieutenant-General Hill and Major-Generals Cheatham and Walker. Hill could not be found, and at daylight orders were sent to Generals Breckinridge and Cleburne of Hill's corps to advance with their divisions at once. The order was received in the presence of General Hill, who, Breckinridge reports, ordered a delay of the movement, and notified General Polk that his troops were getting their rations and could not move for an hour or more. He had alsc delayed his attack in consequence of a misapprehension on his part as to the relation between his line and that of General Cheatham. The reasons for delay were unsatisfactory to the commanding general, who in time relieved Generals Polk and Hill from their commands.

At 10 a. m. the attack was made by Cleburne and Breckinridge, Cheatham by order of General Bragg being held in reserve. The attack was taken up by Stewart, whose division was on the right of the left wing, and soon the whole army was engaged. General Bragg, in his official report, says "the attack on the left met with less resistance, much of the enemy's strength having been transferred to our right."

In the first advance of Cleburne, Wood's brigade lost 500 men killed and wounded in a few minutes, and the brigade was withdrawn. L. E. Polk's left had in turn been driven back, and his entire brigade was ordered to retire. Breckinridge, after a fierce combat at close quarters, routed the first line of the enemy, but found it impossible to break the second, and retired to his original position. Finally, another advance was ordered and Breckinridge dashed over the enemy's breastworks in his front, though the enemy made a stubborn resistance. In this assault he had the co-operation of Jackson's, Maney's and Wright's brigades of Cheatham's division.

Cleburne's attack was upon the point from which he had been repulsed in the forenoon. Lucius E. Polk's brigade, mainly Tennesseeans, charged and carried the northwestern angle of the enemy's breastworks, taking in succession three lines. The enemy fled precipitately and was pursued to the Chattanooga and Lafayette road. In his official report General Cleburne said of General Polk: "It is due to him and to the country which wishes to appreciate its faithful servants, to say that to the intrepidity and stern determination of purpose of himself and men I was principally indebted for the success of the charge on Sunday evening, which drove the enemy from his breastworks and gave us the battle." During this advance Lieut. W. B. Richmond, aide-de-camp to Lieutenant-General Polk, was killed; an active and efficient officer, invaluable to his chief.

Major-General Stewart attacked with Brown's brigade of Tennesseeans, advancing with Wood's brigade. Clayton was moved up, and Bate placed in line with him. The front line, says General Stewart, met "the most terrific fire it has ever been my fortune to witness." Wood broke in confusion, exposing Brown to an enfilading fire. The latter advanced still further, when his two right regiments gave way in disorder, but with his center and left, followed by Clayton and Bate, he pressed on, passing the cornfield in front of the burnt house, and beyond the Chattanooga road, driving the enemy within his intrenchments and passing over a battery of four guns. New batteries with infantry supports opening upon Stewart's front and flank, he retired and reformed on the ground first occupied. In this charge Generals Brown and Clayton were wounded by grapeshot, and General Bate had two horses shot under him. At 5 p. m. of that day the division again advanced, Col. Edmund C. Cook commanding Brown's brigade, and with a yell and at double-quick, dashed on the breastworks with a routed enemy flying in front.

The field officers of the Eighteenth were wounded, and the regiment was commanded in the battle of the 20th by Capt. Gid. H. Lowe. Maj. R. F. Saffell, commanding the Twenty-sixth after the fall of Colonel Lillard, reported a loss of 98 killed and wounded, out of 229 present for duty. The Thirty-second sustained a loss of 82. Colonel Cook reported that Private J. W. Ellis, after marching with his company for six weeks barefooted, went into battle in this condition, and was always with the front until he fell severely wounded. Private Mayfield, simultaneously shocked by a shell and wounded in the thigh by a minie ball, was placed on a litter and carried some distance toward the rear, when recovering consciousness he sprang from the litter and cried out, "This will not do for me," rejoined his company and gallantly performed a soldier's duty. Capt. W. P. Simpson, who succeeded to the command of the Twenty-third battalion after Major Newman was wounded, reported a loss of 43 killed and wounded.

Bate's brigade went into the fight with muskets in the hands of one-third of the men, but after the first charge, says General Bate, every man was supplied with an Enfield rifle and ammunition by the enemy in his retreat. Every field officer in the brigade except three was wounded, and in the two days' battle the brigade lost 607 killed and wounded, out of a total of 1,188. Col. R. C. Tyler, Fifteenth; Lieut.-Col. R. Dudley Frayser, Thirty-seventh; Col. Thomas B. Smith, Twentieth, were wounded; Capt. C. G. Jarnigan, Thirty-seventh, and Lieut. John B Kent, Fifteenth, were killed; Lieuts. J. C. Grayson and J. P. Acuff, Thirty-seventh, were mortally wounded. Capt. W. C. Yancey, of General Bate's staff, was severely wounded in the action of the 20th, and the color-bearer of the Thirty-seventh, a brave lad whose name was not reported, was killed in the final charge of his regiment.

Bushrod Johnson's command was formed at 7 a. m. of the 20th, but it was 10 o'clock when his skirmishers fell back under the advance of the enemy. Johnson opened with artillery and musketry and repulsed the attack, and an hour later a general advance was made by the Confederate army. The enemy in Johnson's front was posted along the road leading from Chattanooga to Lee & Gordon's mills, behind the fence at Brotherton's house, also occupying two lines of breastworks in Johnson's front, and to the left of it in the woods next to Brotherton's farm. Johnson advanced and engaged the enemy, fighting over 600 yards through the woods under a heavy fire of all arms, and finally crossing the road, his command passed on both sides of Brotherton's house. Though Johnson suffered heavy losses, his charge was irresistible, and the enemy fled or was killed or captured at the fences and outhouses.

Johnson advanced his whole line, Gregg's brigade under the gallant Col. Cyrus A. Sugg, Fiftieth, in rear, supported by Brig.-Gen. E. M. Law, then commanding Hood's division, in a third line. The scene now presented, said General Johnson, was unspeakably grand—

the rush of our heavy columns sweeping out from the shadow of the forest into the open fields; the glitter of arms; the retreat of the foe; the shouts of our men; the dust, the smoke; the noise of arms of whistling balls and grapeshot and bursting shells, made a battle scene of unsurpassed grandeur. Here General Hood gave his final order, "Go ahead and keep ahead of everything." The order was obeyed. Gregg's brigade, under Sugg, captured nine pieces of artillery. Four 3-inch rifle pieces were taken from the First Missouri Federal artillery, and turned over to Bledsoe's First Missouri Confederate artillery of that brigade. Pushing forward, the crest of the ridge was occupied and a damaging fire was delivered on the retreating masses, but the enemy reformed and returned to the attack, and without support on his right, Johnson was forced to fall back. At this point, Lieut.-Col. James D. Tillman, Forty-first Tennessee, was severely wounded. The troops rallied in line at the batteries, again repulsed the enemy and held the hill, and when the final charge was made, General Johnson reports, "with a shout we drove the enemy far down the northern slope to the bottom of the deep hollow beyond. We had completely flanked and passed to the rear of his position and thus aided in carrying the heights south of Snodgrass' house." Colonel Fulton, commanding Johnson's brigade, was greatly distinguished. Of Colonel Sugg, General Johnson said: "I feel especially indebted for his gallant, able and efficient services in commanding Gregg's brigade. He is a good and meritorious officer." Johnson's brigade lost 299 killed and wounded. Gregg's brigade lost 585 killed and wounded; of these 109 men were killed on the field.

Lieut.-Col. John L. McEwen, Jr., Forty-fourth; Liout.-Col. Horace Ready and Maj. J. G. Lowe, Twenty-third; Lieut.-Col. Watt W. Floyd and Maj. Samuel Davis, Seventeenth, were wounded. Lieutenant Scruggs, Seventeenth, was wounded and captured on the 19th and recaptured by his own regiment on the 20th. Colonel Floyd relates that in passing the Vidito house, he learned from Mr. Vidito, who was on the outlook, that the four ladies of his family "were lying in a little hole under the kitchen floor, concealed from the enemy, where they had been for two days. As we passed the house he discovered who we were and exclaimed, 'The Confederates have the field!' whereupon the ladies threw off the planks that covered them, rushed out of the house and came bounding toward us with shouts of joy, as women never shouted before.

The Seventeenth sustained heavy losses, the Twenty-third lost 103 killed and wounded, and every member of the field and staff was wounded. Lieuts. Nash L. Kuhn and D. M. Molloy, Twenty-fifth, were killed. Adjt. A. R. Greigg of the same regiment recaptured the colors of the Tenth South Carolina.

The Sixty-third Tennessee, Col. A. Fulkerson, of Gracie's brigade, went into action between 4 and 5 o'clock p. m. of the 20th, supporting Kershaw's brigade. The regiment was on the right of the brigade, and although in battle for the first time, exhibited the steadiness and valor of veterans, and was among the most conspicuous participants in the action fought and won by Preston's division of Buckner's corps, on the heights near 'Snodgrass' house. Out of an aggregate of 404, it lost in killed and wounded 202. General Gracie said in his report of the battle, "Lieut.-Col. A. Fulkerson, Sixty-third Tennessee, commanded the regiment and led it into action. To him it owes its discipline and efficiency. Colonel Fulkerson was severely wounded, making with the one received at Shiloh (as major of the Nineteenth) the second during the war. He is deserving of a much higher position." Others wounded were Capts. W. N. Wilkinson, William H. Fulkerson, Lieuts. Henry Fugate, S. W. Jones, H. J. Barker, W. P. Rhea, James J. Aerec, A. H. Bullock, George H. Neill, J. H. McClure and Layne.

Capt. James T. Gillespie and Lieut. Shelby M. Deaderick were killed and buried on the field made famous by the prowess of their regiment.

According to Maj. Thomas Kennedy Porter, Buckner's chief of artillery, the artillery of the corps was seldom used, the ground over which the battle was fought being so thickly wooded that the officers could not see more than 300 yards to the front, and could not ascertain what damage was inflicted. When Preston's division became hotly engaged and the enemy sent a large force to strengthen the line in his front, three batteries were then posted about 1,000 yards from the Chattanooga road, where the enemy was crossing, which did great execution, silenced the enemy's guns, cut off his reinforcements, and enabled Preston to capture between 500 and 600 prisoners.

In this day's battle, Forrest's cavalry was active and vigilant. Armstrong's division and Dibrell's brigade fought on foot and were always up with the infantry, for which General Forrest commended them with "pride and pleasure." Morton's and Freeman's Tennessee batteries rendered valiant service in resisting the advance of Gordon Granger's column. Forrest's men were without rations, his horses were without water and had only a partial ration for two days, but no complaint was made.

The army of Tennessee bivouacked within the enemy's intrenchments or upon the heights it had so gallantly won.

On the morning of the 20th of September, General Rosecrans reported present for duty, 67,877 officers and men. In his revised statement of casualties he reported a loss of 16,170 killed, wounded and captured, of which 1,657 were killed on the field, 9,756 were wounded, and 4,757 were captured by the Confederates. He had 9,913 serviceable horses and 246 pieces of field artillery. Capt. Horace Porter, his chief of ordnance, reports the loss of 36 pieces of artillery, the same number of artillery carriages, and 22 caissons and limbers, with 8,008 rifled muskets, 5,834 sets of infantry accouterments, 150,280 rounds of infantry ammunition, and a large lot of sabers, carbines and pistols.

At the close of the day, Mr. C. A. Dana, the distinguished editor, then assistant secretary of war, reported to his chief that "Chickamauga is as fatal a name in our history as Bull Run." The field was abandoned by the commanding general and two of his corps commanders, Crittenden and McCook. Thomas held the Federal left until his line of works was assaulted and carried by the brigade of Brigadier-General Polk, and until Bushrod Johnson flanked and passed to the rear of Gordon Granger; about that time Kelly's brigade of Preston's division had captured two entire regiments of Granger's, when the enemy fled precipitately.

In his official report, Lieutenant-General Longstreet, commanding the left wing of the Confederate army, noted the capture by his command of 40 pieces of artillery, over 3,000 prisoners, 10 regimental standards, 17,645 small-arms, and 393,000 rounds of small-arms ammunition collected on the "field." General Bragg reported the capture of 8,000 prisoners and 51 pieces of artillery. Capt. O. T. Gibbes, ordnance officer, army of Tennessee, reported that 66 pieces of captured artillery were received by him at Ringgold, Ga. Gen. U. S. Grant, in a letter to Gen. W. T. Sherman, dated September 30, 1863, says "our loss was 54 pieces of artillery."

It was not until 2 p. m. of the 21st that an advance of the army was made. Cheatham, leading it on the right, bivouacked for the night at the "Mission House," and moving early on the morning of the 22d, reached Missionary Ridge at 10 a. m. He reported that finding the enemy on the crest of the ridge in force, his position was assailed and carried by Maney's and Vaughan's brigades after a spirited engagement of a few minutes. "The position was found to be one of much natural strength, increased by breastworks made of stone and fallen timber, but the enemy, now demoralized by a succession of disasters, made but a feeble resistance, and fled in great haste."

Chickamauga was a great victory for the Confederate army, and yet a great disappointment to Tennesseeans. When the barren victory at Murfreesboro was won, and the State was abandoned, temporarily as it was believed, the criticism of the tactics of the commanding general was guarded and respectful; but when Cheatham's division was halted on the crest of Missionary Ridge, hope ceased to be "an anchor of the soul."

No Tennesseean complained of the burthens put upon his people by a state of war, but official robbery and oppression, insults to the old men and to their mothers, their wives and daughters, taxed the endurance of brave men to the utmost. The rule of the Federal authorities in Tennessee was worse than an iron one. Mr. Dana, under date of September 8, 1863, in a dispatch to E. M. Stanton, secretary of war, said Andrew Johnson, military governor of the State, "complains of the tardiness of Rosecrans, and these long months of precious time wasted. He has fallen under bad influence, and especially under that of his chief of detectives, a man named Truesdall. This man is deep in all kinds of plunder, and has kept the army inactive to enable his accomplices and himself to become rich by jobs and contracts," and he could have added, by the wholesale robbery of the people.

The expulsion of non-combatants from their homes; the appropriation of private property not needed by the army; the indignities offered to people of both sexes; the grasping, domineering, oppressive temper and practices of a class of which Truesdall was a representative, have no parallel in modern history. But in spite of the surrender of the State, and of the unnamed acts of violence and cruelty, the soldiers of Tennessee were steadfast to their colors to the end.

CHAPTER VIII.

THE FATAL PAUSE ON MISSIONARY RIDGE—CHANGES IN COMMAND—CHEATHAM'S DIVISION—THE FIGHT AT LOOKOUT MOUNTAIN—DISASTER ON MISSIONARY RIDGE—GALLANTRY OF TENNESSEE COMMANDS—BATTLE AT RINGGOLD—THE KNOXVILLE CAMPAIGN.

THE army of Tennessee was halted on Missionary Ridge, and remained inactive for two months, until the 25th of November, when it was driven from its position and forced back to Dalton, Ga.

On the 16th of October, General Rosecrans was superseded in the command of the army of the Cumberland by Maj.-Gen. George H. Thomas, and the military division of the Mississippi, consisting of the departments of the Cumberland, Ohio and Tennessee, was created, with Maj.-Gen. U. S. Grant in command.

General Bragg preferred charges against Lieutenant-General Polk for disobedience of orders at Chickamauga, and on the 29th of September, by a special order, suspended him from command. President Davis, "after an examination into the causes and circumstances," ignored the action of General Bragg, and assigned Polk to the command of the department of Mississippi and Louisiana. On taking leave of his army corps and turning it over to Major-General Cheatham the day following his suspension, he said: "I leave my command in the care of the bravest of the brave, who has often led them in the darkest hours of their trials. He and you will have my hopes and prayers to the Ruler of the Universe for your happiness and success."

A large percentage of the four Tennessee brigades

under Cheatham had seen service under General Polk, from Belmont to Chickamauga. Whatever of glory and honor they had won was under his leadership, and they were devoted to him above all men next to their own division general. The men murmured, the officers resented in silence the action of the commanding general, and for this the Tennesseeans were scattered. Maney's brigade was assigned to Walker's division, Strahl's to Stewart's, Vaughn's to Hindman's; Wright's brigade was detached and sent to Charleston, east Tennessee; and the Mississippi brigade, commanded by the gallant Walthall, and the Alabama brigade of John C. Moore, were assigned to Cheatham's division. Cheatham was proud of his new command, but his devotion to the old one "was wonderful, passing the love of woman." His command of Polk's corps was temporary. Lieutenant-General Hardee was restored to the army of Tennessee, and commanded the corps at the disastrous battle soon to be fought.

Cheatham resumed command of his division after dark on the 24th of November and some hours after the capture of Walthall's pickets by Hooker's corps. Why General Walthall "was not sustained is yet unexplained," says General Bragg in his official report; "the commander on that part of the field, Major-General Stevenson, had six brigades at his disposal." When General Cheatham took command he was accompanied by Gen. John C. Breckinridge, and the two, in the presence of Cheatham's chief of staff, were urged by the commanding general to hasten to Lookout mountain, and if possible withdraw Stevenson's division from its summit and conduct our forces across Chattanooga creek. Holtzclaw's brigade relieved Walthall, the enemy retiring before his advance; the danger was not imminent or immediately threatening, and the order was easily executed.

General Bragg, referring to the affair in his official report, says: "Orders were immediately given for the ground to be disputed until we could withdraw our forces across Chattanooga creek, and the movement was commenced. This having been successfully accomplished, our whole forces were concentrated on the ridge." General Walthall reports that at 11 o'clock p. m., "under orders from Major-General Cheatham, I moved my command to McFarland's spring, where I passed the night." Major-General Stevenson reporting his action to the commanding general, stated: "I was engaged in issuing the necessary orders for the retirement of the troops when Major-General Cheatham arrived (at 8 p. m.). He informed me that he had come to consult with me, but not to assume command. I sent the troops from the top of the mountain down, and then proceeded myself to a point near its base where General Cheatham and myself had an appointment to meet. Here, as senior officer, he assumed command, and I gave no further directions with regard to the retirement of the troops except such as I received from him for those of my own division. Here we also met Major-General Breckinridge, who, when Major-General Cheatham took command, returned to his corps."

The First brigade (Brown's Tennessee) crossed Chattanooga creek at 11 p. m., followed at short intervals by the entire force. The movement was conducted successfully and in order by General Cheatham; no ammunition was lost, not a sick or wounded man was abandoned; but no credit was accorded him for his services, and no mention was made of his name in the official report of the commanding general.

Brown's Tennessee brigade was ordered at 4 a. m., on the 25th, to the extreme right of the line as reinforcements to General Cleburne, in whose front the enemy was supposed to be concentrating forces for his main attack. The brigade occupied the position between the left of Cleburne's line of defenses and the railroad. Brown's skirmishers, he reports, were all the while engaged, and so hotly for a time that he reinforced the line until half of the brigade was deployed. The advance of the enemy was checked, many were killed and wounded, and 50 prisoners captured. An hour before sunset the brigade was ordered to report to Major-General Cheatham, the enemy having already penetrated the line on his left, and there the brigade was warmly engaged until ordered to retire across the Chickamauga. In the action in support of Cleburne, Maj. W. H. Joyner, of the Eighteenth, was wounded, Lieut. J. T. Pigg, of the Thirty-second, was killed, and 16 men wounded.

Bate's brigade, Col. R. C. Tyler commanding, was fiercely assailed; the troops on the right gave way, and in attempting to rally the broken line Colonel Tyler was dangerously wounded, when the command devolved on Lieut.-Col. James J. Turner, of the Tenth and Thirtieth. Colonel Turner, in his history of the battle, says he fell back about 1,500 yards and halted and formed across the road, when the division commander, Brigadier-General Bate, directed him to follow on to the pontoon bridge at the Chickamauga, the sun being an hour high. "Cobb's battery and a number of detached soldiers, numbering about 500, came up and fell into our line of battle. As all the generals had left and we were free to act independently, we concluded to stop the Federal forces at this point till darkness should arrest their advance. Cobb's battery opened upon the enemy vigorously, and I directed Major Caswell to deploy his Georgia battalion of sharpshooters to cover our front and feel the enemy, which order was executed to the letter. As soon as the Federals came in range, both sides opened with great spirit. We had the advantage in position, but were outnumbered by at least three to one. The firing was very severe, ammunition was nearly exhausted, and it was quite dark—an hour after sunset. At this juncture, after a battle of two hours, General Breckinridge, the corps commander, came up from the rear, having heard the firing, and inquired, 'What command is this and why are you here?' He added that his entire command had been broken and was in retreat, and ordered me to fall back." The darkness was Turner's protection, and the order from Breckinridge saved him from capture. The regiments on his right, he says, came out to the road within a few yards of the Federal line. (Col. Jas. J. Turner, sketch of Thirtieth Tennessee.)

Turner's command consisted of the Thirty-seventh Georgia, Lieut.-Col. Joseph T. Smith; Fourth Georgia sharpshooters, Major Caswell; Tenth Tennessee, Major O'Neill; Fifteenth and Thirty-seventh Tennessee, Lieut.-Col. R. Dudley Frayser; Twentieth Tennessee, Maj. W. M. Shy; First Tennessee battalion, Maj. Stephen H. Colms; his own gallant regiment, the Thirtieth Tennessee, and Cobb's battalion of artillery, composed of Cobb's, Slocumb's and Mebane's batteries. Turner fought Sheridan's division and held it in check for two hours. It was a gallant action, and the names of the participants will live forever. Turner won promotion, if he did not receive it. The rear alone was open to him, the Federal troops in vastly superior numbers were in front and on both flanks; but the line of retreat was taken up in good order, no pursuit was made, and he reached the pontoon bridge over the Chickamauga at midnight, just before it was removed. Vaughn's brigade (now of Hindman's division), says General Vaughn, "did some of the greatest and most heroic fighting of the war, and though forced to fall back, contested every inch of ground." When flanked on the left, the brigade retired in order.

Maney's brigade of Walker's division was on the extreme right in support of Cleburne, Maney being posted in rear of Smith's line. The First and Twenty-seventh, Col. H. R. Feild, were moved in front of the works to a very exposed position on the right of Warfield's Arkansas regiment. General Cleburne ordered Cumming to charge the enemy in his front, and he advanced with the Fifty-sixth and Thirty-sixth Georgia. "Twice," says General

Cleburne, "he was checked and had to reform, and Warfield's Arkansas regiment and the gallant First and Twenty-seventh Tennessee prepared to share his next effort. At the command, the whole rushed forward with a cheer, and the enemy, completely surprised, fled. Lieutenant-Colonel Sanders, leading the left of Mills' Texas regiment on the enemy's flank, pursued him to the foot of the ridge and nearly across the open ground in front. The column returned with 8 stand of colors and 500 prisoners. The enemy, reinforced, made an attempt to follow, but was met and routed by the Fiftieth Tennessee." In this gallant action of the Fiftieth, its noble colonel, Cyrus A. Sugg, fell mortally wounded. He was greatly distinguished at Chickamauga; no officer of the army had a more promising record, and no Tennessee name deserves greater honor. General Cleburne, referring to him and to Col. McConnell of Cumming's brigade, said: "I did not personally know them, but I saw and can bear witness to their gallant bearing and noble death." Gen. L. E. Polk's Arkansas and Tennessee brigade was not actively engaged, but rendered good service in holding an important position. The same can be said of Wright's Tennessee brigade, which was acting under the orders of the commanding general of the army.

Cheatham's division took position on Missionary Ridge to the left of the road which led down to the right of our fortifications. It was moved to the right and again, under orders, to the left, where it was subjected to a fire of the enemy's artillery and sharpshooters. General Walthall, in his report of the battle, says: "My position was not attacked in front; but about 4 o'clock, when the lines had been forced and broken on the left (of Cheatham), and after the enemy had reached the top of the ridge, the major-general commanding directed me to form my line across the ridge at right angles to the position I then occupied. This change was made under a brisk fire of the enemy, who advanced upon me along the crest of the ridge. The fire was kept up until after dark, but the position was held, the enemy not approaching nearer than 200 yards." General Cheatham considered this action of Walthall's one of the most brilliant of the war, and his report of it excessively modest. The change of position under fire and the repulse of the enemy's repeated assaults were a distinction to the brigade commander and to his veteran troops. If he had yielded, an army corps would have poured down upon Cleburne's left and overwhelmed him. In this combat General Walthall and Maj. John Ingram, of General Cheatham's staff, were seriously wounded; Adjt. John W. Campbell, Twenty-ninth Mississippi, was mortally wounded, and the brigade sustained a loss of 28 wounded. Moore's brigade was on the left of Walthall and the right of Jackson's two brigades, where the enemy made a great effort to drive them from their position, but failed signally.

The general commanding the army seemed to appreciate Walthall's splendid performance. In his official report he says: "Lieutenant-General Hardee, leaving Major-General Cleburne in command on the extreme right, moved toward the left when he heard the heavy firing in that direction. He reached the right of Anderson's division just in time to find it had nearly all fallen back, commencing on its left, where the enemy had first crowned the ridge. By a prompt and judicious movement he threw a portion of Cheatham's division directly across the ridge facing the enemy, who was now moving a strong force immediately on his left flank. By a decided stand here the enemy was entirely checked, and that portion of our force to the right remained intact." In fact, when General Hardee came up from the right, Walthall had already formed across the ridge and driven the enemy back. With enthusiasm Hardee said to Cheatham, "You have saved the right of the army." The "heavy firing" heard by General Hardee was Walthall's resistance to the advance of the enemy.

Strahl's Tennessee brigade, Stewart's division, constituted a part of what General Stewart aptly called "the attenuated line" by which Missionary Ridge was nominally held. It was swept from the crest after a stout resistance and crossed the Chickamauga in order.

Hooker had been sent from Virginia with two army corps to reinforce the Federal army; Sherman's army had been brought up; and two months of inaction enabled General Grant, in command at Chattanooga, to concentrate a great army. On the other hand, Longstreet with his corps and Bushrod Johnson with his division had been detached and sent to east Tennessee, and, says Lieutenant-General Stewart, "the preparation made by General Bragg indicated a purpose to retreat," but it was abandoned. The movement by the enemy on Bragg's right caused an undue concentration in that quarter, while the left and center were strung out into little more than a skirmish line. The movements of the Federal army were in full view of the Confederate troops; the numbers were overwhelming, and "like a spring tide from the mighty ocean, they rushed up the slopes of Missionary Ridge." It was not surprising that parts of Anderson's division, a mere skirmish line, were seized with a panic, and without resistance abandoned the field and lost the battle, and possibly prevented a greater disaster.

General Grant was slow to claim the great victory he had won. At 7:15 p. m. of the 25th of November he advised the general-in-chief of the Federal army, "I have no idea of finding Bragg here to-morrow." It was not until the morning of the 27th that the advance of Thomas' forces under Hooker and Palmer reached the front of the Confederate rear guard of Hardee's corps under Cleburne, less than 20 miles away, at Ringgold, Ga.

Cleburne's command consisted of 4,157 men; his retirement to this place had been leisurely made; he was in position carefully selected, and he received the attack about 8 a. m. of the 27th, by a force many times his superior. The repulse was a bloody and decisive one, from which the enemy made no attempt to advance. Cleburne lost 20 killed, 190 wounded, and Hooker admitted a loss of 65 killed and 377 wounded. Among the wounded of Cleburne's command were Col. W. D. Robison, Second Tennessee, and Lieut.-Col. J. G. Cole, Fifth (Confederate) Tennessee, mortally wounded. Colonel Cole had been a conspicuous figure of Polk's brigade in all of the great battles of the Southwest, and had won commendation and honor on every field.

General Grant reported his losses at Missionary Ridge at 5,616 killed, wounded and missing. The corrected figures show a loss of 5,824. The Confederate loss he estimated "probably less than ours," but claimed 6,142 prisoners, 40 pieces of artillery and 7,000 stand of small-arms by the entire army; while Hooker, commanding the Eleventh and Twelfth army corps, reported the capture by his command of "6,547 prisoners, 7 pieces of artillery, 9 battleflags and not less than 10,000 stand of small-arms." General Grant, in forwarding Hooker's report under date of March 25, 1864, placed this endorsement upon it: "Attention is called to that part of the report giving the number of prisoners and small-arms captured, which is greater than the number really captured by the whole army."

This General Hooker, who was so defiant of historical accuracy, is the same Gen. Joseph Hooker who was the author of a slanderous communication addressed to the Hon. S. P. Chase, dated December 28, 1863, and published in 1890, on page 339, Series 1, Vol. XXXI, Part 2, of "Official Records of the Union and Confederate Armies," in which the following statement was made: "Before the battle of Lookout, I had opened communication with Cheatham's division, holding the summit of the mountain, and had good reason to believe that I would have succeeded in bringing in all the enlisted men with some of the officers but for their untimely removal. They were relieved by Stevenson's division. The only conditions I required were that they should give themselves to me with arms in their hands, and take the oath of allegiance; theirs, that they should be permitted to return to their homes, or go where the conscription could not reach them. You will remember that when Bragg retreated from Tennessee he was compelled to march the Tennessee troops under guard."

No man, living or dead, could have believed that there was the slightest foundation for this story. It was evidently prepared with the expectation that the author of it would be exalted for his supposed zeal in the prosecution of his missionary labor in beguiling Cheatham's division from allegiance to their country and to their honor, and with no expectation that it would be published as a part of the history of those perilous days.

Cheatham's division never occupied the summit of the mountain. The First and Twenty-seventh Tennessee, of Maney's brigade, Walker's division, were there on picket duty for about ten days in October; and this consolidated regiment is the same referred to in handsome terms by General Cleburne for participation in the battle of November 25th, when, uniting with troops from Texas and Arkansas, Sherman's forces in their front were driven from the field.

"You will remember" (said this American Munchausen) "that when Bragg retreated from Tennessee he was compelled to march the Tennessee troops under guard." Judge Chase could remember nothing so idiotic or so impossible. It is a pity that the author of the slander had not remembered the lesson taught in Dickens' "Great Expectations:" "Don't you tell no more lies, Pip; that ain't the way to get out of being common, old chap." When Bragg retired from Tennessee, Cheatham's division constituted the rear guard of the army, and its last service before ascending the mountain was to drive, in inglorious confusion and retreat, the Federal cavalry by which it was assailed at Cowan. When it reached Chattanooga it was stronger than when it retired from Shelbyville; furloughed men and volunteers joined it en route, and in many instances ran the gauntlet of Federal pickets, scouts and cavalry. In addition to the Tennessee brigades of Cheatham, John C. Brown's and Bushrod Johnson's were composed exclusively of Tennesseeans, and Bate's, Polk's and Smith's were largely Tennessee troops; and these, with the artillery and cavalry from that State, constituted a force too strong and too spirited to "march under guard," unless they had been led by the vaunting "hero of the battle above the clouds."

The Knoxville campaign, under Lieut.-Gen. James Longstreet, was participated in by Bushrod Johnson's brigade; the Fourth, Eighth, Ninth and Tenth Tennessee cavalry under Brig.-Gen. W. Y. C. Humes; Dibrell's cavalry brigade; Freeman's, White's, Rhett's and McClung's batteries, and the First Tennessee cavalry, Col. Onslow Bean. General Johnson, with his own and Gracie's brigade, reached the front of Knoxville on the 27th and 28th of November, 1863. On the 29th he moved to the attack on Fort Loudon in support of the assaulting column under Brigadier-General Humphreys, Gracie on the right. The command approached to within 250 yards of the enemy's fortifications on which the assault was made, and was soon under fire. At this time Gracie was withdrawn by the lieutenant-general commanding, and an order made for Johnson to halt. The attack was abandoned, and Johnson occupied, with his skirmishers, the advance rifle-pits, distant 250 yards from the enemy's fort. During the assault on Fort Loudon, Johnson's brigade lost Lieut. S. W. Ross, Forty-fourth, and Private J. P. Hicks, Seventeenth, killed, and 19 officers and men wounded. On December 4th, at nightfall, Johnson's command withdrew from the line of investment in front of Knoxville and moved with Longstreet's corps to Bean's Station and

Rogersville. Major Lane, of the Twenty-third, withdrew the pickets from the enemy's front at 11 p. m.

Johnson's command was not in good condition for a campaign in midwinter; the men were poorly clad and many of them barefooted. On December 14th they participated in a combat at Bean's Station, in which the brigade sustained a loss of 6 killed and 52 wounded. In this affair General Johnson advanced directly against the enemy and drove him to the buildings at Bean's Station, where he met with a stout resistance. During the night the enemy succeeded in making his escape, after sustaining a loss of 100 killed, with many wounded, and the sacrifice of valuable stores.

In the advance on Knoxville the cavalry under General Wheeler attacked the enemy first at Maryville, where Dibrell's Tennessee brigade charged the Eleventh Kentucky cavalry, scattering it into small parties and capturing 151 prisoners. Wolford's Federal brigade, coming up to the rescue, was assailed by Wheeler and driven over Little river in wild confusion, and 85 prisoners taken. The following day Wheeler moved across Little river and attacked the brigades of Federal cavalry commanded by Gen. J. M. Shackleford, Col. Frank Wolford and Col. Charles D. Pennebaker, charging this force with the Eighth and Eleventh Texas, the Third Arkansas, and Dibrell's Tennessee brigade. The enemy's line was broken and the field abandoned in disorder. The pursuit was continued for three miles to the river opposite Knoxville, where the enemy dashed over the pontoon bridge, creating great consternation, while many plunged into the river and some were drowned. In this stampede 140 prisoners were captured and many killed and wounded.

The suffering of the Confederate soldiers in this campaign may be inferred from the fact that General Longstreet, on December 16th, informed the adjutant-general that "we shall be obliged to suspend active operations for want of shoes and clothing."

CHAPTER IX.

THE ATLANTA CAMPAIGN—JOHNSTON TAKES COMMAND —REUNION OF CHEATHAM'S DIVISION—TENNESSEE-ANS AT RESACA—NEW HOPE CHURCH—DALLAS—KENESAW MOUNTAIN—LOSSES OF THE ARMY—BATTLES ABOUT ATLANTA—JONESBORO.

GENERAL JOSEPH E. JOHNSTON assumed command of the army of Tennessee on the 27th of December, 1863. His order announcing the fact was received by the troops with great enthusiasm. He found the army deficient in numbers, arms, subsistence, stores and field transportation. General Bragg had reported to the President after Missionary Ridge, expressing "confidence in the courage and morale of the troops." The courage of the troops was indisputable—recent failures and disasters had not shaken it, and General Johnston's presence revived confidence in themselves and hope for the success of the cause for which so many sacrifices had been made.

One of the earliest orders of General Johnston was the restoration of Maney's, Strahl's and Vaughan's brigades to Cheatham's division, together with Donelson's old brigade, afterward Wright's, Col. John C. Carter, Thirty-eighth Tennessee, commanding. The *esprit de corps* of the division was fully restored, and the old spirit of invincibility was again dominant. The enthusiasm consequent upon this reunion found expression in a serenade to the general-in-chief, in which the men of the entire division were participants, a demonstration not prescribed in army regulations, but so hearty and cordial that the severity of discipline relaxed in favor of the veterans.

General Johnston occupied the next three months in

the training and discipline of his troops. The winter was exceptionally severe; the rations were not the best; fuel and clothing, hats and shoes were not always obtainable; but the approach of spring found the men cheerful and ready for action. On the 1st of May, 1864, the army of Tennessee had of infantry, artillery and cavalry, 42,756 officers and men.

Gen. W. T. Sherman, commanding the Federal army, telegraphed the general commanding at Washington, on the 5th of May, that his forward movement was being made from Ringgold, Ga., with an army 80,000 strong. General Johnston was soon reinforced by the divisions of Major-Generals Loring and French, commanded by Lieutenant-General Polk, and known thereafter as Polk's corps. On the 5th the Confederate troops were formed to receive the enemy; Stewart's and Bate's divisions in Mill creek gap, and Cheatham on Stewart's right, occupying a mile on the crest of the mountain. The assault on Stewart and Bate was repulsed, but Cheatham and Bate were constantly skirmishing until the night of the 12th.

On the 8th an attack was made in force upon the angle where the Confederate right and center joined the crest of the mountain held by Pettus' (Alabama) brigade, but was quickly repulsed. Brown's Tennessee brigade was moved to the left of Pettus, and there sustained and repulsed a vigorous assault on the 9th by a large force advancing in column. General Johnston says "it was met with the firmness always displayed where Pettus or Brown commanded and their troops fought." At 9:40 p. m., Major-General Hooker, reporting his failure at Mill creek gap (defended by Stewart, Cheatham and Bate) to General Sherman, said: "General Geary failed to take it; with his force it is impossible." On the 16th General Hooker reported that his loss up to the 15th was 760 wounded.

On the night of the 12th the army of Tennessee (Hardee's corps in advance) moved to Resaca, Vaughan's brigade of Cheatham's division having already been sent to the support of Brigadier-General Cantey. On the arrival of Hardee's corps it was fiercely attacked by the army of the Ohio, commanded by Major-General Schofield, and Palmer's corps, with the result that Gen. Geo. H. Thomas reported to the commanding general under date of May 14th, that "the position in front of Palmer and Schofield cannot be carried," adding, "Howard's corps is moving in on Schofield's left." With this force, heavy skirmishing with frequent assaults continued for three days. Failing in an attack on Cheatham's line made on the 13th, unsuccessful efforts were made to carry the line held by Cleburne and Bate during the 14th and 15th, and during this time heavy skirmishing was continuous along the line occupied by the army of Tennessee. On the night of the 15th, Gen. W. H. T. Walker, then at Calhoun, reported that the Federal army was crossing the Oostenaula river near that place, and this forced General Johnston's retirement from Resaca.

On the 9th, Major-General Wheeler, with Brig.-Gen. Geo. G. Dibrell's Tennessee brigade of cavalry, composed of the Fourth, Col. Wm. S. McLemore; Eighth, Capt. Jefferson Leftwich; Ninth, Capt. James M. Reynolds; Tenth, Maj. John Minor; and Allen's Alabama brigade, Colonel Cook's Texas Rangers, and the Eighth Confederate regiment, encountered about 5,000 Federal cavalry near Varnell's Station. Dismounting his command except two regiments, he routed the enemy and captured 100 prisoners, among them Colonel La Grange, commanding brigade, 3 captains and 5 lieutenants. After the rout Colonel Cook and Colonel Prather charged into the enemy's ranks, killing and wounding large numbers.

In a dispatch of May 16th, General Sherman stated that his wounded at Resaca numbered 3,375; the number of dead, he added, "will not exceed the usual proportion." There were 1,790 Federal dead buried at Resaca, and 170 Confederates. The latter loss was mainly on the skirmish line, the assaults made by the Federal troops being received behind intrenchments. General Johnston coming on the field observed the skirmish line in front of Vaughan's brigade hotly engaged, having first driven the enemy's advance from the field, then repelled a desperate assault by reinforcements, and he turned to the gallant commander of the brigade and asked, "What command is this in your front?" Vaughan's face was lighted by the enthusiasm of battle, and with pride in his brave fellows he replied, "That is the Thirteenth and One Hundred and Fifty-fourth Tennessee of my brigade, Cheatham's division." "And who," asked the general, "is in command of that line?" The answer was, "Lieut.-Col. John W. Dawson." Turning to the division general, Johnston said: "I never witnessed such a display of skill and courage, and never saw troops under such discipline and control." Every movement of Dawson was under observation, in full view of the commanding generals of the army, the corps, the division and the brigade. Such an opportunity is of rare occurrence. Dawson did not know whose eyes were upon him; his lofty courage, sense of duty and patriotism alone animated him, and this display at Resaca was made by him on every battlefield of the war where he fought. Col. Sidney S. Stanton, Twenty-eighth Tennessee, who fell in this battle, had been conspicuous in many engagements, was greatly distinguished at Chickamauga, had attained State distinction in civil life, and was recognized as a rising man. Though he deprecated war, he carried into it the coolness and courage of his race, and by his personal example stimulated his command to action.

"By his light
Did all the chivalry move
To do brave acts."

At Calhoun, Cleburne reported, he moved to his left and rear to meet a force threatening Walker's right. Polk's

Arkansas and Tennessee brigade met the movement and punished the enemy handsomely, and no further attempt at an advance was made. At nightfall Johnston retired toward Adairsville, and on the morning of the 17th went into position two miles north of that place—Cheatham's division being placed in front of Hardee's corps, supported by Cleburne, Bate on his left. The enemy made a furious assault on Cheatham, but was repulsed and was content to hold his position. At night Johnston retired to Kingston, and after a halt of a few hours the army fell back to Cassville. There General Johnston's battle order was read to the army. Hardee reported that his troops were "wild with enthusiasm and delight." The position was well chosen, and the best occupied during the campaign. But, according to General Johnston's report, Polk and Hood were unwilling to risk a battle there, claiming that a part of Polk's corps was enfiladed by the Federal artillery, and urged Johnston to abandon the place and cross the Etowah river. Hardee, although not so favorably posted, remonstrated against the change. General Johnston yielded his better judgment and lost his best opportunity, and at daylight of the 20th reluctantly crossed the Etowah.

On the 19th, Federal dispatches were sent to Washington stating that "Johnston retires slowly, leaving nothing, and hitting hard if crowded." Sherman, in spite of his heavy losses, reported on the 21st of May that he would move on the following day "with full 80,000 fighting men," and had ordered the Seventeenth army corps, 10,500 strong, to join him.

Hardee's corps spent Saturday and Sunday near Allatoona, on Pumpkin Vine creek; on the following day marched eight miles to meet a reported movement of the enemy; on the 24th marched ten miles below Dallas, and then immediately returned where General Johnston had concentrated the army.

On the 27th, Cleburne fought the battle of New Hope

Church. Being attacked at 4 o'clock p. m. by four army corps, the enemy was repulsed after an obstinate fight of an hour and a half, and Cleburne reported the capture of 160 prisoners, exclusive of 72 sent to his field hospital, and the capture of 1,200 small-arms. His own loss was 85 killed and 363 wounded, and he estimated the Federal loss at 3,000. According to General Hardee, 700 Federal dead were lying within a dozen paces of Cleburne's line. Brig.-Gen. W. A. Quarles, with his Tennessee brigade, received the thanks of General Cleburne for efficient co-operation in resisting the attack. A body of the assailants charged into Quarles' rifle-pits, where most of them were killed or captured.

On the 28th, in a heavy skirmish in which Strahl's brigade was engaged, Col. Jonathan J. Lamb, Fifth Tennessee, was mortally wounded. He was a courageous, vigilant and well-beloved officer, who fought in the ranks as a private soldier at Shiloh, and won promotion from time to time until he reached the command of his regiment. At his fall the gallant Maj. Henry Hampton, of the Fourth, assumed command of the Fourth and Fifth (consolidated). On the same day, Bate's division, on the left of the army and in front of the village of Dallas, was instructed to ascertain by a forced reconnoissance if the intrenchments were still held in force. The brigade commanders mistook the resistance to Armstrong's cavalry as a signal to advance and rushed forward to the attack, but were compelled to draw off after sustaining a loss of 300 killed and wounded.

Skirmishing continued from day to day, and early in June the army had been transferred to a line before Marietta. On June 14th, Lieutenant-General Polk was killed by the enemy's artillery while on the outpost of Bate's division on Pine mountain by a chance shot from a Federal battery distant 600 or 700 yards, at the time being in company with General Johnston and Lieutenant-General Hardee, making an examination of the position.

The death of this eminent man brought great sorrow to the army. He had been a central figure in it from its organization, and the men had discovered at an early day that he was insensible to fear and was just and generous, qualities which secured for him the love and confidence of officers and men.

The battle of Kenesaw Mountain was fought by Cheatham on the 27th of June. The order to attack his position was dated the 26th. It was executed by Newton's division of the Fourth army corps, over 5,000 strong—Harker's brigade on the right in two columns, Wagner's brigade on Harker's left in one column, the regiments being in close column, left in front. Whittaker's brigade of Stanley's division, Fourth corps, followed Harker as a support, in column of deployed regiments. Kirby's brigade of the same division followed Wagner in column with two-regiment front, the two brigades of Stanley also numbering 5,000 men. Wood's division of the Fourth corps sent two brigades, 5,000 strong, in rear and to the left of Newton's division, Kimball's brigade being on the extreme left. Davis' division of the Fourteenth army corps, over 6,000 strong, was on Newton's right and confronted Cleburne's division, with Grose's brigade and other troops in reserve. Cheatham's entire division was hotly engaged, but the salient in his line was the main point of attack. Davis' division, in front of Cleburne, was repulsed. Nearly all of the field officers in McCook's brigade, including the brigade commander, were killed.

General Johnston said in his "Narrative:"

The most determined and powerful attack fell upon Cheatham's division and the left of Cleburne's. The lines of the two armies were much nearer to each other there; therefore the action was begun at shorter range. The Federal troops were in greater force, and deeper order, too, and pressed forward with the resolution always displayed by the American soldier when properly led. An attempt to turn the left was promptly met and defeated by Cheatham's reserve, Vaughan's brigade. After maintaining the contest for three-quarters of an hour, until more of their best soldiers lay dead and wounded than the number of British veterans that fell in General Jackson's celebrated battle of New Orleans, the foremost dead lying against our breastworks, they retired unsuccessful, because they had encountered intrenched infantry unsurpassed by that of Napoleon's Old Guard, or that which followed Wellington into France, out of Spain.

Cheatham lost 195 officers and men, Cleburne, 11. The attempt to turn Cheatham's left was defeated by the prompt action of Brig.-Gen. O. F. Strahl with his brigade. Brig.-Gen. C. G. Harker fell in the attempt to lead his command to a second assault. The "angle" in Cheatham's line, known to the survivors of Harker's division as "dead angle," was held by parts of Maney's and Vaughan's brigades, Maney's brigadc commanded by Col. F. M. Walker, Nineteenth Tennessee. It was the weak point in the line, and when the preparation for the assault was made, the division general instructed his command that the position must be held at any cost; that its loss meant more than the loss of a battle. The First and Twenty-seventh, One Hundred and Fifty-fourth and Thirteenth Tennessee held the post of danger and of honor, and to the order of their chief they responded with a ringing cheer that must have chilled the hearts of the advancing hosts. On the right and left of these two (consolidated) regiments stood their veteran comrades of the division, ready to support them or to take their places and join in the defense. The advancing column came like a great surge of the sea, and the resistance was like that of the rock upon which the billows break; 385 Federal dead were left lying in front of Maney's brigade, and 415 in front of Vaughan's. Gen. Geo. H. Thomas officially reported the loss of the army of the Cumberland during the month of June at 5,747, three-fourths of which must have occurred in front of the "dead angle." On the 29th a truce was agreed to at the request of the Federal commander, to permit the burial of his dead lying near the Confederate breastworks.

The Federal and Confederate armies confronted each other for twenty-six days near Marietta. On July 4th Cheatham's division was sent to the assistance of Hood's corps, and during that day the division sustained a great loss in the wounding and permanent disability of Brig.-Gen. A. J. Vaughan, who lost a leg from a cannon shot while his brigade was resting in the trenches. General Vaughan was a representative of the best type of the Southern soldier, was present and conspicuous at every battle from Belmont down to this date, and never failed in his duty. His judgment was never at fault, his vigilance and reliability proverbial, his courage superb, and in another age he would have been classed with "Hector and all the gallantry of Troy."

Maj.-Gen. Alexander P. Stewart, of Tennessee, was made lieutenant-general, and on the 7th of July assumed command of Polk's corps, a well-deserved promotion won on the battlefield. General Johnston hesitated in his recommendation of a successor to Lieutenant-General Polk. Major-Generals Loring and French commanded divisions in Polk's corps. Cheatham and Cleburne had just won great distinction at New Hope church and Kenesaw Mountain. Without their knowledge their names were considered by the commanding general, but his conclusion to present the name of Stewart was approved by the army.

On the 8th of July two corps of Sherman's army crossed the Chattahoochee and intrenched, and on the night of the 9th the army of Tennessee crossed the river and went into position two miles from it. On the 17th the entire Federal army crossed the river, and that evening General Johnston received notice from the war office at Richmond that he had been relieved and that Hood, now a full general, had been placed in command of the army. General Johnston turned the command over to General Hood on the afternoon of the following day. Lieutenant-General Stewart expressed the opinion of the Tennessee troops when he said that the army gave General Johnston "love and unlimited confidence," and that there was no abatement of it when he retired. The event affected the army like the hush of death.

The loss of the army of Tennessee in killed and wounded from the commencement of the campaign to the crossing of the Etowah, as reported by Medical Director Foard, was 3,384, more than half of it in Hood's corps; between the passage of the Etowah and Lost Mountain the loss was 2,005, more than half in Hardee's corps. During the entire campaign from Dalton to the 18th of July, when General Johnston was relieved, the losses were, killed 1,221, wounded 8,229; total, 9,450. From the 18th of July, when General Hood assumed command, to the 1st of September, 1864, the close of the campaign, the losses were, killed 1,756, wounded 10,267; total, 12,023.

The Third Tennessee, famous as the regiment organized and disciplined by Gen. John C. Brown, lost Maj. F. C. Barber and Capt. D. G. Alexander, killed at Resaca, and later on, at Powder Springs, the gallant Col. C. H. Walker fell. Under his command the Third had maintained the reputation won at Fort Donelson. At Raymond, Miss., under very trying circumstances, he commanded the regiment with unsurpassed skill and courage. Maj. John P. McGuire, Thirty-second Tennessee, was badly wounded, and Lieutenant Waddy killed, at Powder Springs. Capt. J. B. Ward, Fifth, an officer of unusual merit, was killed at Resaca. Lieut. John Talley, Ninth, fell at Resaca; and all along the line from Dalton to Atlanta our brave fellows fell, but on account of the constant movements and change of position of the army no reports were made by regimental commanders. At the close of the campaign in September, there were few of them surviving to record the action of their commands.

Col. Edmund Cook, Thirty-second, fell at Powder Springs. Major-General Stevenson said of him and Colonel Walker that they were "models of the Southern soldier and gentleman." Colonel Cook was commanding Brown's brigade when he fell mortally wounded. His regiment and brigade were exposed for the want of adequate support on the left and sustained heavy losses; but he held his command in place, and by his coolness and noble bearing concentrated upon himself the attention of his entire command. He was a gifted man, endowed with a genius for war as well as for the pursuits of civil life. A great career in either was within his reach.

On assuming command, General Hood reported his strength at 48,750 of all arms, including 10,000 cavalry and 1,500 Georgia militia. General Cheatham was placed in command of Hood's corps, General Maney in command of Cheatham's division. The enemy was in bivouac between Atlanta and the Chattahoochee, and was preparing to advance.

On the evening of July 18th our cavalry was driven across Peachtree creek, and the army of the Cumberland was in the act of crossing it; whereupon General Hood decided to attack the enemy while attempting to cross this stream, and orders were given to advance at 1 p. m. of the 20th. The movement was delayed to 4 p. m. and resulted in failure and heavy losses.

On the following night Hardee was moved south on the McDonough road with orders to attack at daylight on the 22d and turn the left of McPherson's army. The attack was made with great energy, General Hood reporting that Hardee's troops "fought with great spirit and determination, carrying several lines of intrenchments, Wheeler attacking on the right. Hardee held the ground he gained. Cheatham, commanding Hood's corps, carried the enemy's intrenchments in his front and captured

5 guns and 5 stand of colors. Hardee captured 8 guns and 13 stand of colors." This was one of the bloodiest and most desperately-fought battles of the war, and was the last success of the army of Tennessee. The poor result of the combat was the withdrawal of the enemy's left to the Georgia railroad and the investment of Atlanta.

The tribute Tennessee paid was the lives of many of her noblest sons. Among the dead was Col. Frank M. Walker, Nineteenth regiment, commanding Maney's brigade, who had won promotion at Kenesaw Mountain. His commission as brigadier-general, long deserved, arrived the day following his death. Col. C. W. Heiskell, who succeeded to the command of the Nineteenth, said of him: "Here in the forefront of the battle, in the midst of his command, his voice ringing out in words of encouragement and command above the sound of rifles, so close that the muzzles of the guns of the Confederates almost touched those of the enemy, the beloved and chivalrous Walker fell; of him it is impossible to speak too highly." He was an officer of great distinction, of exalted character, and equal to any position in civil or military life.

Among the others who fell on the 22d were the fearless and dashing Capt. Wayne Caldwell and Color-Bearer Ab Dinwiddie, of the Fifth; Capt. J. L. Hall, Lieuts. Jesse Farrell, G. Robinson and W. H. Morgan, Ninth; Maj. P. H. V. Weems, Capt. J. H. Johnson and Lieutenant Divny, Eleventh. Capt. W. C. Bryant and Adjt. W. C. Whitfield, Twenty-eighth, were killed; Col. D. C. Crook and Lieut. William Betty of same regiment were severely wounded. Lieut.-Col. John B. Johnson and Maj. Kyle Blevins, two young and accomplished officers of the Twenty-ninth, were killed. Capt. J. B. Carthell, commanding the Twelfth, was killed; a noble man, deserving promotion, which would have come to him in a few days. Col. W. P. Jones and Lieut.-Col. Henry C. McNeill, Thirty-third, were both killed. To them Brig.-

Gen. Alexander W. Campbell, the first colonel of the regiment, made this tribute: "It may be truly said of them and of their regiment, as of all that immortal band which will be known in history as Cheatham's Tennessee division, none were braver, none more cheerful in the discharge of duty, nor more patriotic in their devotion to the cause they had espoused."

Capt. Richard Beard, of the Fifth (Confederate) Tennessee regiment, published the following statement in relation to the death of Maj.-Gen. J. B. McPherson, the distinguished Federal soldier who fell in the battle of the 22d of July. Captain Beard was in the line ordered by General Cleburne to advance and never halt until the breastworks were captured. "We ran through a line of skirmishers and took them without firing a gun, and suddenly came to the edge of a narrow wagon road running parallel with our line of march, and down which General McPherson came thundering at the head of his staff. He came upon us suddenly. My own company had reached the verge of the road when he discovered us. I was so near him as to see every feature of his face. I threw up my sword as a signal for him to surrender. He checked his horse, raised his hat in salute, wheeled to the right and dashed off to the rear in a gallop. Corporal Coleman, standing near me, was ordered to fire, and it was his shot that brought General McPherson down. He was passing under the branches of a tree, bending forward, when the fatal bullet struck him. It ranged upward and passed near the heart. A volley was fired at his fleeing staff. I ran up to the general, who had fallen upon his knees and face, but no sign of life was perceptible. Right by his side lay a signal officer of his staff whose horse had been shot from under him, who if hurt at all, was slightly wounded. He informed me that the dead man was General McPherson. General Sherman, in his history of the campaign, alleged that McPherson's pocket-book and papers were found in the haversack of a prisoner; but his person and effects were not disturbed by my command." The lines were rapidly changing, and in a few minutes McPherson's body was in the Federal lines. Captain Beard was a gentleman before he was a soldier, and would not have tolerated a robbery or an indignity to the person of the dead general.

On the 26th Lieut.-Gen. Stephen D. Lee assumed command of Hood's corps, General Cheatham returning to his division. In the engagement of the 28th Lieutenant-General Stewart was wounded, and on the 29th Cheatham was placed in command of his corps; Brigadier-General Maney commanding Cheatham's division. On the 13th of August General Stewart resumed command of his corps, and a sick leave was granted to General Cheatham, which continued until after the battle of Jonesboro.

On the morning of July 28th the enemy moved out to our left and gained the Lickskillet road. At 11 a. m. Lee's corps was ordered to check the movement. Brig.-Gen. John C. Brown, commanding Hindman's division, with Clayton's division on his right, advanced and drove the enemy across the road and to a distance a half mile beyond, where he encountered temporary breastworks, from which he was repulsed with heavy loss. Clayton advanced ten minutes later and was driven back; then Walthall's division of Stewart's corps, under instructions from General Lee, assaulted the position from which Brown and Clayton had just been driven.

General Walthall reported that "Brigadier-General Quarles (with his brigade of Tennesseeans) made a bold and bloody assault, but his command was checked by the strong force in his front and the unopposed troops which lapped his left and poured into it a damaging flank fire." "If," said General Walthall, "it had been possible for the daring of officers and the desperate fighting of the men to have overcome such odds in numbers and strength of position as we encountered all along my whole line, the enemy would have been beaten, but double the force could not have accomplished what my division was ordered to undertake."

Among the killed of Quarles' brigade was Col. John R. White, Fifty-third Tennessee. Major Richardson, who succeeded to the command of the regiment, was mortally wounded, and the gallant Lieut.-Col. Joseph D. Wilson was desperately wounded and reported killed by the brigade commander. "They fell," said General Quarles, "in front of their regiments, leading them on the enemy's works. Truer and more earnest patriots never lived, and the purity of their private characters gracefully softened the ruder virtues of the soldier." Col. W. F. Young, Forty-ninth, was so severely wounded that the amputation of his right arm was necessary. The five officers next in rank to him were shot down, and the seventh, Capt. Thomas H. Smith, took command of the regiment. Lieut. Ashton Johnson, aide-de-camp to General Quarles, was killed, and Polk G. Johnson, of his staff, was wounded. The latter, unable to mount his horse, obtained permission to serve one of the guns of Yates' battery then in action. Rev. J. H. McNeily, chaplain of the Forty-ninth, followed his regiment to the field. General Quarles said of him that "he was everywhere to be seen, ministering to the physical and spiritual comfort of the dying and wounded."

Under orders the troops were withdrawn at nightfall within our line of works, upon which, from the 28th of July to the 6th of August, the enemy made gradual approaches and assaults; but all of his attacks were repulsed, the most notable being that made on the 6th on Tyler's Tennessee and Georgia brigade of Bate's division. This brigade, holding an intrenched skirmish line, sustained and repulsed three assaults of the enemy, in which his loss was, in killed and wounded and prisoners from 800 to 1,000 men, besides two colors and 300 to 400 stand of small-arms and all of his intrenching tools.

Tyler's brigade lost 20 killed and wounded. General Lee, to whom Bate was reporting, issued a special order commending the conduct of the division, particularly Tyler's brigade and said: "Soldiers who fight with the coolness and determination that these men did will always be victorious over any reasonable number." The troops engaged in this affair were the Second Tennessee, Col. William D. Robison; Tenth, Col. William Grace; Fifteenth and Thirty-seventh, Lieut.-Col. R. Dudley Frayser; Twentieth, Lieut.-Col. W. M. Shy; Thirtieth, Lieut.-Col. James J. Turner; Thirty-seventh Georgia, Lieut.-Col. Joseph T. Smith; Fourth battalion Georgia sharpshooters, Capt. B. M. Turner; that intrepid soldier, Gen. Thomas Benton Smith, of Tennessee, commanding.

On the evening of the 30th of August the enemy reached the vicinity of Jonesboro. General Hood was deluded into the belief that the movement was made by two corps and that the Federal army was still in front of Atlanta. Hardee's and Lee's corps were ordered to Jonesboro, Hardee in command, Hood remaining at Atlanta. Cleburne, in command of Hardee's corps, was in position at 9 o'clock. Lee was in position at 11 o'clock a. m. of the 31st, after an all-night march, delayed because of the fact that Cleburne had encountered the enemy on his march. General Hood's order was to attack the enemy and drive him across Flint river, but instead of two army corps, Hardee found in his front the Federal army, except the Twentieth corps left at Chattahoochee bridge. Lee attacked the enemy behind works and was repulsed, falling back with a loss of 1,300 killed and wounded. Cleburne carried the temporary works of the enemy. A portion of his corps had crossed Flint river and captured two pieces of artillery, which he was unable to bring over the river. The enemy threatening an attack on Lee's corps, Cleburne's division under Brig.-Gen. M. P. Lowrey was dispatched to support Lee, while Maney, commanding Cheatham's division, occupied

Lowrey's position. Hardee was on the defensive. At night Lee's corps was ordered by General Hood to return, his dispatch stating that "the enemy may make an attack on Atlanta to-morrow." On the 1st of September Hardee's corps received repeated assaults made by Sherman's army, but he succeeded in maintaining his position and enabled General Hood to withdraw from Atlanta. At night Hardee retired four miles to Lovejoy's Station, where the army was concentrated.

On the 1st of September Brig.-Gen. John C. Carter commanded Cheatham's division; on the 31st of August and the 1st of September Col. Geo. C. Porter commanded Maney's brigade, and Col. James D. Tillman commanded Strahl's. Brig.-Gen. George W. Gordon commanded Vaughan's, known hereafter as Gordon's, and on the 1st Col. John H. Anderson commanded Carter's brigade.

On the second day of the battle of Jonesboro, Carter drove the enemy back and retook the works in which a part of Govan's brigade of Cleburne's division had been captured. Gordon's brigade was most exposed, and maintained the reputation acquired under the leadership of Smith and Vaughan. The enemy, in vastly superior numbers, was held in check until night closed the battle, and Gordon covered the retreat to Lovejoy's Station.

Col. A. J. Long, Eleventh Tennessee, was mortally wounded, and Capt. J. H. Darden killed—true and faithful soldiers, said General Gordon, greatly beloved and deeply lamented. The Third lost the gallant Col. Calvin J. Clack, promoted to the command of the regiment after the fall of Colonel Walker near Marietta. The veteran Tenth mourned the loss of Col. William Grace, mortally wounded, who in his last hours gave expression to a single regret, that he could no longer serve the cause he loved so well. The chaplain of his regiment, Father Blieml, was killed while administering the sacrament of extreme unction to the dying on the field.

Tyler's brigade was hurled against the intrenched position of the enemy, protected by an abatis, well-served artillery and two lines of infantry, and it was, said Lieut.-Col. James J. Turner, Thirtieth, a fatal charge, the command losing one-third of its strength in killed and wounded. Capt. J. H. Turner, Thirtieth, gallantly leading his company forward, received four mortal wounds almost in an instant, and Colonel Turner was twice wounded and disabled.

General Hood telegraphed General Bragg on September 5th the following account of the battle: "To let you know what a disgraceful effort was made by our men in the engagement of August 31st, I give you the wounded in the two corps: Hardee's, 539, Lee's, 946; killed, a very small number." Many times during the months of July and August the troops from Tennessee had made fruitless assaults against the enemy's intrenchments; their ranks had been decimated at Peachtree Creek and at the battle of Atlanta, heralded as a great victory, and the right of Quarles' brigade was slaughtered at the affair on Lickskillet road. It took that high order of courage which they exhibited in the face of these disheartening disasters for Long and Clack and Grace and Darden and Turner to lead their men up to the enemy's intrenchments, over his abatis, defended by five times their number, into the very jaws of death—there to die, surrounded by a third of their comrades killed or wounded.

Then, almost before the wounded were gathered from the field or the dead buried in unmarked graves, the general commanding records his displeasure at their conduct because the harvest of death was not more abundant.

CHAPTER X.

THE CAMPAIGN AGAINST SHERMAN'S BASE — ALLATOONA AND DALTON—HOOD'S CAMPAIGN IN TENNESSEE—SPRING HILL—RESPONSIBILITY FOR THE LOST OPPORTUNITY—THE BATTLE OF FRANKLIN —SIEGE OF MURFREESBORO—SIEGE AND BATTLE OF NASHVILLE—RETREAT TO MISSISSIPPI.

GENERAL HOOD continued in position at Lovejoy's Station until the 18th of September, when he moved toward the West Point railroad and formed a line of battle near Palmetto. Here Lieutenant-General Hardee was at his own request removed from command of his corps, and was succeeded by Major-General Cheatham.

On the 29th Hood crossed the Chattahoochee at Pumpkintown and Phillips' ferry, the army being made to understand by the commanding general that this movement was not in retreat, but that his purpose was to draw the Federal army out of Atlanta and force Sherman to attack him in position. Hood continued his march as far north as Dalton, then moved westward to Gadsden and thence to Tuscumbia, Ala., where the army was halted for three weeks. When the Federal army retired from the front of Lovejoy's Station, General Hood's conception of the campaign was embodied in a dispatch to the secretary of war, dated September 6, 1864, "Sherman continues his retreat beyond Jonesboro;" but in fact, after Hood moved across the Chattahoochee, Sherman pursued him to Gaylesville, Ala., then returned to Atlanta, and on the 15th of November began his march through Georgia to the sea.

Stewart's corps captured the garrisons at Big Shanty and Acworth, and General French attacked Allatoona, but when success was near at hand the appearance of heavy reinforcements caused him to withdraw. Cheatham made a demonstration on Dalton with Strahl's brigade, and the garrison, 1,200 strong, surrendered unconditionally; and at the same time General Bate, under orders of Cheatham, demanded the surrender of a formidable blockhouse a few miles distant. The bearer of the flag, the gallant Capt. H. J. Cheney, had his horse killed under him. The flag was not recognized, whereupon General Bate advanced his artillery and opened fire. The first shell entered a porthole, killing fifteen or twenty of the garrison, and the white flag was run up.

General Beauregard, commanding the military division of the West, in forwarding to the war department the report of General Hood's operations in the Tennessee campaign, under date of January 9, 1865, said: "The plan of the campaign into middle Tennessee was correct as originally designed by General Hood, and if carried out without modification, would have compelled General Sherman to return to middle Tennessee to protect and repair his lines of communication before he could have collected enough supplies to march his army from Atlanta to the seacoast. But instead of crossing the Tennessee river at Guntersville, as General Hood had intended when at Gadsden [where General Beauregard had an interview with him], he changed his course while on the march and repaired to Tuscumbia and Florence," where three precious weeks were spent, enabling Sherman to repair the road to Chattanooga and collect his supplies for the march to the sea, at the same time affording time to General Thomas, who had been sent to Tennessee, for the concentration of an army at Nashville strong enough to crush Hood even if he had avoided Franklin.

Marching through the beautiful valley of the Tennessee over which Sherman had carried his army to reinforce Grant at Chattanooga, our army was appalled at its desolation. Sherman's iron hand had destroyed it—old men, non-combatants, women, children, faithful slaves, were reduced to want. General Hood published an order to the troops directing their attention to the ruin of this fair land, and appealing to their manhood to recover the State of Tennessee. The torch, not the sword, had caused this great destitution and made a desert of the valley. In many parts it was unoccupied. The inhabitants, robbed of cattle, horses, mules, and the implements of husbandry destroyed, were fugitives from their own homes without having committed a crime, forced into an "exile without an end, and without an example in story."

On the 21st of November General Hood began his march to Nashville; on the 29th crossed Duck river three miles above Columbia, and then, with Cheatham's and Stewart's corps and a division of Lee's corps, marched to Spring Hill.

Cheatham was in front, and in his official report, dated December 11, 1864, General Hood stated that "Major-General Cheatham was ordered at once to attack the enemy vigorously and get possession of this pike [the road to Franklin], and although these orders were frequently and earnestly repeated, he made but a feeble and partial attack, failing to reach the point indicated." Again, in his history of the campaign ("Advance and Retreat," pp. 285, 286) it is related: "General Stewart was then ordered to proceed to the right of Cheatham and place his corps across the pike north of Spring Hill. By this hour, however, twilight was upon us, when General Cheatham rode up in person. I at once directed Stewart to halt, and turning to Cheatham I exclaimed with deep emotion, as I felt the golden opportunity fast slipping from me, 'General, why in the name of God have you not attacked the enemy and taken possession of the pike?'" Lieutenant-General Stewart, referring to this statement in a published letter, says that "no such exclamation by Hood to Cheatham could have been made in my presence."

Major-General Cheatham gave the following account of the affair at Spring Hill:

In pursuance of orders from army headquarters, my command crossed Duck river on the morning of the 29th of November, 1864, the division of Major-General Cleburne in advance, followed by that of Major-General Bate, the division of Major-General Brown in the rear. The march was made as rapidly as the condition of the road would allow and without occurrence of note, until about 3 o'clock p. m., when I arrived at Rutherford's creek, two and one-half miles from Spring Hill. At this point General Hood gave me verbal orders as follows: That I should get Cleburne across the creek and send him forward toward Spring Hill, with instructions to communicate with General Forrest, who was near the village, ascertain from him the position of the enemy, and attack immediately; that I should remain at the creek, assist General Bate in crossing his division, and then go forward and put Bate's command in to support Cleburne, and that he would push Brown forward to join me.

As soon as the division of General Bate had crossed the creek I rode forward, and at a point on the road, about one and a half mile from Spring Hill, I saw the left of Cleburne's command just disappearing over the hill to the left of the road. Halting there, I waited a few minutes for the arrival of Bate, and formed his command with his right upon the position of Cleburne's left, and ordered him forward to the support of Cleburne. Shortly after Bate's division had disappeared over the same range of hills, I heard firing toward Cleburne's right and just then General Brown's division had come up. I thereupon ordered Brown to proceed to the right, turn the range of hills over which Cleburne and Bate had crossed, and form line of battle and attack to the right of Cleburne. The division of General Brown was in motion to execute this order when I received a message from Cleburne that his right brigade had been struck in flank by the enemy and had suffered severely, and that he had been compelled to fall back and reform his division with a change of front.

It so happened that the direction of Cleburne's advance was such as had exposed his right flank to the enemy's line. When his command was formed on the road by which he had marched from Rutherford's creek, neither the village of Spring Hill nor the turnpike could be seen. Instead of advancing directly upon Spring Hill, his forward movement was a little south of west and almost parallel with the turnpike toward Columbia, instead of northwest upon the enemy's lines, south and east of the village. A reference to the map will show Cleburne's line of advance. General Cleburne was killed in the assault upon Franklin the next day, and I had no opportunity to learn from him how it was that the error of direction occurred.

Meanwhile General Bate, whom I had placed in position on the left of Cleburne's line of march, continued to move forward in the same direction until he had reached the farm of N. F. Cheairs, one and a half mile south of Spring Hill.

After Brown had reached the position indicated to him and had formed a line of battle, he sent to inform me that it would be certain disaster for him to attack, as the enemy's line extended beyond his right several hundred yards. I sent word to him to throw back his right brigade and make the attack. I had already sent couriers after General Bate to bring him back and direct him to join Cleburne's left. Going to the right of my line I found Generals Brown and Cleburne, and the latter reported that he had reformed his division. I then gave orders to Brown and Cleburne that as soon as they could connect their lines they should attack the enemy, who were then in sight; informing them at the same time that General Hood had just told me that Stewart's column was close at hand, and that General Stewart had been ordered to go to my right and place his command across the pike. I furthermore said to them that I would go myself and see that General Bate was placed in position to connect with them, and immediately rode to the left of my line for that purpose.

During all this time I had met and talked with General Hood repeatedly, our field headquarters being not over 100 yards apart. After Cleburne's repulse I had been along my line and had seen that Brown's right was outflanked several hundred yards. I had urged General Hood to hurry up Stewart and place him on my right, and had received from him the assurance that this would be done; and this assurance, as before stated, I had communicated to Generals Cleburne and Brown.

When I returned from my left, where I had been to get Bate in position, and was on the way to the right of my line, it was dark; but I intended to move forward with Cleburne and Brown and make the attack, knowing that Bate would be in position to support them. Stewart's column had already passed by on the way toward the turnpike, and I presumed he would be in position on my right.

On reaching the road where General Hood's field quarters had been established, I found a courier with a message from General Hood requesting me to come to him at Captain Thompson's house, about one and a fourth miles back on the road to Rutherford's creek. I found General Stewart and General Hood. The commanding general there informed me that he had concluded to wait till morning, and directed me to hold my command in readiness to attack at daylight.

I was never more astonished than when General Hood informed me that he had concluded to postpone the attack till daylight. The road was still open—orders to remain quiet until morning—and nothing to prevent the enemy from marching to Franklin.

The following communication, written by Governor (afterward Senator) Harris of Tennessee, then acting as aide to General Hood, is a valuable contribution to the history of this campaign. It is copied from Drake's "Annals of the Army of Tennessee," for May, 1877. A copy was furnished to General Hood:

Gov. James D. Porter:

Dear Sir: In answer to yours of the 12th instant, I have to say that on the night that the army of Tennessee, under command of Gen. J. B. Hood, halted at Spring Hill on its march from Columbia to Nashville, General Hood, his adjutant-general, Major Mason, and myself occupied the same room at the residence of Captain Thompson, near the village. Late at night we were aroused by a private soldier, who reported to General Hood that on reaching the camp near Spring Hill he found himself within the Federal lines; that the troops were in great confusion, a part of them were marching in the direction of Franklin, others had turned toward Columbia, and that the road was blocked with baggage-wagons and gun-carriages, rendering it impossible to move in order in either direction. Upon the receipt of this report, General Hood directed Major Mason to order General Cheatham to move down on the road immediately and attack the enemy. General Hood and myself remained in bed. I went to sleep, and I supposed that General Hood did the same. At daylight on the following morning we learned that the Federal army had left Spring Hill and was being concentrated at Franklin.

On the march to Franklin, General Hood spoke to me, in the presence of Major Mason, of the failure of General Cheatham to make the night attack at Spring Hill, and censured him in severe terms for his disobedience of orders. Soon after this, being alone with Major Mason, the latter remarked that "General Cheatham was not to blame about the matter last night. I did not send him the order." I asked if he had communicated the fact to General Hood. He answered that he had not. I replied that it is due to General Cheatham that this explanation should be made. Thereupon Major Mason joined General Hood and gave him the information. Afterward General Hood said to me that he had done injustice to General Cheatham, and requested me to inform him that he held him blameless for the failure at Spring Hill. And, on the day following the battle of Franklin, I was informed by General Hood that he had addressed a note to General Cheatham, assuring him that he did not censure or charge him with the failure to make the attack.

Very respectfully,

ISHAM G. HARRIS.

Memphis, Tenn., May 20, 1877.

Maj.-Gen. John C. Brown, commanding Cheatham's division, gave the following account of the same affair:

My division comprised four brigades of infantry, commanded respectively by Gen. S. R. Gist, of South Carolina, Gens. O. F. Strahl, G. W. Gordon and John C. Carter, of Tennessee. The whole command on the morning of November 29, 1864, when I left my bivouac on the

Mooresville turnpike in front of Columbia, Tenn., numbered not exceeding 2,750 effective men. Gist's brigade was the largest and Strahl's was next in numerical strength; those of Gordon and Carter being about equal in the number of effective men. We started on the march about sunrise, and after traversing cedar brakes and pathless woods, crossed Duck river by a pontoon previously laid, about four miles above Columbia, at or near what was known as Davis' ferry or Davis' ford. Conforming to the daily alternations, my division was the rear of your (Cheatham's) corps. After crossing Duck river, as I now recollect, at or near Bear creek, the commanding general, apprehending an attack on our left flank, ordered your corps, in its march from that point, to move in two parallel columns, so that it could come instantly into action in two lines of battle if attacked on the flank. Accordingly, my division was ordered to form the supporting column, and for that purpose to leave the road by which the main body was moving, and so conform its movements to that of the other two divisions (Cleburne's and Bate's), that in coming into action to meet an attack on our left flank, it would occupy a place in rear of and about 400 yards distant from the front line of battle. The march thence to Rutherford's creek was made pursuant to these orders, and the whole distance thus traversed (five or six miles) was through fields and woods and over rough ground, adding greatly to the fatigues of the day. About the commencement of this movement, or soon afterward, by the orders of the commanding general in person, the whole of Gist's and about one-half of Strahl's brigade were detached for picket duty, to be relieved by the orders of the commanding general, thus leaving me with about one-half of my division.

When near Rutherford's creek, learning that a crossing was not practicable east of the road, I changed the direction of the march to the left into the road and found Bate's division preparing to cross the stream. After reaching the north bank of the stream, I was ordered to pursue the road leading in the direction of the Caldwell place, while Cleburne's and Bate's divisions moved at an angle to the left; but before reaching the Dr. Caldwell house, I was ordered to change the direction of my column to the left, and we reached the "Lewisburg," or

"Rally Hill" pike, near the toll-gate, a distance of one and a half mile from Spring Hill. This was within an hour or an hour and a half of sunset. I could distinctly see the enemy in force, both infantry and artillery, at Spring Hill, but did not, and perhaps could not at that point, see either troops or wagons, moving on the Columbia pike. Forrest's cavalry were on higher ground northeast of my position. I was ordered to form line of battle and "take" Spring Hill. Gist's brigade and the detachment from Strahl had not reported. I formed my line as speedily as worn troops could move, and after throwing forward a skirmish line, advanced 400 or 500 yards, when I discovered a line of the enemy thrown out of Spring Hill, across and threatening my right flank, and I then discovered for the first time that General Forrest's cavalry, which I had been assured would protect my right, had been ordered to another part of the field, leaving me without any protection on my right flank or support in rear. I had neither artillery nor cavalry, and was left in a position where I must meet with inevitable disaster if I advanced on Spring Hill. A hasty consultation with my brigade commanders resulted in a determination to suspend the advance and confer with the corps commander. I need not remind you that in a very few minutes you were upon the field and fully approved of what had been done, as did also General Hood a little later, when he directed that the attack should be delayed until the arrival of Generals Stewart and Gist, and in the meanwhile, that the whole command should be held under orders to advance at a moment's notice. General Gist's brigade reported a little after nightfall and was immediately placed in position on my right. General Stewart's corps came up later and went into bivouac on the stream in rear of my right, where it remained until the following morning. I received no further orders that evening or during the night to advance or change my position. After daylight on the morning of the 30th I took up the line of march for Franklin, the enemy in the meantime having preceded us under circumstances of which you are fully advised.

On the march to Franklin, General Cleburne, with whom I had long enjoyed very close personal relations, sent a message to the head of my column requesting an interview. Allowing my column to pass on, I awaited his arrival. When he came up we rode apart from the column through the fields, and he told me with much feeling that he had heard that the commanding general was endeavoring to place upon him the responsibility of allowing the enemy to pass our position on the night previous. I replied to him that I had heard nothing on that subject and that I hoped he was mistaken. He said, "No, I think not; my information comes through a very reliable channel," and said that he could not afford to rest under such an imputation, and should certainly have the matter investigated to the fullest extent, as soon as we were away from the immediate presence of the enemy. General Cleburne was quite angry and evidently was deeply hurt, under the conviction that the commander-in-chief had censured him. I asked General Cleburne who was responsible for the escape of the enemy during the afternoon and night previous. In reply to that inquiry he indulged in some criticisms of a command (Bate's division) occupying a position on his left, and concluded by saying that of course the responsibility rests with the commander-in-chief, as he was upon the field during the afternoon and was fully advised during the night of the movement of the enemy. The conversation at this point was abruptly terminated by the arrival of orders from yourself or the commanding general. As he left he said, "We will resume this conversation at the first convenient moment," but in less than three hours after that time this gallant soldier was a corpse upon the bloody field of Franklin.

Major-General Bate, referring to an interview with General Hood between the hours of 10 and 12 of the night of the 29th of November, at which General Bate mentioned a conflict in the orders of the general commanding and the corps commander touching the movement of his division, relates that General Hood said: "It makes no difference now, or it is all right, anyhow, for General Forrest, as you see, has just left and informed me that he holds the turnpike with a portion of his forces north of Spring Hill, and will stop the enemy if he tries to pass toward Franklin, and so in the morning we will have a surrender without a fight." He further said in a congratulatory manner, "We can sleep quietly to-night."

General Forrest reported that after the arrival of Cleburne's division at Spring Hill, "I ordered Brig.-Gen. W. H. Jackson to move with his division in the direction of Thompson's Station and there intercept the enemy. He struck the road at Fitzgerald's, four miles from Spring Hill, at 11 o'clock, just as the front of the enemy's column had passed. This attack was a complete surprise, producing much panic and confusion. Brigadier-General Jackson had possession of the pike and fought the enemy until daylight, but receiving no support he was compelled to retire." Two small brigades, commanded by Brigadier-Generals Armstrong and Ross, constituted Jackson's division. If an adequate force had been sent forward to take advantage of the panic and confusion created by Jackson's attack, a second golden opportunity would not have been lost.

The first intimation of dissatisfaction on the part of the commanding general at the management of the affair at Spring Hill was suggested by the receipt of the following note, written in front of Nashville and dated December 3, 1864:

My Dear General: I do not censure you for the failure at Spring Hill. I am satisfied that you are not responsible for it. I witnessed the splendid manner in which you delivered battle at Franklin on the 30th ult., and I now have a higher estimate of you as a soldier than I ever had. Yours very truly,

J. B. Hood, General.

Maj.-Gen. B. F. Cheatham.

"On the morning of the 4th of December," says General Cheatham, "I went to the headquarters of General Hood, and referring to his note and the criticism that had evidently been made by some one, I said to him, 'A great opportunity was lost at Spring Hill, but you know that I obeyed your orders there, as everywhere, literally and promptly.' General Hood not only did not dissent from what I said, but exhibited the most cordial manner, coupled with confidence and friendship."

At daylight Cheatham's corps passed through the village of Spring Hill, and between 1 and 2 o'clock p. m. the army reached the vicinity of Franklin, and Stewart's and Cheatham's corps were put in positions. The enemy was heavily intrenched and was superior in numbers and equipment. On the morning of the battle, General Schofield, commanding the Federal army, had behind his works 23,734 infantry and artillery, and his cavalry numbered 5,500. Maj.-Gen. J. D. Cox, U. S. A., upon whose authority these figures are given, states in his history of the battle of Franklin that Hood delivered the assault on the Federal lines with "two or three hundred less than 24,000" men, and gives Forrest's strength at 9,000. Maj.-Gen. John C. Brown reported that on the morning of November 29, 1864, he had not exceeding 2,750 men in his division, the largest in Cheatham's corps, and the three divisions did not exceed 6,000. Smith's brigade of Cleburne's division was not present. Stewart's corps after Allatoona was less than 7,000, and with Johnson's division of Lee's corps, the assaulting column did not exceed 16,000 men. General Forrest stated in his official report that the entire cavalry force under his command was about 5,000.

Bate's division was on the left, Brown's in the center, Cleburne's on the right. General Bate says his line "charged the works of the enemy. My right got to the works (the second line) and remained there until morning; the left was driven back. The enemy's works were strong and defiant, constructed on a slight elevation, with few obstructions in front for several hundred yards. The works to the left of Carter's creek turnpike were not strong, and with a vigorous assault should have been carried; a fact, however, not known until next day." Bate's division sustained a loss of 47 killed and 253 wounded.

Capt. Todd Carter, on staff duty with Smith's Tennessee brigade, fell mortally wounded near the enemy's works and almost at the door of his father's house.

No more magnificent spectacle was ever witnessed than the advance of the two divisions commanded by Cleburne and Brown; no two divisions of the army were ever led with greater skill and gallantry; no generals of division were ever supported with better ability by brigade, regimental and company officers. The troops were veterans who had never failed to respond to orders, although discouraged by recent and frequent disasters; and fully alive to the desperation of the assault about to be made, they advanced with noble courage. Before troops of equal numbers in the open field they would have been irresistible, but to attack intrenched troops, superior in numbers, advancing over an open plain without cover, was a disregard of the rules of war, a waste of precious lives, and a wrecking of an army once the pride and hope of the Southwest.

Major-General Stanley, commanding the Fourth Federal corps, in his official report stated that: "In view of the strong position we held, nothing appeared so improbable as that they would assault. I felt so confident in this belief that I did not leave General Schofield's headquarters until the firing commenced." Major-General Cox, commanding the Twenty-third corps, and in active command of the Federal line of battle, undertakes to account for the attack made by General Hood thus: "His exasperation at what he regarded as a hair's breadth escape on our part from the toils in which he thought he had encompassed us at Spring Hill had probably clouded his judgment. He blamed some of his subordinates for the hesitation which he seems himself to have been responsible for, and now, in an excitement which led him astray, he determined to risk everything upon a desperate assault." The same eminent author, referring to the assault made by Cleburne and Brown on the Federal center, says: "They were seen coming in splendid array. The sight was one to send a thrill through the heart, and those who saw it have never forgotten its martial magnificence."

Maj.-Gen. John C. Brown, in a report to General Cheatham of the operations of his command, said:

After we had dislodged the enemy's advance pickets from the chain of ridges in front of Franklin, Generals Bate and Cleburne and myself were summoned to the commanding general at a point very near the Columbia turnpike road, and, as I recollect, both yourself and General Stewart were present. From that point we had an unobstructed view of the enemy's works in front of Franklin, across the turnpike road, and for some distance to the right and left. My position was immediately on the left of the turnpike, while Cleburne was upon the right. General Bate's position was either in my rear or immediately upon my left.

The commanding general, after surveying the field, remarked in substance, "The country around Franklin for many miles is open and exposed to the full view of the Federal army, and I cannot mask the movements of my troops so as to turn either flank of the enemy, and if I attempt it he will withdraw and precede me into Nashville. While his immediate center is very strong, his flanks are weak. Stewart's corps is massed in McGavock's woods on the right, and I will send Bate's division under cover of the hills to the left in advance of the movement of my center; giving him time sufficient to get into position to attack concurrently with the center column. He can connect with Chalmers' right (posted upon the Harpeth below Franklin) and with Brown's left." The policy of General Hood's decision was not discussed, and I cannot recollect any question propounded by him to any one present indicating a desire for an expression of opinion by any one. He thereupon ordered Bate to move at once, and directed Stewart to attack with his corps the enemy's left flank. Cleburne and myself were directed to form in conjunction, Cleburne on the right and I on the left of the turnpike, and threaten and (if not routed before we reached the works) attack the enemy's center; but were instructed not to move until further orders from him, as he desired Bate and Stewart, having a longer distance to march, to move in advance of us.

After the expiration of half an hour or more, at a signal from yourself, Cleburne and myself were directed to commence our movement. We advanced our line, attacking simultaneously the enemy's front line of works (being a lunette some 400 or 500 yards in advance of the main works). We routed and drove that line back upon the enemy's main line with but slight loss to ourselves and without impeding the advance of our line. General Cleburne and myself met several times upon the turnpike road and conferred and acted in harmony in the movement. When we assaulted the main line, we carried the works in many places. General Gordon, commanding the right brigade of my front line, stormed and carried the enemy's works at the turnpike road and advanced a considerable distance within the works, when he and a part of his command were captured. The enemy rapidly reinforced his center from his flanks, and the slaughter in our ranks was frightful, considering the very short time in which we were engaged. The loss was so heavy to my front line that I immediately brought forward the supporting brigades (Strahl's and Carter's), and we held the works in a hand-to-hand fight, with varying fortune, until night closed upon the bloody conflict. The engagement lasted but little more than one hour, during which time the fire of the enemy's infantry was terrific. Generals Gist and Strahl were killed on the field, with nearly all of their staff officers. General Carter received a mortal wound from which he died in a few hours. When I was shot from my horse near nightfall, I had only one staff officer and two couriers on duty.

General Carter, whose command was on my extreme left, reported to me once through a member of his staff, and again in person, that there were no supports on his left and that flank was being threatened, and on personal inspection I found that there were no troops on my left at sunset. I regret very much that the loss of my papers will not allow me to give you in detail the list of casualties and to mention the conduct of very many officers and men conspicuous for their gallantry during the engagement. It is just to say, however, that the entire command did its full duty. The enemy were intrenched in strong works protected in front by an abatis of black locust, which was almost impassable, and our advancing lines were met by successive volleys of musketry that would have repulsed any but well-tried and dauntless veterans.

Gist's and Gordon's brigades reached the outer ditch of the intrenchments, mounted the works and met the enemy in a death struggle. The colors of the Twenty-fourth South Carolina, says its gallant Col. Ellison Capers, were planted and defended on the parapet. Part of both brigades went over the works, General Gordon himself was captured, and Col. Horace Rice, Eleventh and Twenty-ninth Tennessee (consolidated), was wounded inside of the enemy's main line. General Gordon states that "the gallant Ensign-Sergeant Drew, of the Twenty-ninth, bearing the flag of the Eleventh, was killed as he mounted the main line of works, fell inside and died upon his colors, upon whose folds are still seen marks of his blood."

Lieut. James A. Tillman, Twenty-fourth South Carolina, led his company over the works and captured 40 prisoners and the colors of the Ninety-seventh Ohio, this being the only stand of colors captured by the Confederate forces. General Gist, gallant gentleman and soldier, was killed in the advance; Colonel Capers was dangerously, and his lieutenant-colonel, J. S. Jones, mortally wounded. The loss of officers and men in Gist's brigade was very great. On the march to Nashville it was commanded by Captain Gillis, Forty-sixth Georgia. Its senior officer, Colonel Capers, recovered and received a well-earned promotion. At the close of hostilities between the States, he dedicated himself to the church, and in that sacred calling has won eminence and the love of his people.

Cheatham's division was commanded after the battle by the gallant Col. C. C. Hurt, Ninth Tennessee, Gen. John C. Brown being dangerously wounded. Brig.-Gen.

John C. Carter was mortally wounded, Gist and Strahl were killed, Gordon was captured inside the enemy's works. Majs. John Ingram and Thomas F. Henry and Capt. M. B. Pilcher of the division staff were severely wounded; Maj. Joseph Vaulx, always gallant and reliable, alone escaped unhurt. No division of the army ever sustained such a loss in general officers.

O. F. Strahl was born on the banks of the Muskingum, came to Tennessee in his youth, and was as thoroughly identified with the State as any one of her sons. He gave to the Fourth Tennessee its drill and discipline, and made it a noted regiment; and, succeeding A. P. Stewart in command of his brigade, added splendor to the reputation won for it by that accomplished soldier. When General Strahl entered upon the Tennessee campaign he was just recovering from a dangerous wound received at the battle of Atlanta on the 22d of July. He was a very accomplished tactician, and always handled his regiment and brigade with ease and skill. He was most fortunate in his subordinates, with officers like Col. Andrew J. Keller; Col. A. D. Gwynne, distinguished at Mill Creek Gap, and called by his comrades the "Knight of Gwynne;" Lieut.-Col. Luke W. Finlay, severely wounded at Shiloh, Perryville and New Hope church, and Maj. Henry Hampton, dangerously wounded at Perryville. The officers of his staff, Captain Johnston, adjutant-general, Lieut. John H. Marsh, inspector-general, soldiers of experience and gallantry, were both killed.

John C. Carter was a native of Georgia, a citizen of Tennessee, where he was educated, entered the service as a lieutenant in the Thirty-eighth Tennessee, won honorable mention from his colonel at Shiloh, and further promotion and honor until he was made a brigadier-general. He early attracted the attention of his division general, upon whose recommendation his final advancement was made upon his merit. He had a wonderful gentleness of manner, coupled with a dauntless courage. Every field officer of his brigade except Colonel Hurt was killed, wounded or captured on the enemy's works. In one regiment, the gallant Sixth, Orderly-Sergt. W. H. Bruner remained the ranking officer.

Gen. William A. Quarles, of Tennessee, was dangerously wounded and captured. His division general, Walthall, said of him: "Brigadier-General Quarles was severely wounded at the head of his brigade within a short distance of the enemy's inner line, and all his staff officers on duty [W. B. Munford and Capt. S. A. Conley] were killed." Col. Isaac N. Holme, Forty-second Tennessee, and Capt. R. T. Johnson, Forty-ninth, were severely wounded; Lieut.-Col. T. M. Atkins, Forty-ninth, Maj. S. C. Cooper, Forty-sixth, and Capt. James J. Rittenburg, Fifty-third, were wounded and captured, and Maj. J. E. McDonald, Fifty-fifth, and Capt. R. T. Coulter, were killed, leaving a captain in command of the brigade.

Brig.-Gen. John Adams, of Tennessee, was killed after leading his command up to the enemy's main line of works. Gen. Jacob D. Cox says of him: "In one of the lulls between these attacks, when the smoke was so thick that one could see a very little way in front, the officers of the line discovered a mounted officer in front forming for another attack or rallying them after a repulse. Shots were fired and horse and rider both fell. The horse struggled to his feet and dashed for the breastworks, leaped upon it and fell dead astride it. The wounded officer was Gen. John Adams. He was brought in and soon died."

General Hood reported the loss of the army of Tennessee at 4,500. The loss of Schofield's army numbered 2,326 killed, wounded and missing. Of this number, 1,104 were captured by the Confederates, about 600 of them by Brown and Cleburne from the enemy's line in advance of his intrenchments.

Gen. J. D. Cox says the Federal loss in killed was "trifling everywhere but near the center," the point assailed by Cleburne and Brown. No report with list of casualties was ever made, and no data exist for the ascertainment of the actual losses of these two divisions, but it must have been 40 per cent in killed, wounded and missing. In Quarles' Tennessee brigade of Stewart's corps, the loss was just as great, and the death rate in Stewart's and Cheatham's corps was out of the usual proportion. It was great enough to make Tennessee a land of mourning.

The attacks of the Confederates were repeated at intervals until dark, and on part of the line until 9 o'clock. At midnight the Federal forces were withdrawn and marched to Nashville.

After our dead comrades were buried and the wounded of both armies provided for, the army of Tennessee moved forward to the front of Nashville, where on the 2d of December a line of battle was formed and intrenchments provided. Smith's brigade of Cleburne's division came up, and Ector's brigade of Stewart's corps rejoined the army, which was now 23,053 strong, opposed to an army under Gen. George H. Thomas of more than three times that number.

On the morning of December 2d, Major-General Bate was ordered by the commanding general to go "over to Murfreesboro" with his division, with instructions to destroy the railroad, and burn the bridges and blockhouses from that place to Nashville. His three brigades and Slocum's battery did not exceed 1,600 men; Col. B. J. Hill with 150 mounted men was to co-operate with him. It was discovered that Murfreesboro had not been evacuated, as Bate was led to believe from the character of his orders, and on the morning of the 4th he notified General Hood that the place was strongly fortified and held by from 8,000 to 10,000 troops, commanded by Major-General Rousseau. Bate had a sharp combat that evening in which the enemy was punished and driven with loss from the field of attack, Bate sustaining a loss of 15 killed and 59 wounded. On the morning of the 5th he captured and burned three blockhouses and the bridges they guarded, and at this time Major-General Forrest arrived with two divisions of cavalry and Sear's and Palmer's brigades of infantry, assumed command and initiated offensive operations under Hood's orders against Murfreesboro.

General Forrest reported that on the morning of the 6th the enemy declined his offer of battle, but on the next morning moved out on the Salem turnpike in force and drove in his pickets, when the infantry, except Smith's (Tennessee) brigade, made a shameful retreat with the loss of two pieces of artillery. Failing with Bate's assistance to rally the troops, he called for Armstrong's and Ross' brigades of Jackson's division, who charged the enemy and checked his advance. On the 9th, Smith's brigade of Cleburne's division, under Colonel Olmstead, relieved Bate, who joined his proper command. On the 13th, Brig.-Gen. W. H. Jackson captured a train of 17 cars and the Sixty-first Illinois regiment of infantry, with 60,000 rations intended for the garrison at Murfreesboro.

Forrest was pushing his investment of Murfreesboro with great vigor when he was advised by Hood of the disaster at Nashville. He then withdrew at once and rejoined the army at Columbia. On the 18th he wrote, "Most of the infantry under my command were barefooted and in a disabled condition. My march over almost impassable roads was therefore unavoidably slow."

The army of Tennessee rested in position before Nashville from the 2d to the 13th of December. Two brigades left in the rear joined their commands, but three were in front of Murfreesboro with Forrest and did not participate in the battle of the 16th. From Ridley's Hill on the Nolensville pike, the center of Cheatham's corps, there was an unobstructed view of Federal movements and preparations for battle. The arrival of troops, the concentration of Wilson's cavalry, was all in plain view. The weather was very severe and the suffering of the men was great. There was no supply of shoes, and the men covered their bare feet with raw hide taken from animals freshly slaughtered. Hundreds of Tennesseeans passed their own doors on the march without halting, and many were in sight of their homes when the guns opened.

On December 15th the enemy, having completed his preparation, moved out to attack the left held by Stewart and the right held by Cheatham. The enemy, says General Stewart, appeared in force along his entire line with the purpose of turning the left flank of the army. The commanding general dispatched Manigault's and Deas' brigades of Johnson's division, Lee's corps, to Stewart's assistance, and they were placed in line parallel to the Hillsboro pike, opposite redoubt No. 4. Under attack the two brigades made but a feeble resistance, and the enemy captured redoubts No. 4 and No. 5, with all artillery in them, and killed and wounded many of our men. A battery from Loring's division was brought over and placed in position and the same brigades brought up to its support, but they again fled, causing the capture of the battery, after which the enemy pressed forward and gained the rear of Walthall and Loring. Walthall, after a gallant resistance, retired his line, when the entire corps formed between the Granny White and Franklin turnpikes, night closing the conflict.

The attack on Cheatham was made by Major-General Steedman with the Twelfth, Thirteenth and One Hundredth regiments of colored troops, under command of Col. Charles R. Thompson of the Twelfth colored; the Fourteenth, Seventeenth (commanded by Col. William R. Shafter), Forty-fourth and a detachment of the Eighteenth colored under Col. T. J. Morgan of the Fourteenth colored; the Sixty-eighth Indiana, Eighteenth

Ohio, and the Second battalion, under command of Lieut.-Col. C. H. Grosvenor, Eighteenth Ohio, and the Twentieth Indiana and Eighteenth Ohio batteries. The assault was received by Cheatham in the forenoon of the 15th, Granbury's brigade having been placed by the corps commander in a lunette with a section of Turner's battery. Lieutenant-Colonel Grosvenor with his brigade assaulted the salient angle of this field work, and claimed in his official report that one of his captains with 100 men gained the interior of the work, but the men of Granbury's brigade, 300 strong, reserved their fire under orders until the assaulting column was in short range. The volley was terrific, and to escape it part of Grosvenor's force doubtless undertook to seek the cover of the ditch in front of the field work and were there killed. No attempt was made to gain the interior of the work; it would have been an impossible undertaking. It was held and defended by a body of trained veterans, who possessed a capacity for successful resistance against five-fold the number reported to have effected the entrance. If it had been possible there would have been no survivors, and there were no Federals killed inside the work. Cheatham's entire line was well intrenched and no impression was made upon it, and no losses sustained by its defenders except from sharpshooters.

Colonel Morgan, commanding the two colored brigades, reported that his line "advanced very close to the enemy's line." His troops did come forward as if on dress parade. Our men had never before encountered them on the battlefield, and were amazed at their soldierly bearing. There was no cover to conceal the advance, and it was difficult to restrain our men from mounting the works to witness the novel and imposing spectacle. Morgan's line was permitted to advance "very close," but when a volley was delivered it was a race between the poor, deluded blacks and their officers for a place of safety.

The description by Lieutenant-Colonel Grosvenor of the conduct of his own command answers for that of the whole attacking column. He said: "The troops were mostly new conscripts, convalescents, and bounty-jumpers, and on this occasion behaved in the most cowardly and disgraceful manner. The enemy, seeing the men hesitating and wavering, fired a heavy volley and stampeded the whole line, and nearly all the men fled from the field." The hillside in our front was covered with the Federal dead and wounded. No effort was made to succor the wounded after this "sham battle" was determined. Orders were received from General Hood to move Cheatham's corps to the left of our army, and after a volley was delivered at Morgan's command, the movement was begun, and very soon completed. In spite of the abandonment of the entire line, Captain Osborne, of the Twentieth Indiana battery, who had "passed to the rear" with Morgan's, Thompson's and Grosvenor's brigades, reports officially that he maintained "a continual fire until night." Before that hour Cheatham's corps had marched two or three miles and gone into position to the left of Stewart's corps. That the wounded were not cared for was no fault of the Confederates, as they retired from the hill immediately after the stampede. The Federal loss was 825 killed, wounded and missing, and of this number 120 were killed.

On the morning of the 16th, Thomas made a general attack on the Confederate line of battle, but was repulsed at all points. About noon an attempt was made to turn Hood's left, held by Govan's brigade of Cleburne's division; the attack being made by Wilson's dismounted cavalry. It was vigorously prosecuted and the position carried, but not until General Govan, and Colonel Green, the officer next in rank, were severely wounded. So soon as the result was ascertained, Col. Hume R. Feild, First Tennessee, commanding Carter's brigade, was dispatched to the left with orders to retake the position at any cost. It could be said of him: "Thou bearest the highest name for valiant acts." In four years of war he had never known failure. It was a critical period, the enemy's shots were taking us in reverse, and before many minutes a lodgment would be made in our rear; but Feild's advance was equal to the emergency, and in a few minutes the ground was recovered and the enemy forced to retire. Colonel Feild immediately reported the result to the corps commander through his gallant aide-de-camp, Charles H. Thompson, with the information that he had deployed his brigade as a skirmish line to cover the enemy's front, and if the assault was repeated he could not maintain himself against a line of battle, and asked for reinforcements. General Cheatham replied: "The colonel must not expect reinforcements; there are no reserves. I sent him to the left because I can trust him to hold any position." But in a short time Gist's brigade, commanded by Col. John H. Anderson, Eighth Tennessee, was sent to his assistance. In the afternoon there was a concentration of artillery in Cheatham's front, with a furious cannonade upon the hill occupied by Bate's division.

Col. A. J. Kellar, Fourth Tennessee, commanding Strahl's brigade, held the right of Cheatham's division, commanded by Brig.-Gen. M. P. Lowrey. In a report made to General Hood on the 18th, he states that the hill occupied by Bate's division "was given up to the enemy without a struggle." Colonel Kellar was on Bate's immediate left. General Hood, referring to the disaster, said: "A portion of our line to the left of the center suddenly gave way, causing in a few minutes our line to give way at all points, our troops retreating rapidly down the Franklin pike." This assault was made by the troops commanded by Generals Schofield and A. J. Smith. Referring to it, Major-General Thomas reported, "Our loss was remarkably small, scarcely mentionable."

When the line gave way, Cheatham dispatched a staff

officer to the commanding general, to report the condition of the left and to ask that some body of troops should be halted east of the Granny White pike to cover the withdrawal of his left. There was no panic there, but he decided not to attempt to bring out the organizations, and directed the men to retire without order and cross the hills to the Franklin road. Lowrey's and Granbury's brigades of Cheatham's division, under Brig.-Gen. J. A. Smith, who had been sent in the forenoon to support the center, were ordered back to the left just as the disaster occurred, halted and put into position, and they checked the advance of the enemy long enough to enable the troops on the extreme left to retire in safety. Brig.-Gens. Henry R. Jackson and Thomas B. Smith, Bate's division, were not affected by the panic and were captured. Col. M. Mageveny, Jr., One Hundred and Fifty-fourth Tennessee, unable to climb the hills when his regiment was ordered to retire, was captured, and the gallant Col. W. W. Shy, Twentieth Tennessee, was killed.

The casualties were inconsiderable in numbers. There was no serious resistance to the Federal advance; it was a battle without an engagement or a contest; and the wonder is that Thomas, with a large and well-appointed army, more than treble the strength of Hood, did not press his right, seize the Franklin turnpike and capture the entire army. Hood's army was in a wretched state, the clothing of the men was scant, and the per cent of the barefooted was distressing. On the retreat out of Tennessee the weather was very severe, rain, sleet and snow falling upon the army after the second day's march; but the spirit of endurance seemed to rise as difficulties multiplied.

Maj.-Gen. George H. Thomas in his official report says of Hood's army: "With the exception of his rear guard, his army had become a disheartened and disorganized rabble of half-armed and barefooted men, who sought every opportunity to fall out by the wayside and desert their cause to put an end to their suffering. The rear guard, however, was undaunted and firm, and did its work bravely to the last." This report was prepared more than a month after the battle, and assumed to be historically correct.

Hood's field return, made on the 10th of December, 1864, shows his effective strength at 23,053, and General Thomas states that "during the two days' operations there were 4,462 prisoners captured," leaving Hood in retreat with an army 18,591 strong. The first return of strength after the campaign was made at Tupelo, Miss., on the 20th of January, 1865, showed an effective total of 16,913, after every soldier from west Tennessee had been furloughed at Corinth, Miss., for thirty days. They represented the One Hundred and Fifty-fourth, Second, Fourth, Fifth, Sixth, Ninth, Twelfth, Thirteenth, Fifteenth, Twenty-first, Twenty-second, Thirty-first, Thirty-third, Thirty-eighth, Forty-sixth, Forty-seventh, Fifty-first, Fifty-second, Fifty-fifth Tennessee regiments, which would not average more than 100 men to the regiment; adding these to the last report, the army would have shown an effective total of 18,813. It was evident that while we had large numbers of poorly-clad and barefooted men, the accusation that they "sought every opportunity to fall out by the wayside and desert their cause" was without foundation.

Immediately after the break in our line the troops sought their own organizations, reformed under their officers, and marched out of the State in perfect order. The formation was made just south of the hills in the rear of our left, a few hundred yards from the abandoned line of battle, where, on account of the timid policy of the Federal commander, and his proverbial want of enterprise, our army was not molested. The men, with an occasional exception, had arms in their hands. At Franklin there were several thousand stand of arms, a very large proportion captured from the enemy; and after the loss of fifty pieces of artillery, the army retired with fifty-nine field pieces and an ample supply of ammunition. The successful resistance to the assault of the Federal cavalry near Franklin by the rear guard of Lee's corps, repeated at Spring Hill the next day by the rear guard of Cheatham's corps, does not sustain the Federal general's report that our army was a "disorganized rabble."

While disasters had multiplied and the suffering was great, the spirit of the men was unbroken. It was well illustrated by Colonel Kellar, Fourth Tennessee, who in his report to Hood said: "For the first time in this war we lost our cannon. Give us the first chance and we will retake them." In the loss of artillery at Nashville, that of three 12-pounder Napoleon guns by Turner's Mississippi battery caused infinite regret in Cheatham's division. With other pieces they had been captured at Perryville, and had been served in all the subsequent battles of the Southwest with the greatest distinction by the company of noble Mississippians who manned them.

General Hood had been over-confident and too enthusiastic. When he retreated from Nashville his only hope was to save the remnant of his army, and he looked to the indomitable Forrest to accomplish this result. The cavalry had suffered from constant exposure to the trying winter weather and was not in condition unaided to check the advance of the enemy long enough to secure Hood's retreat, therefore it was decided to detach Major-General Walthall with instructions to organize a rear guard 3,000 strong, and report to Major-General Forrest. Walthall selected the brigades of Reynolds, Ector and Quarles, of his own division; Featherston's, of Loring's division; Carter's (formerly Maney's), of Cheatham's division, commanded by Col. H. R. Feild; Strahl's, of Cheatham's division, commanded by Col. C. H. Heiskell, and Smith's, of Cleburne's division. Instead of 3,000 men, the effective total was

1,601, but it was a splendid command, led with consummate skill and courage. "Walthall was the youngest division general in the army of Tennessee, and when he drew his sword in command over the rear guard to cover its retreat, there was not a soldier in it, from the commanding general down, who did not believe he would do it or perish in the effort." General Forrest said of him: "He exhibited the highest soldierly qualities; many of his men were without shoes, but they bore their sufferings without murmur, and were ever ready to meet the enemy."

General Walthall said of his command, "For several days the ground was covered with snow, and numbers of the men made the march without shoes, some had no blankets, and all were poorly clad for the season;" but despite these difficulties and privations there was no complaint. Every day there was a skirmish or a combat, in which the cavalry and artillery of Forrest participated with the infantry of Walthall. The danger was a common one, and the two arms of the service were alike conspicuous for courage and endurance. The Federal advance was beaten and punished day by day so thoroughly that General Thomas was forced to admit that "the rear guard was undaunted and firm, and did its work bravely to the last." The rear guard recrossed the Tennessee on the 27th of December, Ector's brigade under Col. D. Coleman, Thirty-ninth North Carolina, in the rear.

General Forrest, in his report of the campaign, said that from the 21st of November to the 27th of December his command was engaged every day with the enemy. "I brought out three pieces of artillery (taken from the enemy), more than I started with. My command captured and destroyed 16 blockhouses and stockades, 20 bridges, 4 locomotives, 100 cars, 10 miles of railroad, and have turned over to the provost-marshal 1,600 prisoners, besides the capture of several hundred horses, mules and cattle." In an address to his troops issued by Forrest on his return to Corinth, Miss., he said: "During the past year (1864) you have fought 50 battles, killed and captured 16,000 of the enemy, captured 2,000 mules and horses, 67 pieces of artillery, 4 gunboats, 14 transports, 20 barges, 300 wagons, 50 ambulances, 10,000 stand of small-arms, 40 blockhouses, destroyed 36 railroad bridges, 200 miles of railroad, 6 engines, 100 cars, and $15,000,000 worth of (Federal) property. Your strength never exceeded 5,000, 2,000 of whom have been killed or wounded; in prisoners you have lost about 200."

This summary of his operations doubtless stimulated General Sherman to advise the assassination of Forrest and to commit other atrocities. An order, or letter of instructions, dated Savannah, Ga., January 21, 1865, addressed to Gen. George H. Thomas (see Vol. XLV, War Records, Part 2, page 621), giving "such instructions as fall within my province as commander of the division," General Sherman advised him to march on Columbus, Miss., Tuscaloosa and Selma, "destroying farms, gathering horses, mules (wagons to be burned), and doing all possible damage, burning Selma and Montgomery, Ala., and all iron foundries, mills and factories," and adds: "I would like to have Forrest hunted down and killed, but doubt if we can do that yet." If the Spanish Captain-General Weyler, of Cuba, had issued and published this letter of instructions to a subordinate officer, the press, the pulpit, the halls of Congress of the United States would have rung with fierce denunciation of the savage spirit of its author, and public opinion would outlaw his memory.

The remnant of the army of Tennessee retired from Corinth to Tupelo, Miss., on the 23d of January, 1865. General Hood was relieved and Lieut.-Gen. Richard Taylor assigned to command.

After a few days of needed rest and preparation, the troops of Lee's, Stewart's and Cheatham's corps, in the order named, were moved by rail to South Carolina.

During the month (January) the Congress adopted this resolution: "That if the President will appoint Gen. J. E. Johnston to the command of the army of Tennessee it will, in the opinion of the Congress of the Confederate States, be hailed with joy by the army and will receive the approval of the country." President Davis did not at once make the appointment himself, but a month later, on the 22d of February, Gen. R. E. Lee, having been made general-in-chief, called General Johnston to the command of the army of Tennessee and of all troops in the department of Georgia, South Carolina and Florida, with instructions to concentrate the troops "and drive back Sherman," but it was too late. The change imparted a sense of relief, gave hope to the country, and revived the spirit of the troops; but Atlanta, Franklin, Nashville and the retreat from Tennessee with its untold horrors, had forced the conviction upon the mind of the soldiers that success was not attainable. Nevertheless, to the honor and glory of the South, the troops entered upon the final campaign with loyalty and unmatched constancy. Cheatham, with the mass of the Tennesseeans, except the West Tennesseeans on furlough, arrived at Augusta, Ga., on the 9th of February, and halted to meet a threatened advance of the enemy at that place. On the 14th, orders were received to move to Columbia, S. C., and after a march of forty miles in two days the command was halted at Newberry. On the 21st, a march of twenty-one miles was made to the Ennoree river, where orders were received from General Beauregard to return to Newberry. In a day or two the command was ordered to Chester, S. C., and halted there for several days. After another detention at Charlotte, N. C., and another provoking delay at Salisbury, occasioned by a change of gauge of the railroad tracks and the want of cars, orders were received to unite with General Johnston. At noon of the 21st the troops joined him and went into position on the field of Bentonville.

Lieut.-Gen. A. P. Stewart commanded the troops of the army of Tennessee, numbering 8,731 effective men, and General Johnston treated Stewart's command as one corps. There were present, of Cheatham's corps, detachments from Cleburne's and Bate's divisions (only engaged in the battle of the 19th), and 406 effective men under the command of Major-General Bate. Stewart's corps had 890 effective men, and 2,660 of Lee's corps were present; with this force and the North Carolina troops under Gen. Braxton Bragg, and the forces under Lieutenant-General Hardee, numbering 15,000 men of all arms, General Johnston fought the battle of Bentonville. Cheatham's arrival on the 21st increased the strength of the corps to 2,602, and Lieutenant-General Lee joined General Johnston in a few days with about 3,000 troops, composed of detachments from his own, Stewart's and Cheatham's corps, united in one body at Augusta, Ga.

The attack was begun upon our left (Hoke's division) by General Slocum with the Twentieth army corps. General Johnston reported that the attack continued about thirty minutes and was repulsed with heavy loss to the enemy. In a few minutes "another attack was made upon Stewart's corps, commanded by Major-General Loring, by which the enemy was quickly driven back." Hardee was in position at 3 o'clock and made a vigorous attack on the right, well and gallantly (said the commanding general) seconded by Stewart, Hill, Loring and the officers under them. Slocum was badly beaten but was heavily reinforced and assumed the offensive, with little effect. After burying the dead and removing our own and the Federal wounded, the Confederates resumed their first position. On the 20th, the enemy had three of his four corps present well intrenched, but made no general attack. During the day General Bragg's line was several times attacked and the enemy repulsed and severely punished. On the 21st, heavy skirmishing was renewed on the whole front of our line, and at 4 o'clock

Mower's division of the Seventeenth corps penetrated the cavalry line on our extreme left and moved upon Bentonville. General Sherman, reporting the incident to General Grant, said: "Yesterday we pushed him (Johnston) hard and came very near crushing him." But General Hardee met the movement with Cumming's Georgia brigade under Colonel Henderson, while the cavalry, directed by Generals Hampton and Wheeler, charged his left flank, with Hogan's Alabama brigade under General Allen; while the Eighth Texas and the Fourth Tennessee, the gallant Col. Baxter Smith commanding the brigade, bore down upon the enemy's left and front. The enemy was routed and driven back in disorder upon his reserves, and our only line of retreat over Mill creek was made secure.

This action of the 21st was one of the most gallant of the war, the last one in which the troops of the army of Tennessee participated. It was an exhibition of the dash and courage and the best qualities of the Southern soldier, and will forever be an example of what brave men can accomplish. The future was very dark to them, hope of success and independence had faded, the distant home had been abandoned to the spoiler, they had endured four years of hardship, privation and all the perils of battle, but at the last moment every sense was subordinated to that of duty. Sherman had on the field, when Mower attempted to seize Johnston's line of retreat, just three times the force of the Confederates, with Schofield's army in supporting distance, the combined force exceeding 75,000 men. In the early morning of the 22d, General Johnston retired across Mill creek and formed line again, but the enemy made no effort to advance. In the three days' fighting, Johnston's army lost 223 killed, 1,467 wounded, 653 missing; and captured 903 prisoners, with their arms, and 3 pieces of artillery. Sherman must have lost 400 in killed and wounded, as the Confederates fought behind intrenchments. In a dispatch to General Grant, General Sherman states his entire losses in the Carolina campaign at 2,500; but his own official return of casualties fixes his loss at Kinston at 1,337; at Averasboro, 682; at Bentonville, 1,527; total, 3,546. The Federal authorities give the number of missing at Bentonville only 214; General Johnston reports the number of prisoners captured 903. Counted among the Confederate missing were several detachments of men who went through the Federal line in the charge of the 19th. Referring to this, Brig.-Gen. J. B. Palmer of Tennessee reported that Col. Anderson Searcy and Lieutenant-Colonel Hall of the Forty-fifth Tennessee, and Major Joyner of the Eighteenth, "with fifty of my men and small detachments from other commands of our army, after having remained in rear of Sherman's army for nine days, made their way around the enemy's left flank and rejoined the brigade on the 28th of March, with four stand of colors belonging to the Tennessee regiments. This action required great adroitness, patient courage and endurance, and justly entitles them to high distinction as soldiers." The incident was referred to by Gen. D. H. Hill, commanding Lee's corps, and Palmer and his brigade were warmly commended both by him and General Stevenson, the division commander.

In the operations culminating in the battle of Bentonville, Wheeler's cavalry bore a conspicuous part. Brig.-Gen. W. Y. C. Humes of Tennessee commanded two brigades of cavalry. The Fourth Tennessee, Col. William S. McLemore, the Thirteenth and Shaw's Tennessee battalion, Capt. R. V. Wright, constituted the brigade commanded by Gen. George G. Dibrell of Tennessee, one of the noblest of men, and the equal in every soldierly quality of any son of his State. Always reliable, trusted in council and on the field, he won the confidence of all under whom he served. He survived the war and was rewarded by his countrymen with distinguished and well-earned honors.

The First Tennessee, Lieut.-Col. James H. Lewis; the

Second, Lieut.-Col. John H. Kuhn; the Fifth, Col. George W. McKenzie, and the Ninth battalion, Maj. James H. Akin, constituted the brigade commanded by the gallant Col. Henry M. Ashby. The Fourth and Eighth were commanded by Col. Baxter Smith, and brigaded with the Eighth Texas. Among our losses, Major-General Bate reported the fall of Maj. W. H. Wilkinson, and refers to him as "the young, gallant and lamented commander of Tyler's brigade." He fell leading his brigade in a memorable and final charge upon the enemy's line. In Palmer's brigade, Col. R. M. Saffell and Lieut.-Col. A. F. Boggess, Twenty-sixth regiment, were killed. Colonel Saffell volunteered with Ashby's cavalry when the enemy attempted to turn our left, on the 21st, and was killed, gallantly leading a successful charge. Lieutenant-Colonel Boggess, said General Palmer, "fell in the gallant discharge of his duties, a noble specimen of the man, officer and soldier."

Johnston's army changed position on the 24th to a point four miles north of Smithfield, and there halted until the 10th of April. Under orders from army headquarters, the 8th and 9th were spent in the reorganization of an army in which regiments were now reduced to the strength of companies, and many companies were without representatives. A pathetic incident occurred when the roll of Company G, of the One Hundred and Fifty-fourth Tennessee, was called. It had one representative present, and he disabled from wounds received in battle. He walked out of line, and addressing General Cheatham, said: "General, there was near a hundred of us when we mustered into the service in April, 1861, under our brave Capt. Marsh Patrick. We have been with you from Belmont down, we have never had a desertion, and only two or three captured, and those on picket line. We have had over 50 per cent killed in battle, many have died from disease, and some have lost a leg or an arm or are otherwise permanently disabled, but I am here to follow you to the end." Of all the noble bands of Tennesseeans who once swelled the ranks of the army, there was just a sufficient number remaining to organize four regiments. The First was composed of the First, Sixth, Eighth, Ninth, Sixteenth, Twenty-seventh, Twenty-eighth and Thirty-fourth (consolidated), Col. Hume R. Feild, Lieut.-Col. Oliver A. Bradshaw, Maj. W. D. Kelly. The Eleventh, Twelfth, Thirteenth, Twenty-ninth, Forty-seventh, Fiftieth, Fifty-first and One Hundred and Fifty-fourth (consolidated), constituted the Second, Col. Horace Rice, Lieut.-Col. George W. Pease. The Fourth, Fifth, Nineteenth, Twenty-fourth, Thirty-first, Thirty-third, Thirty-fifth, Thirty-eighth and Forty-first (consolidated), constituted the Third Tennessee, Col. James D. Tillman. The Second, Third, Tenth, Fifteenth, Eighteenth, Twentieth, Twenty-sixth, Thirtieth, Thirty-second, Thirty-seventh and Forty-fifth, and Twenty-third battalion, constituted the Fourth Tennessee, Col. Anderson Searcy. The four regiments constituted one brigade, and Brig.-Gen. Joseph B. Palmer was assigned to its command. This, with Gist's South Carolina and Georgia brigade, Col. William G. Foster commanding, constituted a division, commanded by Maj.-Gen. B. F. Cheatham. Maj.-Gen. John C. Brown was placed in command of Cleburne's division. Lieutenant-General Stewart resumed command of his army corps, and no other general officer from Tennessee was assigned to duty. The army continued the march from the 10th, through Raleigh, crossed the Haw and Alamance rivers, on the 15th making a march of 15 miles; marched 12 miles on the 16th on the New Salem road and bivouacked. Richmond had been evacuated, the army of Northern Virginia under General Lee had surrendered, and on the 17th Johnston's army was confronted by overwhelming numbers. The troops were excited and full of suspense, but never more alert or obedient to orders. On the 19th it was known that a truce had been agreed upon by the commanding generals of the two armies, and terms of peace negotiated. The authorities at Washington refused to ratify the terms of settlement. On the 26th the army marched 10 miles on the Center and Thomasville road, and on the following day it was officially announced that terms had been agreed upon by which the troops under General Johnston would be surrendered.

This announcement brought sorrow, but no surprise. The humblest man in the ranks felt that it was inevitable. There had existed a bare hope that the union of the armies of Lee and Johnston might be productive of good for the country, but this was dispelled by the surrender of Lee. Tennesseeans accepted the situation in a manner befitting a people who had made so many sacrifices and endured so many wrongs without complaint, and whose heroic sons had won glory and honor on every battlefield of the war.

Thirty-nine thousand and twelve officers and men of Johnston's army were paroled at Greensboro, N. C., and other points, in accordance with the military convention of April 26, 1865, and among them were 2,000 Tennesseeans, all in Cheatham's division. The paroled soldiers, maintaining their organizations, retired to Salisbury, where rations were distributed and $1.25 in coin was paid to officers and men. This fund constituted the military chest of the army and had just come under the control of General Johnston, under orders from President Davis. It was the first payment in coin made to the troops, and the first of any description for many months. A touching farewell to the troops was published by General Johnston, and the Tennessee brigade marched to Greeneville, Tenn., under command of Gen. J. B. Palmer, and took the cars for their homes.

CHAPTER XI.

TENNESSEEANS IN VIRGINIA—RECORDS OF ARCHER'S AND JOHNSON'S BRIGADES.

WHEN Brig.-Gen. W. W. Loring took command of the "Northwestern army," then distributed at various points in West Virginia, in July, 1861, he was joined at Huntersville by Brig.-Gen. Daniel S. Donelson's Tennessee brigade, composed of the Eighth and Sixteenth regiments under Cols. Alfred Fulton and John H. Savage, and by Brig.-Gen. Samuel R. Anderson's Tennessee brigade, composed of the First, Col. George Maney; the Seventh, Col. Robert Hatton, and the Fourteenth, Col. W. A. Forbes. Early in August, Gen. R. E. Lee assumed command of the forces in West Virginia, and Brig.-Gen. W. S. Rosecrans became his opponent in command of the Federal forces. In preparing the well-laid scheme to destroy the Federal forces at Cheat Mountain pass, General Lee moved Donelson's and Anderson's brigades to the right and left of the Federal position by circuitous mountain paths, which enabled them to penetrate the rear of the enemy. General Lee said: "With great effort the troops intended for the surprise had reached their destination, having traversed 20 miles of steep, rugged mountain paths, and the last day through a terrible storm which lasted all night, and in which they had to stand drenched to the skin in the cold rain. When morning broke I could see the enemy's tents on Valley river at the point on the Huttonsville road just below me. It was a tempting sight. We waited for the attack (by Rust) on Cheat mountain, which was to be the signal, till 10 a. m. But the signal did not come. All chance for surprise was gone, the opportunity was lost and our plan discovered."

During these operations Col. John H. Savage, of the Sixteenth Tennessee, with a guide, captured an entire company of Federal infantry with their arms and accouterments. The Savannah, Ga., Republican published an account of Colonel Savage's bold action in a communication dated September 21, 1861:

A Bold Capture.—After marching about three miles from Tygart river, Colonel Savage of the Sixteenth Tennessee regiment, desiring to make a reconnoissance, sallied off from his regiment at least a quarter of a mile, and while alone he suddenly and unexpectedly came up to where a company of Yankee pickets were stationed. Both he and they were considerably surprised, but the gallant colonel, changing not a color in his countenance, in a bold and defiant manner, standing erect in his stirrups, looking in his rear and then quickly facing the pickets, exclaimed in a stentorian voice: "You rascals, if you don't ground arms and surrender immediately, my men shall surround you and shoot you to pieces in a minute." They did surrender and he made them prisoners. The company consisted of three commissioned, four non-commissioned officers and sixty privates. (Head's History Sixteenth Tennessee.)

After the withdrawal of the troops from Sewell mountain, Donelson's brigade was sent to South Carolina and Anderson's remained with Loring until after Stonewall Jackson's winter campaign.

On the 1st of January, 1862, Anderson's brigade moved from its encampment near Winchester, Va., in the direction of Bath, as part of the expedition commanded by Gen. Stonewall Jackson. Approaching Bath on the morning of the 4th, General Jackson directed Loring, commanding his advance, to move a regiment to the left along the mountain which commanded the town. Colonel Maney was directed to execute the order, and General Jackson reported that "it was undertaken with a patriotic enthusiasm which entitles the First Tennessee regiment and its commander to special praise." Subsequently, the Seventh under Colonel Hatton, and a section of Shumaker's battery under Lieutenant Lanier, were ordered to co-operate with Maney. The troops had not advanced far before the enemy fled, leaving his baggage and stores. General Jackson was entirely successful in the expedition, though the weather was intensely cold, and snow and sleet made the roads almost impassable to wagons and teams, and very trying to the men.

On the 13th of February, Anderson's brigade was ordered to Aquia creek, except the First regiment, which was ordered to Tennessee.

In the organization of the army of Northern Virginia, on the peninsula, April 30, 1862, the Tennessee brigade, composed of the First, Col. Peter Turney; the Seventh, Col. Robert Hatton, and the Fourteenth, Col. W. A. Forbes, 2,030 strong, was commanded by Brig.-Gen. Samuel R. Anderson, and constituted a part of Whiting's division of the reserve corps under the command of Maj.-Gen. G. W. Smith.

On the 8th of May this brigade participated in the affair at Eltham, which, General Smith stated, "forms one of the most interesting incidents of the march of my command in retiring from Yorktown out of the peninsula." Having learned that the enemy had anchored off West Point and was landing troops, General Smith attacked on May 7th with Hood's and Hampton's brigades. Two attempts were made to flank the Confederates, but the appearance of Gen. S. R. Anderson with the Tennessee brigade (said the division general) on our left, made that flank secure. The enemy was driven a mile and a half through a dense forest, in which it was impossible to see over 30 or 40 yards, until he took refuge under the cover of his gunboats, leaving many dead and wounded on the field, while the Confederate loss was but 8 killed and 32 wounded, a few of the latter belonging to the Tennessee brigade.

General Whiting said: "I take occasion to make my acknowledgments to Brigadier-General Anderson of Tennessee, who, arriving on the field at a critical moment to the support of General Hood, and placing two of his regiments in the fire of the enemy, courteously waived the command, although senior to us all."

Soon after this affair General Anderson was relieved at his own request, and on the 23d, Col. Robert Hatton of the Seventh Tennessee was made brigadier-general. Lieut.-Col. John F. Goodner was promoted to the command of of the Seventh, Maj. John K. Howard was made lieutenant-colonel, and Capt. John A. Fite was made major.

At 12:30 o'clock on the morning of May 31st, Whiting's, Hood's and Pettigrew's brigades were placed near the fork of the Nine-mile and New Bridge roads, Hatton's and Hampton's in reserve near Mrs. Christian's farm. Between 4 and 5 o'clock p. m. Longstreet opened the battle of Seven Pines.

General Whiting was ordered to move his command by the Nine-mile road to Longstreet's assistance, and as they came up they were at once hotly engaged. Gen. G. W. Smith stated that when Hatton came up, his brigade was formed on the edge of the field near the road. It moved across the field with alacrity, and the precision of its movement in line of battle has been seldom equaled, even on the parade ground. Instructions were given for putting the brigade in close action. At the same time it was already under a deadly fire in a dense, entangled wood, struggling through a morass covered with logs and thick bushes. The men continued to advance without firing a shot until coming up with the front line of troops already engaged, when they, too, commenced firing, advancing upon the left to within 15 or 20 yards of the line of fire of the enemy, which came from the low bank of an old ditch. The thickness of the woods and undergrowth prevented the officers from seeing their men except in limited numbers, while the roar of musketry was almost deafening. Very seldom, if ever, did troops in their first battle go so close to a covered line under so strong a fire and remain within such short distance so long a time. On no part of the line did the enemy leave their cover or advance one single foot. Our troops held their position until it was too dark to distinguish friend from foe. The engagement lasted one hour and a half. It was the first battle for Hatton's brigade, and as it moved into action in the presence of President Davis, Gen. J. E. Johnston, commanding the army, and Gen. R. E. Lee, then military adviser of the President, it is not remarkable that its movements, under such an inspiration, excited the admiration of the division general. Three fresh brigades were ready to move forward into close action, and there is no reason to doubt that with one short hour of daylight the enemy would have been driven into the swamps of the Chickahominy. As it was, darkness compelled the abandonment of an unfinished task, and the troops were withdrawn from the swamp and bivouacked within musket range of the enemy. When General Smith withdrew his troops, he was informed that General Johnston had been severely wounded and disabled, which misfortune devolved on him the temporary command of the army. On the following day at 2 o'clock p. m. Gen. Robert E. Lee was assigned to the command of the army.

Seven Pines would have been a fatal day for Tennessee if no other casualty had befallen Hatton's brigade than the fall of its commander. "The personal bearing and conduct of the lamented General Hatton upon the field were gallant, and true to his high social and official character," said General Smith. "He fell while bravely and skillfully leading his brigade in the extreme front of the battle." Robert Hatton carried into the military service of the country the good wishes and affections of a greater number of people of his State than any other one of its citizen soldiers. Young and gifted, of the noblest character, he gathered about him the largest personal and political following. An ardent adherent and lover of the Federal government and Union of the States up to the date of President Lincoln's proclamation calling for troops, he then espoused the cause of the South, and the influence of his action stimulated many thousands of Tennesseeans to abandon all allegiance to the Washington government.

No officer of the brigade reported its action on the battlefield or furnished lists of casualties. Capt. J. H. Moore, Seventh Tennessee, is authority for the statement that "Adjt. G. A. Howard and eight out of the ten company commanders and half of the privates of the Seventh were killed or wounded." The losses were heavy in the First and Fourteenth. Dr. John Martin, assistant surgeon of the Fourteenth, was killed on the field while in the act of giving succor to a wounded man of his regiment.

A short time before the battles of Mechanicsville and Gaines' Mill, Brig.-Gen. J. J. Archer was assigned to the command of the Tennessee brigade which became part of A. P. Hill's division. This organization was maintained to the end. General Archer was distinguished at Seven Pines as colonel of the Fifth Texas, and there he won his promotion.

In referring to his part in the battle which preceded the great fights around Richmond, Gen. A. P. Hill said it was never contemplated that his division alone should receive the shock of battle at Mechanicsville, but such was the case, the only assistance received being from the division commanded by Brigadier-General Ripley. It was the intention of General Lee to attack the Federal right in the early morning of the 26th of June. Gen. Stonewall Jackson was expected to be in position at the dawn of day, but receiving no intelligence from him at 3 o'clock p. m. General Hill determined, in pursuance of General Lee's original orders, to cross the Chickahominy with a brigade, push on, and clear the Meadow bridge. At 3 o'clock General Hill crossed the bridge with his entire division, encountering slight opposition, the enemy falling back to Mechanicsville.

The Tennessee brigade, reduced at Seven Pines to 1,228 muskets, marched into the town and thence up the Mechanicsville turnpike, in line of battle, the Nineteenth Georgia on the left, the First Tennessee, Lieut.-Col. J. C. Shackelford commanding, on the right, the Fifth Alabama and Seventh Tennessee supporting, the Fourteenth Tennessee co-operating with Field's brigade. The brigade moved steadily forward to Beaver Dam creek under a heavy fire of all arms, the enemy being heavily intrenched on the opposite bank. Night closed before a crossing could be effected, and before morning the enemy abandoned their works and the battlefield. The Tennessee brigade lost 43 killed and 171 wounded, among the latter the gallant Maj. John A. Fite. The object of this attack, clearing the way for Longstreet's corps, was fully accomplished.

General McClellan, commanding the Federal army, stated that at the time of this battle he was satisfied that he had to deal with at least double his numbers. McClellan's army was about 100,000 strong, with 40,000 under McDowell covering Washington. The field returns of the army of Northern Virginia show a strength of 81,000, and of this force 30,000 under Magruder were covering Richmond.

On the morning of the 27th, Hill's division crossed Beaver Dam creek, and under orders of General Lee, took the route to Cold Harbor or Gaines' mill.

Arriving at the creek upon which Gaines' mill is located, half a mile from Cold Harbor, the enemy was discovered upon the opposite bank. At 2:30 p. m. of the 27th, General Hill advanced his division to the attack, and soon discovered that the whole force of the enemy was in his front.

The Tennessee brigade, now reduced to less than 1,000 men, says General Archer, advanced alone and unsupported across an open field to attack the enemy posted and protected in the wood beyond by the works, which a short time afterward it required seven brigades to carry. The Tennesseeans advanced at a double-quick to within twenty steps of the breastworks, when they fell back before an irresistible fire of artillery and small-arms. A half hour later they moved forward to the attack of the same position and entered the works in the front line of attack, the enemy now being swept from the field.

Archer's brigade lost in this action 49 killed and 271 wounded, a loss in the two days' battles of 542. Among the killed was the intrepid Lieut.-Col. J. C. Shackelford, commanding the First Tennessee. Capt. William P. Tolley of the same regiment was dangerously wounded and disabled for life. He was one of the most gallant soldiers of the war, and enjoys the distinction of commanding the first company organized in Tennessee. All the field officers of this regiment and of the Seventeenth Tennessee were killed or wounded. The gallant Col. John F. Goodner and Maj. W. H. Williamson of the Seventh were severely wounded. Lieut.-Col. John K. Howard of the same regiment received a mortal wound. A noble gentleman, a gifted orator, a valiant soldier, he fell in the first charge of his regiment, close up to the enemy's works. It was not the fortune of many regiments to have two field officers so richly endowed intellectually as Hatton and Howard. In a notice of Hatton, written a few days after his fall, Colonel Howard said: "A whole community will assemble around the stricken widow of our general; and the mothers of the noble boys who fell by his side will mingle their tears with hers"; words prophetic of a scene to be re-enacted in a few short weeks by the same community of people when intelligence of his own untimely death was received.

Sunday, June 29th, Hill's division recrossed the

Chickahominy, and on Monday, the 30th, it moved up by the cross made by the Long Bridge road and the Quaker road near Frayser's farm. Longstreet was warmly engaged when, Hill's division coming up, one after another of his brigade was sent forward whenever assistance was wanted. General Hill stated that "on our extreme right, matters seemed to be going badly. Two brigades of Longstreet's division had been roughly handled and had fallen back. Archer was brought up and sent in, and, in his shirt-sleeves, leading his gallant brigade, affairs were soon restored in that quarter." At dark the enemy made a desperate pressure on the Confederate line, but a part of Wilcox's brigade moved into the fight at a critical moment with a "loud and long rebel yell," and the contest was ended by the retirement of the enemy. The trophies of Hill's division this day were fourteen pieces of artillery and two stand of colors.

The next evening was fought the battle of Malvern Hill. Hill's division was placed in line of battle near the scene of action and under fire, but was not actively engaged. At night the Federal army continued its retreat to Harrison's landing on the James river. Here McClellan took position under the protecting guns of the fleet, fortified, and renewed his call for reinforcements.

McClellan's losses in these operations were reported officially to be 22,686 killed, wounded and captured; but more than this, his army lost its prestige, and the Washington authorities were dissatisfied and disgruntled at his failure to capture Richmond. The army of Northern Virginia lost 16,782 killed, wounded and missing, but it won the confidence and stimulated the hopes of the country, and achieved imperishable honor for its commanding general.

On the 26th of June, Maj.-Gen. John Pope of the United States army was assigned to command of the Federal army of Virginia. In President Lincoln's order making the assignment, he stated that the object was to protect "the national capital from danger of insult, to attack and overcome the rebel forces under Jackson and Ewell, and render the most effective aid to relieve General McClellan and capture Richmond." Under date of the 14th of July, General Pope in an address to his army said: "I have come to you from the West, where we have always seen the backs of our enemies; I presume that I have been called here to pursue the same system." Pope had under his command 77,779 men of all arms, soon reinforced by Burnside's command with 12,000, and by Cox from the Kanawha with 6,000. McClellan's army, strong and well appointed, remained inactive for a month.

On the 13th of July, General Jackson was ordered to Gordonsville, Pope's advance having reached the Rapidan. A. P. Hill, with his division, was ordered on July 27th to join General Jackson. On the 21st of July, Pope, writing to Banks, one of his corps commanders, said, "Let Bayard amuse Ewell with cavalry." He felt himself master of the situation until on the morning of the 9th of August, Jackson (greatly inferior in numbers) burst upon him with great fury, and pushed him from the field in retreat, capturing 400 prisoners, including a brigadier-general, 5,300 stand of small-arms, one piece of artillery, several caissons and three colors. On the 11th he sued for permission to bury his dead. General Jackson remained in position during the day of the 12th, and at night returned to Gordonsville. The next morning Pope telegraphed General Halleck, "The enemy has retreated under cover of the night;" but the general-in-chief, wiser than his redoubtable lieutenant, briefly answered, "Beware of a snare. Feigned retreats are Secesh tactics." On the 13th, General Lee congratulated General Jackson on his victory.

In this action at Cedar Run, the Tennessee troops participating were the First, Col. Peter Turney; the Seventh, Col. John A. Fite, and the Fourteenth, Col. W. A. Forbes, of Archer's brigade. General Archer reported that he found General Jackson's division already engaged when he arrived at 5 p. m., and pushing forward to engage the enemy, he crossed a field under heavy fire, where he lost 19 killed and 116 wounded, after which he met with no "opposition, but took a number of prisoners and continued the pursuit until night." The Tennesseeans lost 11 killed, 81 wounded; among the wounded, Col. John A. Fite and acting Maj. James C. Franklin; among the killed, Lieuts. Alexander Hogan and John Wise, Seventh Tennessee. Lieut.-Col. G. A. Harrell, Fourteenth Tennessee, was mortally wounded.

Gen. Stonewall Jackson reported that "the conduct of officers and men during the battle merits great praise," and in concluding his report to General Lee, he said: "In order to render thanks to God for the victory of Cedar Run and other past victories, and to implore His continued favor in the future, divine service was held in the army on August 14th."

Of the affair at Warrenton Springs ford, August 24th, General Archer says: "My brigade remained in bivouac in reserve, and although exposed to heavy shelling from the enemy's batteries, sustained no loss." After this the brigade marched to Manassas Junction, arriving there on the 26th of August, advanced in line, and soon came in sight of the enemy. Gen. Stonewall Jackson riding up with a battery, ordered General Archer to support it, and the enemy was soon broken and forced to retreat toward the railroad bridge of Bull run. In this action Archer reported a loss of 4 killed and 17 wounded.

August 28th the brigade marched through Centreville, up the Warrenton turnpike, and across Bull run, and formed in line nearly parallel with the railroad cut. When the engagement opened, about 5 p. m., Archer moved forward to support the batteries, and remained under a heavy fire of shot and shell until twilight. The next morning he was posted on the extreme left of Hill's division. At 3 p. m. the brigade was moved to the right, and an hour later it advanced to the railroad cut, to the relief of Pender's brigade. As the last regiment, the First Tennessee, entered the cut, it was ordered to fire on the enemy, "which it did with great effect," the enemy answering with a furious assault upon the brigade front. The attack, however, was firmly and gallantly resisted and the enemy driven back, but reinforced he made a second vigorous attack which was repelled by a countercharge. General Archer says of this second charge: "Many of my men were out of ammunition and charged with empty rifles. I did not average two cartridges to the man. A third assault was repulsed in the same manner, my brigade charging upon the enemy with loud cheers and driving them back with their empty rifles." The next morning he relieved General Early's pickets with 130 men under "the brave Col. N. J. George, First Tennessee, who is always ready and anxious for the most daring service." Soon the brigade was attacked, the enemy was driven back into the woods, and Archer's men "obtained a fresh supply of ammunition from the cartridge boxes of the dead Yankees." At 5 o'clock p. m. Archer and Pender advanced into the open field where the enemy was posted with one battery of six guns, with two other batteries in supporting distance, and with infantry supports to all. The two brigades moved directly on the six-gun battery, but the enemy stood to his guns and continued to fire until the Confederates were within 75 yards. At this juncture the enemy began to break, but Archer captured three pieces, while Pender overtook and captured the other three. This action was hotly contested, the loss in Archer's brigade being 17 killed and 196 wounded. Among the dead, Tennessee mourned Col. W. A. Forbes, Fourteenth, who was killed near the battery captured in another moment by his comrades. A. P. Hill referred to him as "the brave Colonel Forbes." General Archer commended in his report two Tennesseeans, of whom he said: "Among the officers whose gallantry I especially noticed in this action was Lieut.-Col. N. J. George, First Tennessee; also F. M. Barnes, private of Company A, Fourteenth Tennessee, who seized the colors from the hands of the wounded color-bearer and bore them bravely through the fight." Capt. Young T. Stubblefield and Lieut. W. E. Forbes, First Tennessee, were among the killed. Major Morris, Fourteenth Tennessee, was mortally wounded.

General Lee reported, in the series of engagements on the plains of Manassas, 7,000 Federal prisoners taken in addition to 2,000 wounded and abandoned by Pope's army, and the capture of 30 pieces of artillery and upward of 20,000 stand of small-arms. At Cedar Run and the combats and battles here recited, Archer lost in killed and wounded 369, out of a brigade of 1,200 strong, or nearly one-third of his effective total. At the battle of Second Manassas, Jackson reported that at one time pending the engagement "the opposing forces delivered their volleys into each other at the distance of ten paces."

The Federal army fell back on Washington City and General Pope was at once relieved of his command.

In the brief campaign against Pope, the Fourteenth Tennessee lost three field officers, Forbes, Harrell and Morris; Maj. William McComb succeeded Lieutenant-Colonel Harrell, and on the fall of Colonel Forbes, succeeded to the command of the regiment. Capt. J. W. Lockert was made lieutenant-colonel, and Capt. J. H. Johnson became major.

When General Lee started on his Maryland campaign, he dispatched Gen. Stonewall Jackson with about one-third of his army in the direction of Harper's Ferry, which was invested on the evening of September 14, 1862. Tennesseeans participating in the series of battles from Warrenton ford to Shepherdstown, inclusive, were the First Tennessee, Col. Peter Turney; Seventh Tennessee, Maj. S. G. Shepard; Fourteenth Tennessee, Lieut.-Col. Lockert of Archer's brigade, A. P. Hill's division. Archer advanced toward the southern defenses of Bolivar heights, in rear of Harper's Ferry, and was halted for the night within 400 yards of the enemy's guns. The next morning, while he was struggling through a well-constructed abatis in the immediate front of the enemy, the garrison, 11,000 strong, was surrendered to General Jackson. Archer's brigade lost 1 man killed and 22 wounded.

The capture of Harper's Ferry with the garrison and 73 pieces of artillery, 13,000 stand of small-arms, 200 wagons with large quantities of stores and supplies, was a brilliant achievement and a shock to the Federal authorities. At once a commission, presided over by Major-General Hunter, was organized to inquire into the causes of the surrender. After a long and tedious investigation the responsibility was fixed upon Col. Dixon S. Miles, commanding the garrison. He was mortally wounded in the attack made by General Jackson's forces, and died in a few hours; he could not appear before any earthly tribunal, still Major-General Hunter announced in his official report that his "incapacity, amounting to almost imbecility, led to the shameful surrender of this important post."

The morning after the surrender, the Tennesseeans marched 17 miles to the field of Sharpsburg. It was a long and fatiguing march. Arriving on the field, Archer was placed on the left of Hill's division and was immediately engaged. General Archer reported that "in passing over the distance, 250 yards, I lost nearly one-third of my already greatly-reduced command, but it rushed forward, alone, at double-quick, giving the enemy but little time to estimate its small numbers, and drove him from his strong position." The enemy was posted in force behind a stone fence. It was now near sunset.

Archer remained in position all of the next day. The following morning General Lee retired across the Potomac, Archer's brigade constituting part of the rear guard. At Sharpsburg the Seventh Tennessee was commanded by Lieut. George A. Howard, adjutant of the regiment. The brigade lost 14 killed and 90 wounded, among the latter, Col. William McComb, Fourteenth. General Archer said of him that his gallant conduct attracted his attention, "though where all who were engaged behaved so gallantly, it is difficult to select examples of particular merit."

Gen. R. E. Lee, referring to the conduct of Archer's and four other brigades of Hill's division, said: "By this time, between 3 and 4 p. m., Gen. A. P. Hill with five of his brigades reached the scene of action, drove the enemy immediately from the position they had taken, restoring our right and maintaining our ground." Gen. A. P. Hill, in his report, states that when General Lee placed him in position he was not a moment too soon. The enemy had already advanced in three lines, had broken through D. R. Jones' division, captured McIntosh's battery, and were in full tide of success. With a yell of defiance Archer charged them, retook McIntosh's guns and drove them back pellmell.

When General Lee recrossed the Potomac he left Brigadier-General Pendleton on the Virginia side with the reserve artillery and 600 infantry to guard the crossing. During the day Gen. Fitz John Porter of the Federal army, with his corps, appeared on the opposite side, and that night (the 19th) crossed several brigades over. After a short engagement Pendleton's infantry support gave way and four of his guns were captured. Orders were now sent to General Hill to return with his division and dislodge the enemy, who had taken position on the right bank of the river under cover of their artillery on the commanding hills on the opposite side. General Hill, who had bivouacked five miles in front of Shepherdstown, returned in the early morning of the 20th, made his formation, and advanced to attack the enemy, who had lined the opposite hills with 70 pieces of artillery, and posted the infantry who had crossed on the crest of the high banks of the Virginia shores. General Hill stated that his troops advanced in the face of the most tremendous fire of artillery he had ever witnessed, and too much praise could not be awarded the regiments for their steady, unwavering step. General Pender, with three brigades, became hotly engaged, and Archer, commanding his own, Lane's and Brockenbrough's brigades, moved by the left flank, and after forming on Pender's left, a simultaneous daring charge was made which drove the enemy in mad confusion in the river. "Then commenced the most terrible slaughter that has yet been witnessed. The broad surface of the Potomac was blue with the floating bodies of our foe. But few escaped to tell the tale." General Archer reported that many of the enemy's troops were killed, and many driven down the precipitous banks into the river. Two hundred prisoners were taken. Archer and Pender had 30 killed and 231 wounded. In this affair, Col. Peter Turney commanded the First, Colonel Lockert the Fourteenth, and Adjt. George A. Howard the Seventh Tennessee.

At nightfall the brigade returned to the bivouac of the previous night. General Lee marched his army to the Opequon near Martinsburg, and after a few days to the vicinity of Winchester, marching thence after a long rest a distance of 175 miles in twelve days. Archer's brigade reached the Massaponax hills near Fredericksburg on the 3d of December.

"The history of the achievements of the army from the time it advanced from Gordonsville leaves nothing to be said in commendation of the courage, fortitude and good conduct of both officers and men," said General Lee in his official report.

On the 5th of November, 1862, President Lincoln relieved Major-General McClellan and assigned Major-General Burnside to the command of the army of the Potomac. General Burnside assumed command and concentrated the army, 113,000 strong, at Fredericksburg. General Lee, discovering his purpose, rapidly concentrated the army of Northern Virginia, and when the Federal army crossed the Rappahannock, he was in position ready for Burnside's attack. Burnside crossed the river on the night of the 11th of December, 1862, with a division, and occupied Fredericksburg. On the 13th his troops were all over the river, and at 9 a. m. his advance was made on the right wing of our army commanded by Gen. Stonewall Jackson. A. P. Hill's division, on Jackson's right, was fiercely assailed.

General Archer, commanding the Tennesseeans, reported that when the enemy advanced upon his brigade, several batteries were brought forward and placed in position, about 1,000 yards distant; at 10:30 they turned all their guns on his line, and after thirty minutes Meade's and Doubleday's divisions boldly came forward to the attack. This advance was met with such a destructive fire that the enemy in front hastily fell back and took shelter in a railroad cut, where he remained during the action. In the meantime another column of troops entered the point of wood on Archer's left, passing around his flank, and attacked the Nineteenth Georgia and Fourteenth Tennessee in rear with a superior force, and compelled these regiments to retire, leaving 160 prisoners in the enemy's hands. A part of the Seventh Tennessee, seeing the regiments on the left give way, left the trenches in disorder. The First Tennessee, said General Archer, with Lieuts. F. A. Timberlake, O. H. Foster, B. Wilmouth and Wm. T. Baird of the Seventh Tennessee, with a portion of their regiment, held the ground gallantly, and after ammunition was exhausted, charged with empty guns under Lieut.-Col. N. J. George (Colonel Turney having been wounded early in the action) across the railroad track, with Hoke's brigade of Early's division, and forced the enemy to retire in confusion. Gen. R. E. Lee, referring to this action in his official report, said Archer and Lane repulsed that portion of the line in their immediate front, but before the interval between these commands could be closed, the enemy passed through in overwhelming numbers and turned the left of Archer and the right of Lane, attacking in front and flank the two regiments of Archer and the brigade of Lane, which after a brave and obstinate resistance gave way. Archer held his line with the First Tennessee and with the Fifth Alabama battalion, assisted by the Forty-second Virginia and the Twenty-second Virginia battalion, until reinforcements arrived. It was at this point that Lieutenant-Colonel George made the brilliant and effective charge, in connection with Hoke's brigade, that contributed largely to the general success.

General Archer stated that Lieut. Z. G. Gunn, Fourteenth Tennessee, fell in the most gallant performance of duty. Colonel Turney, Lieutenant-Colonel George, Maj. F. G. Buchanan and Capt. M. Turney, First Tennessee, were wounded.

General Lee had 20,000 troops engaged, of which he lost 4,101 killed and wounded. Burnside reported 1,152 killed and 9,000 wounded. The official returns give his loss at 12,658. General Lee captured 900 prisoners and 9,000 stand of arms.

The 14th and 15th passed without an attempt at an advance, and during the night of the 15th, Burnside retreated across the Rappahannock.

General Burnside stated in his official report of the battle that he had made "four distinct efforts" (to cross the Rappahannock) between November 9, 1862, and January 25, 1863. The first failed for want of pontoons; the second was the battle of Fredericksburg; the third was stopped by President Lincoln, and the fourth was defeated by the elements. On the 25th of January he was relieved and Maj.-Gen. Joseph Hooker was assigned to the command of the army of the Potomac.

After the battle of Fredericksburg, the army of Northern Virginia under General Lee remained encamped on the south side of the Rappahannock until the latter part of April, 1863, the Federal army, then under General Hooker, occupying the north side of the river opposite Fredericksburg, extending to the Potomac. On the 28th, the enemy crossed the river in force at Fredericksburg, but no advance was attempted. General Lee learned that Hooker was moving a large force up and across the Rappahannock and across the Rapidan, following routes near Chancellorsville, with the purpose of gaining the rear of the Confederate army. On the 1st of May, Jackson's corps moved in the direction of Chancellorsville, at 8 a. m. began preparation for battle, and the enemy now advancing was easily pushed back to Chancellorsville.

At 11 a. m. on the 2d, Archer's brigade was withdrawn from the plank road and was ordered to the left of the Welford Furnace road; but after marching two miles the brigade commander learned that a large body of the enemy had attacked our army train in his rear and driven off the troops guarding it. On receiving this important information he at once returned and found that the enemy had been repulsed by Lieut.-Col. J. T. Brown of the artillery, assisted by detachments of infantry, among them Capt. W. S. Moore with two companies of the Fourteenth Tennessee. Captain Moore, who had just been relieved from picket duty, was returning to his regiment, and thus was opportunely at the right place when the train was attacked and bore a conspicuous part in its protection. In his official report, General Lee made honorable mention of Captain Moore and his command.

The next morning General Archer moved forward to the attack, driving the enemy's skirmishers. The brigade attacked at a double-quick and drove the enemy in confusion, capturing four pieces of artillery and 100 prisoners. Referring to this incident, General Heth, commanding the division (General Hill having been wounded), said General Archer advanced with his brigade, conforming his line of battle to that of the enemy, charged the works in his front, and without the least halt or hesitation carried them, driving the enemy before him, who outnumbered him five to one. General Archer captured a four-gun battery. By his gallant attack he secured the key to the enemy's position, clearing a hill and open space in his front and gaining for our artillery a position from which they were enabled to silence the 29-gun battery of the enemy which had inflicted so much loss on our lines. From this position our artillery had also a raking fire on the enemy's works on our right. Archer, after carrying the hill, advanced beyond the open space and attacked the enemy on his right, at which time he was joined by Anderson's division. Reinforcements were brought up, a general advance took place, the enemy's works were cleared, and he fell back in the direction of the United States ford. The field was won, but the fall of Stonewall Jackson made Chancellorsville a dearly-bought victory."

The Tennessee regiments of Archer's brigade were commanded as follows: The First by Lieut.-Col. N. J. George, the Second by Lieut.-Col. John A. Fite, and the Fourteenth by Lieut.-Col. Wm. McComb until, being wounded, he was succeeded by Capt. R. C. Wilson. Capt. W. W. Thompson, Fourteenth, and Lieut. Andrew T. Paul, Seventh, were killed. The three Tennessee regiments lost 189 killed, wounded and missing, of which number 16 were captured. The Federal army of the Potomac lost during the Chancellorsville campaign in killed, wounded and missing, 17,287 officers and men, and retreated across the Rappahannock after signal defeats at Chancellorsville, Marye's hill, and Salem heights. With a conspicuous absence of modesty, under date of the 6th of May, General Hooker issued a general order in which he tenders "to this army my congratulations on its achievements of the last seven days."

After General Lee's decisive victory at Chancellorsville he determined to draw the Federal army from its position on the Rappahannock, and at the same time expel the Federal general, Milroy, from the valley of Virginia. In execution of this purpose, Hill's division was left in front of Hooker and the other two corps commenced the movement resulting in the victory at Winchester on the 13th of June, which was followed by the march into Pennsylvania. Hooker, seeming to become bewildered by these movements, and uncertain as to the whereabouts of Lee's army, abandoned his position on the Rappahannock. As late as the 17th of June he telegraphed the general-in-chief at Washington: "In your opinion is there any foundation for the report that the Confederates are at Chambersburg, Pa.?" On the 27th he was relieved and Maj.-Gen. George C. Meade was assigned to the command of the army of the Potomac. The army was already in motion.

When General Hill advanced on Gettysburg on the morning of the 1st of July, he found it in possession of Buford's Federal cavalry and the First, Third and Eleventh army corps under Major-General Reynolds. Major-General Heth, in advance, stated that his division was disposed as follows: Archer's Tennessee brigade on the right, with Davis' brigade on the left, both in line of battle, Pettigrew's and Brockenbrough's in reserve. On the right of the turnpike Archer encountered heavy masses in his front, and his gallant little brigade, after being almost surrounded by superior forces in front and on both flanks, was forced back. The service at this time, said the division general, "lost that most gallant and meritorious officer, Brig.-Gen. James L. Archer," who, with 60 or 70 of his men, was captured. A second advance was made by Heth's and Pender's divisions, and Lieutenant-General Ewell, coming up with two of his divisions, joined in the engagement, and the enemy were driven through Gettysburg with heavy loss, including about 5,000 prisoners and several pieces of artillery. Of the action of Archer's brigade, Col. B. D. Fry, Thirteenth Alabama, commanding, General Heth said: "This brigade, the heroes of Chancellorsville, fully maintained its hard-won and well-deserved reputation." During the night and the next day Archer's brigade was in position on the right of Hill's corps. This success and the partial successes of Longstreet's and Ewell's corps on the 2d, determined General Lee to continue the assault the next day, the enemy in the meantime having strengthened his lines with earthworks.

On the afternoon of the 3d of July, after the necessary preparation had been completed, the assault on Cemetery hill was made by Pickett's and Heth's divisions in the front line, Heth's division commanded by Brigadier-General Pettigrew (General Heth having been wounded in the affair of the 1st). The glory and fame of this charge, one of the most famous of modern times, belong alike to Pickett's and Heth's divisions. They went forward supported by Wilcox's brigade of Anderson's division, and Lane's and Scales' brigades of Pender's division, under Major-General Trimble, the gallant Pender having received a mortal wound. Lieut.-Col. S. G. Shepard, commanding the Seventh Tennessee, who succeeded to the command of Archer's brigade after the capture of Colonel Fry, in an official report stated that his brigade was on the right of Heth's division in the following order: First Tennessee on the right, next the Thirteenth Alabama, next the Fourteenth Tennessee, on its left the Seventh Tennessee, and the Fifth Alabama battalion on the left of the brigade.

The brigade was on the left of Pickett's division. The enemy reserved his fire until the line was in close range, and then opened a terrible and well-directed volley. "Within 180 or 200 yards of his works," said the brigade commander, "we came upon a lane running between two fences made of stout posts and plank. This was a great obstruction to us, but the men rushed over as rapidly as possible, and advanced directly upon the enemy's works, the first line of which was composed of rough stones. The enemy abandoned this, but just in rear was massed a heavy force. By the time we reached this work, our lines all along, as far as I could see, had become very much weakened. Archer's brigade remained at the works fighting as long as any other troops on the right or left. Every flag in the brigade except one was captured at or within the enemy's works." The First Tennessee had three color-bearers shot down, the third one at the works; the Thirteenth Alabama lost three; the Fourteenth Tennessee had four shot down; the Seventh Tennessee lost three, all under the same circumstances, except when the third color-bearer of the Seventh fell, the colors were torn from the staff by Capt. A. D. Norris of that regiment, and concealed upon his person and restored to the regiment. Of seven field officers of the brigade, five were wounded and captured inside of the enemy's works. Colonel Fry, Lieut.-Col. N. J. George, First Tennessee, Major (afterward lieutenant-colonel) Fite, Seventh Tennessee, the noble Capt. W. H. Williamson, afterward major of the Seventh, who lost an arm, were among the number. The loss in company officers and men (their names were not reported) was in the same proportion.

Capt. John H. Moore, of the Seventh Tennessee, one of the most distinguished officers of his rank in the service, in a communication published in the Philadelphia Times, stated that he lost 40 killed and wounded out of a total of 47 of his company, and that one company of North Carolina troops, of Pettigrew's brigade, 84 strong, lost every officer and man killed or wounded. Captain Moore added, that "in justice to the hundreds of Heth's division who fell in the works on Cemetery hill, in the lane and open fields, in the advance or retreat, I cannot be indifferent when the story of that grand charge is told, unless honors are divided with Heth's division." The brigade, in the battles of the 1st and 3d, out of a total present of 1,043, lost 677 killed, wounded and captured. After the repulse of our attacking column, General Lee remained in position in front of the enemy, awaiting an attack until the night of the 4th, when he retired and fell back beyond Hagerstown, Md., without molestation.

Gettysburg was a victory for the enemy, but it was won at great cost,—his return of casualties showing a loss of 23,049 killed, wounded and captured. The returns also show a great Confederate loss, 20,451. The killed in the Federal army was 307 in excess of the killed in General Lee's army, and the wounded exceeded that of the Confederates by 684. In prisoners, the excess in favor of General Lee was 32. General Lee's prisoners were captured on the battlefield. Except the captures made on Cemetery hill and a few on the afternoon of the 1st, the prisoners lost by the army of Northern Virginia were barefooted and foot-sore stragglers, captured after the battle.

Leaving Hagerstown, Heth's and Pender's divisions constituting the rear guard of the army, Lee took position between that point and Williamsport, then retired on the evening of the 13th to a point one mile and a half from Falling Waters, and formed line of battle. About 11:30 a. m., says General Heth (now sufficiently recovered to command his division), a small body of cavalry numbering 40 or 55 men dashed up and charged his line, and in less than three minutes all of this reckless squad were killed but two or three. The noble General Pettigrew and one man of the Seventh Tennessee were mortally wounded. The charge by this body of Federal cavalry was made upon the First, Seventh and Fourteenth Tennessee and Thirteenth Alabama. A few minutes later, a large body of dismounted cavalry with artillery made a vigorous attack on Brockenbrough's brigade, which was repulsed; but the enemy being heavily reinforced, Brockenbrough retired under orders.

On the 14th of July, General Meade telegraphed General Halleck at Washington, that Brig.-Gen. Judson Kilpatrick, of the Federal cavalry, had captured a brigade of Confederate infantry, two pieces of artillery, two caissons, and a large number of small-arms at Falling Waters. This telegram was given to the public prints, and called forth an official reply and denial from General Lee, dated the 21st of July, 1863, in which he said: "The enemy did not capture any organized body of men. It rained without cessation, rendering the road very difficult to pass, and causing much delay. While the column was thus detained on the road, a number of men, worn down with fatigue, lay down in barns and by the roadside, and many were in this way left behind. The two guns were left in the road, because the horses that drew them were exhausted." The attack made by the redoubtable Kilpatrick was upon Archer's Tennessee brigade and Brockenbrough's Virginia brigade, and not a man was captured. Stragglers representing all commands were taken between Hagerstown and Falling Waters; but every advance made by Kilpatrick was repulsed. General Heth reported that "the enemy made two cavalry charges, and on each occasion I witnessed the unhorsing of the entire party." Concluding his report, made in October, 1863, he said: "I desire to brand upon its perpetrator a falsehood and correct an error. General Meade reported to his government that Kilpatrick had captured a brigade of infantry in the fight at Falling Waters. After General Lee's denial, General Meade reaffirmed his first statement upon the authority of Kilpatrick. General Kilpatrick, in order to glorify himself, has told a deliberate falsehood." Heth had no artillery present, and seeing the necessity for it, an application was sent forward to General Hill for a battery, but his staff officer returned with an order to withdraw and cross the Potomac.

The Tennessee brigade, of Heth's division, began the battle of Gettysburg and fought the combat at Falling Waters, the last one of the army of Northern Virginia north of the Potomac. General Archer suffered a long imprisonment, and was one of the victims of that barbarous action on the part of the Federal authorities which placed him, with a shipload of Confederate officers, under the fire of our own guns in Charleston harbor. He was exchanged in the autumn of 1864, and was promoted to major-general, but was unfit for duty, and died from disease contracted in Charleston harbor. He was greatly beloved by his Tennessee brigade, at the head of which he had won distinction.

Gen. U. S. Grant, promoted lieutenant-general and assigned to the command of the armies of the United States, on May 4, 1865, crossed the Rapidan at Ely's and Germanna fords with an army 140,000 strong. General Lee confronted him with 64,000 men of all arms. In the battles which followed, Brig.-Gen. H. H. Walker commanded the Tennessee brigade; the First Tennessee was commanded by Maj. Felix G. Buchanan, the Seventh by Lieut.-Col. Samuel G. Shepard, the Fourteenth by Col. William McComb. On the 5th of May, Major-General Warren, with the Fifth Federal corps, attacked Ewell's corps, and was repulsed with a loss of many prisoners and four pieces of artillery. At the same time Getty's division, of the Sixth Federal corps, was sent out on the Orange plank road, reinforced by Hancock's corps, and a combined assault was made upon Heth's and Wilcox's divisions of Hills' corps, which, said General Meade, "was done at first successfully;" but these two divisions, said General Lee, "resisted successfully repeated and desperate assaults" made by a very superior force. Heth and Wilcox inflicted such serious injury on the attacking force that Wadsworth's division and Baxter's brigade of Warren's corps were hurried forward as reinforcements, but no advance was attempted, and night suspended hostilities. The next morning General Grant telegraphed to Halleck, "So far, there is no decisive result. Our loss to this time, 11:30 a. m., I do not think exceeds 8,000."

Heth's division opened the battle of the Wilderness. The Tennessee brigade was in line of battle for eighteen hours without rest. It was in good form and never delivered battle with greater intrepidity. At 5 a. m. of the 6th the enemy advanced, now reinforced by Burnside's corps. The attacks made by the Fifth and Sixth corps, said General Meade, were "without any particular success." He claims that Hancock's corps, with Wadsworth's and Getty's divisions, forced Heth and Wilcox to fall back for a mile in confusion, and states that "Longstreet's corps coming up, the tide of battle was turned and our victorious line was forced back." At the close of the day, Longstreet, with a part of his corps, turned the right of the Sixth corps, capturing the general officers and many men, and this terminated the battle of the Wilderness.

On the 8th, Gen. R. H. Anderson, with the advance of the Confederate army, repulsed the enemy with great slaughter and took possession of Spottsylvania Court House. Receiving reinforcements, General Grant renewed the attack and was handsomely driven back. On the 10th, General Early, commanding Hill's corps, drove the enemy from a position he had taken between Shady Grove church and the court house, taking one gun and a few prisoners, in which engagement Brig.-Gen. H. H. Walker, commanding the Tennessee brigade, was severely wounded, losing a leg. Colonel McComb, of the Fourteenth Tennessee, succeeded to the command. On the evening of the 11th, Heth's division was on the extreme right of our army. "The works occupied by the Tennessee brigade extended about 50 yards in front of the general direction of our line, and terminated in an acute angle with 50 yards of open space between the line and the pine woods. Our skirmish line was engaged in the early morning of the 12th, the Federal artillery opening at the same time. At 9 a. m., in the midst of a heavy rainfall, our skirmishers were driven in, and soon Warren, with the Fifth corps, emerged in three lines from the woods into the open space. We poured volley after volley into their well-dressed ranks and drove them to the cover of the pines; in a few minutes the enemy reformed and made another advance to the open space, but another volley forced him to retire and fall back far into the pine woods. The two assaults made on the angle held by the Tennessee brigade were less than an hour in duration, yet the Federal dead and wounded were as thick on the ground as if a battle had raged for a day." (Capt. J. H. Moore, Seventh Tennessee.) Lieut. F. S. Harris, Seventh Tennessee, commanding the division of sharpshooters, and Lieut. Byrd Wilmouth, commanding the skirmish line, pursued the enemy with vigor. Both officers were conspicuous for valor—the gallant Wilmouth was killed; Harris survived the war and seven wounds received in battle.

General Grant changed the position of his army from time to time, but invariably found the army of Northern Virginia in his front. Frequent skirmishes and combats without results occurred until the armies met at Cold Harbor. On the 1st of June, Major-General Pickett rejoined General Lee with 5,000 men, increasing his strength to 45,000. Grant was reinforced by 12,000, increasing his effective strength to 112,000. General Grant said: "We assaulted at 4:30 a. m. to-day (June 3d) without gaining any decisive advantage." General Lee reported that the Federal attack was met with great steadiness and repulsed in every instance. Later in the day it was twice renewed against Heth's division on the left and repulsed with loss. In these two attacks, the Tennessee brigade under McComb added luster to its already splendid reputation.

Grant reported a loss at the Wilderness of 17,666, at Spottsylvania 18,399, at North Anna and other combats 3,986, at Cold Harbor 12,738, a total of 52,789 killed, wounded and captured in a campaign of a month. The army under General Lee lost during the campaign 20,000 killed, wounded and captured. In a dispatch to Halleck, dated the day of his signal defeat at Cold Harbor, General Grant confessed to the failure of his plan of campaign, and soon began the siege of Petersburg and the attack on Richmond.

The battle of Drewry's Bluff was fought by the Federal army of the James, composed of the Tenth and Eighteenth army corps and a division of cavalry under command of Gen. Benjamin F. Butler, and a Confederate force under General Beauregard, consisting of three small divisions under Major-General Hoke, Major-General Ransom and Brigadier-General Colquitt, in all ten brigades and three battalions of artillery. The Seventeenth and Twenty-third Tennessee, under Col. R. H. Keeble, the Twenty-fifth and Forty-fourth, under Col. John S. Fulton, and the Sixty-third, under Col. Abraham Fulkerson, constituted Bushrod Johnson's brigade, of Hoke's division.

From his headquarters at Drewry's farm, General Beauregard issued orders dated the 15th of May, concentrating his forces at that point, his purpose, as stated, being to cut off the army of the James from its base of operations at Bermuda Hundred, and capture or destroy it. Ransom's division moved out at 4:45 of May 16th, in line of battle, and soon encountering the Federals, carried the enemy's breastworks in his front by 6 a. m., and after resting a moment, reinforced by one of Colquitt's brigades, advanced to the attack. At this hour a part of Hoke's division was actively engaged. Bushrod Johnson's and Hagood's brigades were soon thrown forward, and Hagood, said General Beauregard, "with great vigor and dash, drove the enemy from his outer lines, capturing a number of prisoners and, in conjunction with Johnson, five pieces of artillery. Johnson, meanwhile, had been heavily engaged. The line of the enemy bent round his right flank, subjecting his brigade for a time to fire in flank and front, but with admirable firmness he repulsed frequent assaults of the enemy moving in masses against his right and rear. Leader, officers and men alike displayed their fitness for the trial to which they were subjected. I cannot forbear to mention Lieutenant Waggoner, of the Twenty-third Tennessee, who went along through a storm of fire and pulled down a white flag which a small, isolated body of our men (stragglers from another command) had raised, receiving a wound in the act. The brigade, holding its ground nobly, lost more than one-fourth of its entire number. At length, Johnson, having brushed the enemy from his right flank in the woods, cleared his front and rested his troops in the shelter of the outer works." Col. H. R. Keeble, Seventeenth and Twenty-third Tennessee, a veteran soldier of great distinction, in his official report dated May 22, 1864, stated: "My orders from General Johnson were to move down the turnpike by the left flank until I reached the outer line of fortifications, when I would halt, front and move forward in connection with General Ransom's division. Long before I reached the outer line of fortifications, I discovered that the enemy were still occupying our works (heretofore constructed and occupied), with a battery of five pieces (Parrott guns) planted in the center of the turnpike, a little beyond the fortifications. We, however, continued to move forward under a shower of grape, canister and minie balls, which swept up the turnpike. Reaching the trenches, line was immediately formed confronting the enemy, and here commenced and raged for two hours one of the most desperate actions in which I have ever been engaged. The enemy were in strong force in our trenches, and their battery, already named, played upon us furiously. They were vastly outnumbering me, and nothing but the thickness of the wall between us. They had also succeeded in throwing a force upon my right flank and rear, from which we received a galling fire. Having thus, in a measure, surrounded us, they frequently demanded our surrender, which was met by yells of defiance and volleys from my regiment. With their battery in our front, their infantry in front, upon my flank and rear, the case seemed desperate to the last degree; but by causing the rear rank of my regiment to face about, we thus met and fought them on all sides; succeeded in driving them off and holding our position, silenced and captured their battery of Parrott guns. One of the pieces was brought to the rear by a detail from my own regiment. Some other brigade or command passed over the ground where the other pieces were left, and I understand, claimed to have captured the battery." General Beauregard accorded the honor to another, "in conjunction with Johnson," but the gallant Keeble, with his Seventeenth and Twenty-third Tennessee, drove the enemy from the battery after one of the fiercest contests of the war and fairly carried off the honors.

General Butler, commanding the "army of the James," in his official report, makes this light reference to the battle: "The enemy, taking advantage of a very thick fog, made an attack upon the right of General Smith's line (the Eighteenth army corps), and forced it back with some confusion and considerable loss. The troops having been on incessant duty for five days, I retired at leisure within my own lines." He reported his losses during the month of May at Port Walthall, Swift creek and other skirmishes, including Drewry's Bluff, at 5,958 killed, wounded and captured. In spite of Butler's flippant report, the battle was a disastrous one to him. Major-General Gilmore, commanding the Tenth corps, at 7:25 a. m. asked General Butler in a written dispatch if it were true that General Brooks' (commanding division in Eighteenth corps) right was turned and a 20-pounder battery lost. General Butler answered, "No truth in report." Very soon after this, Butler dispatched Gilmore: "Brooks is falling back to second line; Weitzel is also falling back." In a little while, at 9:30 a. m., General Gilmore states that he received a dispatch from Butler informing him that "the enemy is pressing around our right; Smith has fallen back to near Halfway house; the enemy is near Dr. Howlett's. You must fall back, press to the right, and get in rear of Smith's corps. He will try to hold his ground until you get in his rear, and clear the road to the intrenchments so that we may get back behind the defenses. Push vigorously." General Butler's heroic soul was "in a flame of zeal severe." At 10 a. m. he again dispatched Gilmore to "get there at once; the troops at General Ames' old position are forced back. We will lose the turnpike unless you hurry." Brigadier-General Weitzel reported officially that "the four regiments of Heckman's brigade were crushed by the (Confederate) attack. This was no surprise on account of the fog, as the whole division was in line of battle and prepared for the shock, having several times received warning." Heckman's brigade held the position assailed by Johnson's Tennessee brigade. General Weitzel reported that Heckman's brigade was crushed by a very large and overwhelming force. Johnson assailed him with 871 muskets. Col. G. A. Stedman, Jr., Eleventh Connecticut, was on Heckman's right. In his report he stated that "finding myself unsupported and in danger of annihilation or capture, I faced the regiment about and marched to the rear, constantly obliquing to the right to avoid the enemy, who were following the regiment with yells." General Weitzel reported that "toward evening the army started for home." He could have added—badly beaten by an inferior force (in numbers and equipments) of ragged, barefooted Confederates. The French emperor's theory that poverty and deprivation make good soldiers was illustrated at Drewry's Bluff.

"The army of the James" left in the hands of General Beauregard 1,400 prisoners, 5 pieces of artillery, 5 stand of colors, 3,936 stand of small-arms, and 60,000 to 70,000 rounds of ammunition. Among the Tennesseeans who fell were Lieut.-Col. John L. McEwen, Forty-fourth;

Lieut.-Col. Matt Floyd, Seventeenth; Lieut.-Col. John Alfred Aiken, Sixty-third; Maj. S. H. Carver, Twenty-fifth; Capt. R. A. Rutledge and Lieut. Wm. T. Battles, Sixty-third. In the list of severely wounded were Captain Cortner and Lieutenant Patrick, Twenty-third; Capts. J. H. Curtis, Twenty-fifth, and C. R. Milliard, Sixty-third. "Frank A. Moses, the gallant standard-bearer of the Sixty-third, while bearing the flag to victory was three times severely wounded, whereupon Private James A. Lindamood seized the flag, and bearing it aloft, called loudly for the men to go forward. Sergt. Thomas Morrell was wounded nine times and killed. Adam Harr, a brave private, was shot in the head and left side; calling for help, he was asked where he was shot, and replied, 'Right through the heart and brain.' Yet he survived the war." (Col. A. Fulkerson, Sixty-third.)

Not many days after Drewry's Bluff, Gen. Bushrod Johnson was made a major-general, and the command of Johnson's famous brigade devolved upon the gallant John S. Fulton, Forty-fourth Tennessee, who had led it with distinction at Chickamauga and Knoxville. Justice in General Johnson's case was tardy and cruel. He commanded brigades as brigadier-general at Fort Donelson, Shiloh, Perryville, Murfreesboro, a division at Chickamauga and Knoxville, and won promotion on every field. At Chickamauga he pierced the enemy's lines and won the battle, but he was a modest man who never learned the trick of "cowering low with blandishment."

At dawn on the 16th of June, Bushrod Johnson with his command abandoned the Bermuda Hundred line, under orders from General Beauregard, and arrived at Petersburg about 10 o'clock a. m. General Beauregard had now about 10,000 men of all arms to meet the Second and Eighteenth army corps, commanded, respectively, by Hancock and Smith. Burnside's corps (the Ninth) came up at noon. The Federal forces now outnumbered Beauregard by six to one. At nightfall Warren's corps, the

Fifth, reached Petersburg, swelling the Federal force to over 90,000 men. Late in the afternoon Beauregard's line of defense was assaulted, only a few hours having been occupied in preparing temporary earthworks, hastily constructed, in the absence of intrenching tools, with bayonets and all manner of substitutes. Yet three hours were occupied by the Federal army in efforts to break the Confederate line; assaults were made, repeated, and repulsed time and again, until finally a part of Hancock's corps made a lodgment. The Tennessee brigade (Johnson's), now reduced to less than 600 men, occupied the extreme right of the line, which it held in the several assaults made upon it, the enemy being driven back with heavy loss.

The most notable event of the day was the action of Lieut. F. M. Kelso, Forty-fourth and Twenty-fifth Tennessee. In an official report to General Johnson he stated that "Between Batteries 14 and 15 there was a space between the right of the brigade occupied by the Forty-fourth Tennessee and Battery 15 of about 100 yards. Colonel Fulton, Forty-fourth, said this space was to have been filled by other troops. About 5 p. m. the enemy made two charges. The first was repulsed; the second was made bearing upon the extreme right, moving right-oblique. I took seventeen men and occupied the interval between the right of the Forty-fourth and Battery 15, and engaged the enemy, who was rapidly advancing. I deployed my command, covering about 50 yards of the unoccupied space. The enemy continued the advance until within 50 yards of our intrenchments. One of the enemy's colors was shot down six times. There was a ravine about 50 yards distant, in which the force in my front lay down and raised the white flag. I ceased firing and called upon them to surrender. After a few minutes I marched out of the works and received the surrender of 400 to 700 men, and marched them inside of our works. I captured the flags of three regiments. One was the splendid banner of the Excelsior One Hundred and Thirteenth regiment of New York; another was a white bunting flag, in the center of which was emblazoned in red the ace of clubs, the badge of the Second corps." It was facetiously said that stout hearts were trumps and Kelso took the trick. Colonel Fulton reported that he was cognizant of the facts, and General Johnson stated that as many prisoners were taken as he had men engaged in his brigade. The names of some of Kelso's seventeen heroes are recalled, and deserve preservation for all time: Sergts. G. W. D. Porter and J. J. Martin; Corp. Turner Goodall (mortally wounded); Privates George Crabtree, Ira Lipscomb, Thomas Lenehan, W. Harvey McGuire, Rufus Button, and Tom Smith and Aaron Triff, Company B, Forty-fourth Tennessee. The victory of the 16th was a splendid one and reflected great honor upon General Beauregard and his troops.

General Meade, in reporting this affair to General Grant, said: "Our men are tired, and the attacks have not been made with force and vigor."

On the 17th, at dawn, the battle was renewed by the attacks made by Grant's entire army, which were three times repulsed, but a part of our lines was broken and a considerable number of Johnson's brigade was killed or captured. Col. A. W. Fulkerson, of the Sixty-third, was captured. He was an officer full of intelligence, and his loss was seriously felt by the command. Johnson's division maintained in this action the line occupied on the 16th, with a skirmish line in the space so bravely defended by Lieutenant Kelso. At night, General Beauregard retired a part of his line of defense, but not until he had first driven Ledlie's division from the position it had carried.

General Gilmore, commanding Tenth army corps, who had volunteered to capture Petersburg and failed, was relieved from command. It is an incident sustaining the charge that spurious money was used by the Federal army;

that on the 10th, Mr. C. A. Dana, secretary of war, telegraphed for $5,000,000 in Confederate money for use of General Grant "in a cavalry expedition, on which he proposed to pay for everything taken." Was the money genuine?

On the 18th, General Meade advanced his forces and made a general assault. Mr. Dana telegraphed to Washington that "Birney with nine brigades had failed; Martindale made an attempt to advance and failed; at 7 p. m., Wilcox of the Ninth corps, and Warren's corps again assaulted, but in vain." He lost in three days 9,500 men killed and wounded. Under orders of General Grant no more assaults were to be made.

On the 30th of June, Col. R. H. Keeble, Seventeenth and Twenty-third Tennessee, was killed, and Col. John S. Fulton, Forty-fourth Tennessee, commanding Johnson's brigade, was mortally wounded. Colonel Keeble attracted the attention of his superior officers on every field where his regiment was engaged, and always won commendation for skill and gallantry. He had won promotion in all grades from lieutenant to colonel. At Drewry's Bluff and in the battles of the 16th, 17th, 18th and 30th of June, he made his name and regiment famous. Colonel Fulton belonged to a family of heroes. He fought in the ranks at Shiloh, and commanded the Forty-fourth at Perryville, Murfreesboro and Chickamauga, where he was noted for soldierly bearing; and thenceforward was identified with Bushrod Johnson's famous brigade and often in command of it. He never failed to confer distinction upon his regiment and brigade, and to reflect honor and glory upon the State of Tennessee. After the fall of Colonel Fulton, Col. John M. Hughs, Twenty-eighth Tennessee, commanded the brigade.

The mine sprung by Burnside's corps, and the "crater" created by the explosion, on the morning of the 30th of July, 1864, was in that portion of Bushrod Johnson's line, 200 yards north of the Baxter road, known as Pegram's salient. "The astonishing effect of the explosion," said General Johnson, "bursting like a volcano at the feet of the men, and the upheaving of an immense column of more than 100,000 cubic feet of earth, to fall around in heavy masses, wounding, crushing or burying everything within its reach," was the most appalling event of the war. Pegram's battery and the Eighteenth and Twenty-second South Carolina lost 278 men killed and wounded. But the men on the right and left rallied in the face of this great explosion of 8,000 pounds of powder, and instead of the capture of the crest in the rear of Johnson's line and the fall of Petersburg, Burnside sustained defeat and heavy loss. The disappointment was so great that a court of inquiry was provided, at which Burnside and several of his subordinates were censured for what General Grant stigmatized as "the miserable failure of Saturday." General Meade admitted a loss of 4,400 killed, wounded and captured. Gen. Bushrod Johnson, a very conservative authority, estimated the Federal losses at between 5,000 and 6,000. On the 31st, General Meade asked for and obtained a cessation of hostilities to enable him to bury the Federal dead in front of Johnson's division. Lieutenant-General Ewell, commanding the department of Richmond, reported to the secretary of war from Chaffin's farm that "Johnson's brigade of Tennesseeans are the only troops of field experience permanently stationed at this point," for the protection of the city from a *coup de main.*

After the close of the year, Johnson's brigade was transferred to the brigade commanded by Brig.-Gen. William McComb of Heth's division, A. P. Hill's corps, which then included all Tennesseeans in the army of Northern Virginia. The regiments were the First, Maj. Felix G. Buchanan; the Seventh, Lieut.-Col. Samuel G. Shepard; the Fourteenth, Maj. James H. Johnson; the Seventeenth and Twenty-third, Col. Horace Ready; the Twenty-fifth and Forty-fourth, Capt. Jonathan E. Spencer, and the Sixty-third, Capt. A. A. Blair. After the fall of Lieut.-Gen. A. P. Hill on April 2, 1865, his corps was attached to Longstreet's, with which McComb's brigade, 480 strong, was surrendered at Appomattox Court House, on the 9th of April, 1865.

McComb's brigade was constantly engaged during the last months of the war, and sustained many unreported losses; in the last battle, on the 2d of April, when General Lee's lines were broken on the right, the Tennesseeans bore an honorable and conspicuous part. In trying to reach Heth's division, which was supporting Pickett on the right, that noble gentleman and soldier, A. P. Hill, received his death-wound, and with him fell many sons of Tennessee who had constituted a part of the Light Division from its organization.

That part of McComb's brigade which formerly constituted Hatton's, afterward Archer's brigade, had served with the army of Northern Virginia from Seven Pines to Appomattox. That part of it which formerly constituted Bushrod Johnson's brigade was distinguished in all the great battles of the Southwest up to and including Chickamauga, where it won great honor; and from Drewry's Bluff to the 9th of April, 1865, it maintained its great reputation. Every battlefield of the South is identified with the names of the two brigades, and no history can be written that does not accord to them honor and praise for enterprise, for powers of endurance, for courage and constancy, and for obedience to orders. The survivors were few when the end came; their comrades slept wherever brave men had fought and died; to the State of Tennessee they will be ever living men of heroic memory.

. . . . Never shall the land forget
How gushed the life-blood of her brave—
Gushed, warm with hope and courage yet,
Upon the soil they sought to save.

CHAPTER XII.

TENNESSEE CAVALRY — WEST TENNESSEE EXPEDITION — STREIGHT'S RAID — FORREST'S NEW COMMAND AT JACKSON—BATTLES OF OKOLONA AND YAZOO—WEST TENNESSEE AGAIN—FORT DONELSON, FORT PILLOW AND OTHER BATTLES—FORREST IN NORTH ALABAMA AND TENNESSEE.

THE greatest achievements of the cavalry of the State were under the leadership of Gen. Nathan B. Forrest. He had rendered conspicuous service at Donelson and at Shiloh, but his career fairly began in June, 1862, when, from Tupelo, Miss., he was ordered by General Beauregard to proceed to north Alabama and middle Tennessee and assume command of the cavalry of Colonels Scott, Wharton and Adams. Forrest, himself, held the rank of colonel.

On the 9th of July, Forrest, now a brigadier-general, left Chattanooga with 1,400 men, including his own regiment under Major Smith; the Eighth Texas, Col. John A. Wharton; the Second Georgia, Colonel Lawton, and two companies of Kentuckians under Captains Taylor and Waltham. He made forced marches to Murfreesboro, arriving at 4:30 a. m. of the 13th in front of that place, then held by the Ninth Michigan and Third Minnesota regiments of infantry, 200 Pennsylvania cavalry, 100 of the Eighth Kentucky cavalry, and Hewett's battery of four guns—1,400 men, commanded by Brig.-Gen. Thomas Crittenden.

The attack was made with characteristic energy and continued for several hours, when the entire Federal force was surrendered as prisoners of war. Forrest lost 25 killed and 60 wounded; the Federals, 75 killed and 125 wounded. Among the Confederates killed was Lieutenant Green of the Tennessee battalion. The fruits of the victory were the four-gun battery complete, sixty wagons and teams, the cavalry horses, arms, ammunition and equipments of the garrison, and a large supply of quartermaster and commissary stores.

After Forrest had leisurely retired with his prisoners and captured property to McMinnville, a great hue and cry was raised. Troops were hurried to Nashville for its defense, others were sent to Readyville, Statesville, Wilton, and to a point on the old Franklin road, others toward Lebanon, all charged with the same duty—to "cut Forrest off." Under date of July 24th, the famous Gen. William Nelson, then at Murfreesboro, informed General Buell that he had ordered a battalion of Wolford's cavalry and a battalion of Beard's to join him. "When they do come I will have about 1,200 cavalry, and Mr. Forrest shall have no rest. I will hunt him myself." Fortunately for General Nelson, he never found him.

Forrest rested a few days at McMinnville, then left there on the 18th with 700 effective troops and moved on Lebanon, Tenn., which he occupied unmolested for two days, the Federal forces having hastily retired. On the 21st he moved to within a few miles of Nashville, destroyed the railroad bridges across Mill creek, skirmished with the garrison at Antioch, captured 97 prisoners, frightened the garrison at Nashville and retired in order. On his return to McMinnville he sent a flag of truce to Murfreesboro. But "he could not be found."

Gen. Frank C. Armstrong reported from Middleburg, Tenn., on the 1st of September, 1862: "Just finished whipping the enemy in front of Bolivar. Ran him in town and captured 71 prisoners, of whom 4 were commissioned officers. Among the Federal dead were two colonels." After this affair, General Armstrong crossed the Hatchie river, passed between Jackson and Bolivar, and destroyed the bridges and trestles between the two places. On his return toward the village of Denmark he encountered two regiments of infantry, two squadrons of cavalry, and a section of artillery at Britton's lane, under command of Col. E. S. Dennis of the Thirtieth Illinois. Colonel Dennis reports the battle to have been of four hours' duration, and claims that his force numbered 800, that he was surrounded by 5,000 Confederates, and in this long struggle sustained a loss of 5 killed and 55 wounded. General Armstrong's account was that he captured Dennis' artillery, destroyed a portion of his wagon train, and captured 213 prisoners, whom he sent to the rear and paroled on the 3d of September. General Armstrong had the co-operation of Col. W. H. Jackson, Seventh Tennessee, whose command, he stated, deserved an equal share of credit with his own.

In an expedition to west Tennessee, Forrest crossed the Tennessee river on the 15th of December and on the 18th, at Lexington, Tenn., attacked the enemy, consisting of a section of artillery and 800 cavalry, Col. R. G. Ingersoll commanding. The Federals were easily routed, with the loss of their 2 guns and 148 prisoners with their horses and equipments. The balance of the force fled in the wildest disorder in the direction of Jackson and Trenton, Tenn. Among the prisoners was Col. Robert G. Ingersoll, the eminent lawyer and agnostic, of the Eleventh Illinois cavalry. Col. G. G. Dibrell, Eighth Tennessee cavalry, being pushed forward in the direction of Jackson, at Webb's or Carroll Station captured 101 prisoners, destroyed the railroad for miles, exchanged 100 of his flint-lock muskets for improved arms, burned the stockade, and rejoined Forrest at Spring creek. On the 20th, Dibrell, with his regiment and one field gun under Capt. John W. Morton, attempted to destroy the stockade and bridge across the Forked Deer river, but was repulsed by a large infantry force, losing several men killed and wounded.

On the 19th, Forrest, with two companies commanded

by Col. T. G. Woodward, Kentucky cavalry, and Col. J. B. Biffle's Nineteenth Tennessee cavalry, with a section of Freeman's battery, drove the Federals, reported at 9,000, inside of their fortifications at Jackson, and then moved rapidly on Humboldt and Trenton. The gallant Col. J. W. Starnes, Fourth Tennessee, was sent against Humboldt, where he captured 100 prisoners and destroyed the stockade and railroad bridge. Colonel Biffle was sent to the rear of Trenton, while Forrest took Maj. N. N. Cox's Second battalion Tennessee cavalry, his escort company, and Freeman's Tennessee battery, and made a bold dash at Trenton, which he captured after a brief engagement, taking over 700 prisoners with arms, horses and stores. The garrison was composed of the Second Tennessee Federal regiment, commanded by Col. Isaac R. Hawkins, which a few days earlier had escaped Forrest at Lexington, and detachments from Ohio, Illinois and other States. In this affair the Confederate loss was 2 killed and 7 wounded.

Col. A. A. Russell, Fourth Alabama cavalry, who was guarding Forrest's rear pending these operations, skirmished for parts of two days with a column of Federal infantry 3,000 strong, and finally dismounted half of his regiment, moved up, delivered one volley and charged the line with his mounted companies. The enemy retreated in a panic across Spring creek, burned the bridge in his rear, and was not again heard of.

At Trenton the Eighth Tennessee completed its armament with improved guns captured from the enemy. On the afternoon of the 21st, Forrest moved north, capturing at Rutherford's Station two companies of Federals, among them Col. T. G. Kinney, One Hundred and Twenty-second Illinois. At Union City 106 Federals were captured without resistance, and the railroad bridges over the north and south forks of the Obion river, with four miles of trestle between them, were destroyed. Forrest dispatched to General Bragg, "We have made a clean sweep of the Federals north of Jackson." To this date Forrest lost 22 killed and wounded, and 2 missing, while the Federal loss in killed and wounded was over 100, in prisoners over 1,200, including 4 colonels, 4 majors, 10 captains and 23 lieutenants.

Brigadier-General Sullivan, commanding the Federal forces in west Tennessee, telegraphed General Grant under date of the 18th, "My cavalry was whipped at Lexington to-day." The next day, after he had been driven to his fortifications at Jackson, he telegraphed General Grant, "Cheatham's brigade is on this side also," a ridiculous piece of misinformation, given, doubtless, as an excuse for his own shortcomings. Cheatham's division was with the army of Tennessee. Colonel Ingersoll's report shows that he was poorly supported, had untrained troops, and was an easy victim to Forrest.

The expedition of Forrest to west Tennessee was undertaken to create a diversion in favor of our army in Mississippi, and was accomplished, said General Bragg, in the "most brilliant and decisive" manner. He was now under orders to recross the Tennessee river. Leaving Middleburg on the 25th, he moved toward McKenzie, Tenn., thence in the direction of Lexington. The Federal commander of the department had in the meantime concentrated large bodies of troops at various points, intending to capture this bold rider who had dared to invade a territory now claimed as their own. On the 31st Forrest moved from Flake's store, sixteen miles north of Lexington, in the direction of that point, and met the advance of the enemy after a march of four miles, at Parker's cross-roads. Here he engaged and fought the brigade commanded by Col. C. L. Dunham, Fiftieth Indiana, composed of two companies of the Eighteenth Illinois infantry, the Fiftieth Indiana, the One Hundred and Twenty-second Illinois, the Thirty-ninth Iowa and three pieces of the Seventh Wisconsin battery, reported by Colonel Dunham at 1,554 rank and file.

General Forrest, with an inferior force (in numbers), reported that he soon found that he could "whip the enemy" dismounted. At the same time moving on Dunham's flank and rear, "we drove them," he said, "through the woods with great slaughter." The Federals retreated to Parker's cross-roads after being punished by Freeman's battery, and, said Colonel Dibrell in his report, "we advanced rapidly at a double-quick and began our first regular battle as cavalry. The enemy made three efforts to charge us, but the galling fire of our small-arms and from a 12-pound howitzer under Sergt. Nat Baxter of Freeman's battery, drove them back. They had six pieces of artillery and we but one. The battle raged with great fury until I was joined on the left by Capt. John W. Morton with one field gun, supported by Cox and Napier's battalions and Starnes' regiment. Forrest moved to the rear with the Nineteenth Tennessee (Biffle's) and Woodward's Kentucky battalion, when the enemy fled in confusion, leaving their dead and wounded and six pieces of artillery in our hands. We had about 300 prisoners, and while parleying for a surrender, General Sullivan came up with another brigade of infantry, attacked our horse-holders before we were aware of his approach, opened on our rear, stampeded the horse-holders and forced an immediate retreat." General Forrest lost the guns and all prisoners except 83 taken from the enemy, with 8 caissons.

Colonel Dunham admitted the loss of 23 killed, 139 wounded and 58 captured. Col. E. F. Noyes, commanding the Thirty-ninth Ohio regiment of Sullivan's brigade, says, when he reached the field he found Dunham's brigade "surrounded on three sides by Forrest's troops. Firing had ceased, flags of truce were passing, and a part, if not all, of Dunham's artillery had been captured, together with several hundred prisoners."

Forrest withdrew in good order, leaving his dead and wounded in the hands of the enemy. He had taken the precaution to send four companies to Clarksburg, seven miles in his rear, to watch for Federal reinforcements, but the command failed to discover Sullivan's approach and the first notice of his presence was the opening of his guns. Colonel Biffle returned from the rear in time to participate in the affair at Parker's cross-roads; and before rejoining Forrest he captured and paroled 150 Federal prisoners within six miles of Trenton. Forrest reported a loss of 60 killed and wounded and 122 captured. Among the dead was Col. T. Alonzo Napier, Tenth Tennessee cavalry, who fell while leading his command in a charge on foot. He was a young officer of great promise and of indomitable courage and energy. Forrest recrossed the Tennessee river without being molested. Col. W. K. M. Breckinridge's regiment of Federal cavalry interposed between Colonel Dibrell and the river, but after skirmishing a few minutes, said the gallant Dibrell, "we charged and routed the regiment, killing and capturing fifteen or twenty of them."

General Sullivan telegraphed that he had "met Forrest 7,000 strong, and after a contest of four hours completely routed him, with great slaughter." Forrest had less than one-fifth of the force attributed to him, but the fierceness and vigor of his attack caused the Federal commander to multiply his numbers many times.

The attack on Fort Donelson of February 3, 1863, was made by Maj.-Gen. Joseph Wheeler, with the brigades of Forrest and John A. Wharton. Forrest's command consisted of detachments from the Fourth Tennessee, Fourth Alabama, Cox's, Napier's and Holman's Tennessee battalions, Woodward's Kentuckians and Morton's battery, in all about 800 men. Wharton's brigade was about 2,000 strong; but General Wheeler reports that only about a thousand men from both brigades participated in the action. The fort was defended gallantly and successfully by Col. A. C. Harding, Eighty-third Illinois, with about 750 men of all arms, fighting under cover. The Confederates were dismounted and made several brave assaults, when, seeing the enemy retiring, as he supposed, Forrest mounted his command and charged through the streets of Dover, but was repulsed and forced to retire.

Forrest, with his aide, Maj. C. W. Anderson, and a detachment of his escort, charged up to within thirty yards of the enemy's works, leading his command close enough to fire upon the enemy behind his parapets, but success could not be won—the men behind the works were as valorous as his own. Lieut.-Col. D. W. Holman, an officer of great dash and enterprise, was severely wounded. Lieutenants Summers and A. S. Chapman of Holman's battalion were killed, and Capts. D. F. Alexander, W. J. Hobson and N. J. Robinson of Napier's battalion were badly wounded and captured. Lieutenant-Colonel Haines, Fourth Tennessee, was severely wounded and permanently disabled. By a strange oversight which cannot be explained, Wheeler's command had no adequate supply of ammunition.

At 8 o'clock p. m. General Wheeler retired and moved south of Duck river. He reported a loss of 100 killed and wounded, and the capture of 80 prisoners, one field gun, a lot of horses and mules, and the destruction of a transport loaded with provisions. Colonel Harding reported his loss at 13 killed, 51 wounded, 46 captured.

On the 15th of March, 1863, the forces under Maj.-Gen. Earl Van Dorn captured the Federal troops at Thompson's Station, Col. John Coburn's brigade, numbering 1,221, including 73 commissioned officers and many arms.

The Tennesseeans engaged were the Nineteenth, Colonel Biffle; the Tenth, Lieut.-Col. Wm. E. De Moss; Col. J. H. Edmundson's regiment; the Fourth, J. W. Starnes; McCann's battalion, Maj. Richard McCann, Freeman's battery, Capt. S. L. Freeman, all under Gen. N. B. Forrest. Other troops under General Van Dorn were the division commanded by Brig.-Gen. W. H. Jackson, composed of Brig.-Gen. F. C. Armstrong's and Col. J. W

Whitfield's brigades, with King's battery of four guns, and General Cosby's brigade of Martin's division.

Colonel Coburn made a determined fight. General Van Dorn stated that "Forrest and Armstrong, and General Jackson with his entire division, charged in the most gallant manner upon the enemy on the hill, from which they had previously repulsed the Texas brigade. After a fierce struggle for the crest of the hill, our troops were driven down it, and with considerable loss." In the mean time, "Forrest with two regiments, the Nineteenth and Tenth Tennessee, had now gained the enemy's rear and charged them, when, after firing a few volleys, they threw down their arms and surrendered." "In the final charge by General Forrest, deciding the fate of the day, Lieut.-Col. E. B. Trezevant, Tenth Tennessee, Capt. Montgomery Little of Forrest's escort, and Capt. A. A. Dysart, Fourth Tennessee, were mortally wounded."

Van Dorn lost 357 killed, wounded and missing. General Forrest reported that when the men saw the gallant Trezevant and Little fall, they "raised a shout and pushed the charge to within twenty feet of the Federal line of battle." The colors of the Nineteenth Michigan were captured by Capt. J. M. Reynolds, Nineteenth Tennessee. Lieut. J. R. Johnson, Nineteenth Tennessee, was killed bearing the colors of his regiment. Upon his fall, Clay Kendrick, one of the color-guard, seized the colors, and when his right arm was shattered by a musket ball, he was seen to transfer the flag to his left hand and bravely carry it until the surrender.

From his headquarters at Tullahoma, March 27, 1863, General Bragg telegraphed the war office at Richmond: "Forrest made a successful attack on Brentwood with his division, burned the bridge, destroyed and took all property and arms, and captured 800 prisoners, including 35 officers."

General Forrest reported that "a flag of truce was sent in, demanding an immediate and unconditional surrender.

The colonel commanding replied that we must come and take him." These were heroic words without meaning. Major De Moss, Tenth Tennessee, drove the enemy within his works, and Forrest's escort was in the act of charging when he raised a white flag and surrendered. Brig.-Gen. Robert B. Mitchell, reporting to General Rosecrans, said the affair "was a very disgraceful one for the commanding officer of our forces, Lieutenant-Colonel Bloodgood, Twenty-second Wisconsin. With a position easily reached from his encampment he could have held the enemy at bay until the arrival of reinforcements; but with a loss of one man killed and four wounded, he seems to have surrendered without an effort to change position, or to make a resistance worthy of the name of fight." The troops captured at Brentwood were the same who had deserted Colonel Coburn at Thompson's Station.

After the surrender, Forrest detached Colonel Lewis, First Tennessee, to make a demonstration on Nashville, and he made important captures and returned safely to headquarters. General Forrest, with the Tenth Tennessee and one gun of Freeman's battery, dashed down the road toward Franklin and demanded the surrender of the garrison occupying the stockade provided as a defense of the railroad bridge. To Maj. C. W. Anderson, of his staff, the surrender was refused, but one shot from Freeman's gun brought out a white flag and the surrender of 230 prisoners.

On the 9th of April, Forrest's command encountered the Federal forces under General Stanley. The Fourth United States cavalry charged and captured Freeman's battery and thirty men, but Colonel Starnes, Fourth Tennessee, dismounted the Nineteenth Tennessee and made a counter attack, recapturing the guns of Freeman's battery and some of the men. The gallant Freeman was left in the enemy's hands. As his captors were retiring from the field, they ordered him to break into a run to prevent his recapture, and as he was unable to do this, an officer rode up and shot him through the head. General Forrest is authority for this statement. The history of the war does not show an act of greater infamy. No murder by poison, or lying in wait, was ever attended by circumstances of greater atrocity—an unarmed man, a prisoner of war, assassinated by an officer! Captain McIntyre, commanding the Fourth regulars, reported that he recrossed the river, "bringing with me a captain, one second lieutenant and 34 prisoners."

On the 8th of April, 1863, General Rosecrans notified Col. A. D. Streight, Fifty-first Indiana volunteers, that he had been assigned to the command of an independent provisional brigade, including his own and the Seventy-third Indiana, Eightieth Illinois, Third Ohio, and two companies of the First Middle Tennessee cavalry raised in north Alabama, with orders to proceed south and cut the railroad south of Dalton, Ga., so as to prevent troops being sent by that route to the army of Tennessee. Streight was supplied with a pack-train of commissary stores and ammunition, and his command, 1,700 strong, was mounted generally from horses and mules taken from citizens.

After elaborate preparation, Streight moved out from Moulton, Ala., on the night of the 28th of April. The next day he marched to Day's gap, 35 miles, and found himself in the midst of "devoted Union people," with no foe to molest him. But very soon an unexpected enemy attacked his rear guard and the "boom of artillery was heard." "I soon learned," he said, "that the enemy had moved through the gaps on my right and left." Forrest was upon him. At Driver's gap, of Sand mountain, he fought the Federals day and night, with two regiments, with a loss of 5 killed and 50 wounded. Streight left on the field 50 killed and 150 wounded, burned his wagons, and turned loose 250 mules and 150 negroes.

On the 3d of May, between Gadsden and Rome, after five days and nights of fighting and marching, General Forrest captured Streight's entire command with arms and horses. The Federal commander handled his command with skill and judgment, and fought it bravely. Forrest was fruitful of resource, and every action abounded with daring and enterprise. He seemed insensible to fatigue or to hunger, and his example encouraged his men to steadiness and constancy. The result of his expedition was an inspiration to the army and the country. To his own escort company, to the Fourth Tennessee under the gallant Maj. W. S. McLemore, to the always reliable Colonel Biffle, Nineteenth Tennessee, and to Morton's battery, the honor belongs for the final triumph; but to his own personal prowess and wise leadership, with one acclaim the country accorded the glory.

Forrest entered west Tennessee on the 4th of December, 1863, and arrived at Bolivar on the 5th. He took with him McDonald's battalion and a section of Morton's battery, numbering 250 trained soldiers, and was joined en route by Richardson's partisans, increasing his command to 500. He established his headquarters at Jackson, and began the organization of the troops gathered together at different points with such success that when he retired from west Tennessee on the 27th, he reported to President Davis that he had 3,000 new troops. In this communication he stated "that the difficulties attending organizing regiments by consolidating the odds and ends of proper commands into full regiments" were very great. That division of the State was crowded with young men ambitious for command, and it required address and firmness on the part of General Forrest to consolidate the several detachments, and to secure efficient regimental organizations. General Hurlbut, commanding the Federal forces of the district, numbering about 20,000 men of all arms, sought to encompass Forrest and destroy him, and was vigilant and energetic in his efforts, but Forrest was equally so. He had successful combats at Jack's creek,

Estanaula, Somerville, Lafayette and Collierville, eluded his pursuers and took out this large force of unarmed men, well mounted, with a wagon train loaded with supplies, and a good stock of beef cattle and hogs.

Brig.-Gen. W. Sooy Smith, commanding the Federal cavalry forces of the department of Tennessee, numbering 7,000, which General Sherman stated was "superior and better in all respects than the combined cavalry which the enemy has in all the State of Mississippi," was ordered to move on Pontotoc and Okolona, Miss., thence down the Mobile & Ohio railroad, destroying it and all resources of the Confederates, and join Sherman at Meridian on February 10, 1864. General Smith reported to General Grant that he reached West Point on the 21st, but could not force his way through to Sherman. He stated that he fought the Confederates "at four points severely and skirmished with them, as we retired, for sixty miles. We had the best of them at all points except Okolona, where our loss was very severe, including a battery of small howitzers." The Confederates, he stated, "pitched into us (at Okolona) and gave us a pretty rough handling, inflicting upon us a loss of perhaps 300 or 400 men killed, wounded and missing."

General Forrest reported that his brigade, commanded by Col. Jeffrey Forrest, successfully disputed Smith's crossing of the Sakatonchee creek, forced him to retire toward West Point, and drove him from that place to within ten miles of Pontotoc, in two days. Forrest pursued the retiring enemy with his escort, a section of Morton's battery, a detachment of Faulkner's regiment, and a regiment from McCulloch's brigade, and never gave them rest until the Federal forces reached Okolona, where Forrest charged the enemy with Bell's brigade under Colonel Barteau, and forced him from the field in great confusion and with heavy loss. It was here that General Smith confessed to a "rough handling."

Five miles out from Okolona, General Smith reformed

and awaited the Confederate attack, soon made by McCulloch's and Forrest's brigades and Hoole's battery. General Forrest stated that "after a short but obstinate resistance the enemy gave way." After the Federal forces reached the hills between Okolona and Pontotoc, the Second Tennessee, Colonel Barteau, and the Seventh Tennessee, Lieut.-Col. W. F. Taylor, Colonel Duckworth commanding brigade, received the repeated charges of seven Federal regiments in open ground, drove them back time after time, and finally forced them from the field, capturing three stand of colors and one piece of artillery. After this, for want of ammunition, General Forrest abandoned the pursuit.

In the combat at Okolona, Col. Jeff. E. Forrest, commanding brigade, fell in the gallant discharge of his duty. By his side, and almost at the same moment, fell George M. Porter, a youthful Tennessee soldier who had seen only a few days' service. In the pursuit of Smith, Forrest lost 144 men killed, wounded and missing, whose names are not reported. Colonel Barteau, commanding Bell's brigade, was wounded, and the command devolved on the gallant Col. R. M. Russell. Colonel Duckworth commanded Forrest's brigade after the fall of Colonel Forrest.

Maj.-Gen. Stephen D. Lee, reporting the operations of his command in this period, stated that on March 5th, Brig.-Gen. R. V. Richardson of Forrest's cavalry, commanding Tennessee brigade, 550 strong, and Brig.-Gen. L. S. Ross of Jackson's division, attacked Yazoo City, drove the enemy from all the redoubts except one and took possession of the city, capturing many stores and a few prisoners. The enemy having concentrated in the strongest redoubt, it was not considered prudent to assault it, as it was surrounded by a ditch and defended by 400 infantry. This, said General Lee, was a gallant affair, and caused the enemy to withdraw from the Yazoo river.

In this affair Col. J. J. Neely, commanding the Fourteenth Tennessee, and Col. Thomas H. Logwood, Fifteenth Tennessee, rendered conspicuous and valuable service. Maj. J. G. Thurmand, Fourteenth Tennessee, fell dead at the head of his regiment. His brigade commander named him as "one of the bravest of brave men." General Ross reported that "the fighting was very desperate. The hardest and hottest part of the engagement was made by the Fourteenth Tennessee, under Major Thurmand, in driving the enemy and the gunboats from town." The Confederates lost about 60 killed and wounded, among the latter, Captain Thrall of the artillery.

Another expedition into west Tennessee was inaugurated on the 9th of March, 1864, by an order to the Seventh Tennessee, Colonel Duckworth, and to McDonald's battalion, Colonel Crews, to prepare rations and ammunition for a movement in the direction of Corinth. A few days thereafter General Forrest advanced with a division commanded by Brig.-Gen. A. Buford. The Third Kentucky, Lieutenant-Colonel Holt; the Seventh Kentucky, Colonel Crossland; the Eighth, Colonel Lyon; Faulkner's Kentucky regiment, Colonel Faulkner, and Wisdom's Tennessee regiment, Lieut.-Col. D. M. Wisdom, constituted the Third brigade, Col. A. P. Thompson commanding. Col. T. H. Bell commanded the Fourth brigade, composed of the Second Tennessee, Col. C. R. Barteau; Sixteenth, Col. A. N. Wilson, and Russell's Tennessee regiment, Col. R. M. Russell. The division was 2,800 strong. The Second brigade of Chalmers' division, commanded by Colonel Duckworth, composed of the Seventh Tennessee, Lieut.-Col. W. F. Taylor; the Twelfth Tennessee, Col. John U. Green; the Thirteenth Tennessee, Col. J. J. Neely; the Fourteenth Tennessee, Col. F. M. Stewart; was ordered to form a part of the expedition.

At this time, west Tennessee was dominated by certain Federal troops, notably the Sixth regiment United States cavalry, recruited in Tennessee and elsewhere and commanded by Col. Fielding Hurst. It was disputed territory, but when a Confederate soldier was captured, no regard was paid to the usages of civilized warfare. The captive was shot and mutilated in the most barbarous and inhuman manner, no trial by court-martial was permitted, no respect was paid to age or calling, and no mercy was accorded to prisoners.

Lieut.-Col. W. M. Reed, an eminent minister of the gospel (who fell in the gallant discharge of his duty in the assault on Fort Pillow), after a careful investigation, submitted a report to General Forrest (see page 118, Vol. XXXII, Part 3, Official Records of the War), in which he recited a series of atrocities that should have brought their authors to the gallows.

General Forrest enclosed the report to Major-General Hurlbut at Memphis, commanding the district of West Tennessee, and asked for the surrender of Hurst for trial. This demand was refused, and thereupon Forrest issued an order declaring Hurst and his officers outlaws. For private gain he had extorted over $5,000 from the citizens of Jackson, Tenn., under a threat of burning the town. He was, said the order, "guilty of house burning, guilty of murder of both citizens and soldiers of the Confederate States." The victims were comrades, or kinsmen and friends of Forrest's cavalry, and yet with a full knowledge of these gross outrages, no Federal prisoner (and hundreds were captured) received other than humane treatment. General Hurlbut was relieved from command on the 16th of April, not because he tolerated Hurst and his kind, but, said General Sherman, "You are relieved because there has been marked timidity in the management of affairs since Forrest passed north of Memphis." Brutality to citizens and barbarity to prisoners called forth no protest; "timidity" in the face of danger was the only sin.

On the 29th of March, Colonel Neely, Thirteenth Tennessee, engaged Hurst near Bolivar, capturing his entire wagon train, routing and driving him on the wings of the wind to Memphis and killing 30 and capturing 35 prisoners, who received honorable treatment. This gallant officer pursued to the vicinity of Memphis, and succeeded in holding Hurlbut at Memphis (with an army at his command) until Forrest covered west Tennessee and southern Kentucky, and assaulted and captured the Federal forces wherever located. On the 22d of March, Forrest was at Trenton. On the following day he detached the Seventh Tennessee, McDonald's battalion and Faulkner's Kentucky regiment, and ordered Duckworth (in command) to assault and capture Union City. The commander there, Colonel Hawkins, Second (Federal) Tennessee regiment, who in December, 1862, had been captured at Trenton, after some parleying and skirmishing, surrendered to Duckworth, with 475 men and their arms, ammunition and horses. In the skirmish preliminary to the surrender, Lieut.-Col. W. D. Lannom of Faulkner's regiment was severely wounded. Lannom had served at Shiloh as lieutenant-colonel of the Seventh Kentucky. He survived the war and fell a victim to a private quarrel.

Three days later, Forrest was in front of Paducah. Colonel Thompson, anxious for his own home and friends, made a gallant attack on Fort Anderson, a well-protected earthwork invincible to a cavalry attack, and lost his life. A serious attack on this fort was not contemplated, and the fall of the gallant and lamented Thompson made it a grave disaster. Forrest took possession of the city of Paducah, and after holding it for nine hours, retired with prisoners, 400 horses and mules, and a large supply of quartermaster and commissary stores.

Fort Pillow was invested April 11 and 12, 1864. It was garrisoned by about 550 troops, black and white, under the command of Major Booth of the Federal army. Major Booth fell early in the action by a shot from a sharpshooter, and the command was then assumed by Major Bradford, of the Thirteenth Tennessee (Federal) cavalry.

The investing force was composed of Bell's brigade of Buford's division, and McCulloch's brigade of Chalmers' division, both commanded by Brig.-Gen. James R. Chalmers. Under date of the 28th of June, General Forrest said in an address to his command, "In the face of a murderous fire from two gunboats and six pieces of artillery on the fort, you stormed the works and either killed or captured the entire garrison."

On the 12th of April, after Chalmers had driven the Federals inside the fort and had established his sharpshooters in the buildings in front, with a close investment of the fort by a superior force, Forrest arrived on the field and immediately demanded the surrender of the garrison, assuring the commanding officer that the Federal forces would be treated as prisoners of war. This demand was refused. The assault was ordered, and in a few minutes the fort was carried. When it became apparent that they could not maintain a successful defense, the garrison, with arms in their hands, sought safety on a Federal gunboat lying in the Mississippi river. In their effort to reach it, as they ran the gauntlet of McCulloch's and Bell's brigades, many were killed and wounded. The commander of the gunboat, anxious for his own safety, pushed off and left the men of the garrison to their fate. The flag over the fort was not lowered, and the resistance continued in a desultory way until nearly half of the garrison were killed or wounded. Forrest captured 7 officers and 219 enlisted men, with the garrison equipage, arms and ammunition, and returned to his headquarters at Jackson, where he found orders to proceed to Mississippi to meet a movement of the enemy.

At Tishomingo creek, or Brice's cross-roads, Forrest won a notable victory over the Federal forces commanded by General Sturgis. Maj.-Gen. C. C. Washburn of the United States army, commanding the district of West Tennessee, fitted out an expedition under orders from Major-General McPherson to engage General Forrest and, if possible, whip and disperse his forces; also to destroy the Mobile & Ohio railroad, which had been placed in complete running order from Corinth to Mobile. General Washburn reported under date of July 20, 1864, that the forces moved out on the 1st of June under the command of Brig.-Gen. Samuel D. Sturgis, consisting of 3,300 cavalry under Brig.-Gen. B. H. Grierson, 5,000 infantry under Colonel McMillen, Ninety-fifth Ohio, and 16 pieces of artillery. General Washburn stated that "the force sent out was in complete order and consisted of some of our best troops." The expedition was provided with eighteen days' rations, the "supply train consisted of 181 wagons, which, with the regimental wagons, made up a train of 250." The troops left the railroad on the 2d of June and reached Brice's cross-roads, a distance of 60 miles, on the 10th; but the return trip was made in one day and two nights.

General Forrest met and fought Sturgis with his entire available force, numbering 3,500 officers and men of all arms. In the early morning of the 10th, the Confederate commander, reaching Brice's cross-roads, formed the commands of Colonels Lyon, Rucker and Johnson, and attacked Grierson's cavalry, driving it back for some distance. A hot skirmish with the enemy was maintained until 1 o'clock, when Brigadier-General Buford arrived with the artillery, followed by Bell's brigade. Forrest at once advanced his line of battle, leading Russell and Wilson of Bell's brigade, with Duff's regiment of Rucker's brigade, and Newsom on the left. The artillery opened with great spirit, the engagement became general, and, said General Forrest, "on the left raged with great fury." At this time the Federal cavalry was alone engaged. At 1:30 the infantry began to arrive. Grierson's cavalry was already whipped. Colonel Winslow, Fourth Iowa cavalry, commanding brigade, General Sturgis reported, was "especially clamorous to be relieved, and permitted to carry his brigade to the rear." Finding, he said, that his troops were being hotly pressed, he ordered a section of artillery to open on the Confederates, but their "artillery soon replied, and with great accuracy, every shell bursting over and in the immediate vicinity of our guns." These shells were from Morton's battery, whose terrible execution, in close proximity to the Federal line, caused "frequent calls for reinforcements" and great confusion in Grierson's ranks. "Order," said Sturgis, "gave way to confusion, and confusion to panic." Without the knowledge of the Federal general, the cavalry had been withdrawn from his left, and he was forced to occupy the abandoned line with his escort company of 100 men of the Nineteenth Pennsylvania cavalry, under the gallant Lieutenant-Colonel Hess, until the arrival of the infantry.

Upon the arrival of the infantry, General Grierson requested authority to withdraw his entire division of cavalry, upon the plea that ' it was exhausted and well-nigh out of ammunition." Grierson's force was 3,500 strong. In Waring's brigade his loss was 22 killed and 51 wounded; in Winslow's brigade, 12 men killed and 52 wounded. A battle was lost and the field abandoned in panic and wild disorder, with a loss almost too insignificant to be reported Winslow sustained other serious losses—189 carbines, 68 pistols, 121 sabers, 68,450 rounds of ammunition, 2 field guns and caissons, and 228 horses, abandoned in a mere panic close of kin to cowardice.

Forrest had now fought a distinct battle with the Federal cavalry and driven it from the field. The Federal infantry occupied the line so ingloriously abandoned, but the impetuosity of the Confederates received no check, and the strong line soon began to yield and reform in a new position. Morton pushed his guns almost in their faces, Bell's brigade assaulted at the distance of 30 paces, the gallant Barteau with his Second regiment of Tennesseeans gained the rear of the enemy, Buford, with

Lyon and Johnson and Rucker, all rushed to the attack, while Faulkner's Kentucky regiment, commanded by Major Tate of Tennessee, and the Seventh Tennessee, Colonel Duckworth, charged the line mounted. "At last," said General Sturgis, "overpowered and exhausted, the roads became crowded and jammed with Federal troops. No power could now check or control the panic-stricken mass as it swept toward the rear, led off by Colonel Winslow at the head of his brigade of cavalry, who never halted until he had reached Stubb's plantation, ten miles in the rear."

Grierson, with a humor akin to that of the late Artemus Ward, in an address dated June 16, 1864, to the officers and soldiers of his cavalry division, said: "Your general congratulates you upon your noble conduct during the expedition under General Sturgis. Fighting against overwhelming numbers for hours on foot, you repulsed the charges of the enemy's infantry and turned his assaults into confusion."

Tishomingo creek was one of the best fought battles during the war between the States, and the most complete victory. Forrest's tactics were perfect. He held Sturgis' well-appointed cavalry, 3,500 strong, with a skirmish line until he could concentrate his troops; then he forced the fighting and routed Grierson in time to attack and crush 5,000 infantry, regiment by regiment, as they came into action. The fruits of the victory were the capture of 1,618 prisoners, of which number 150 were commissioned officers; the entire supply train of the enemy, numbering 168 uninjured wagons; 16 pieces of artillery, with the caissons and limber, harness and fixtures, and a full supply of ammunition; 300,000 rounds of ammunition for small-arms, and 3,000 muskets and carbines abandoned by the flying enemy. General Sturgis reported a loss of 215 killed, 379 wounded. The Confederates lost 492 killed and wounded, of whom 96 were killed. Among the latter were Capt. John Bell, of the staff of Bell's brigade; Capt.

J. R. Hibbitt, Fifteenth Tennessee; Lieuts. J. Robert Arnold and J. P. Revely, Sixteenth Tennessee; Lieut. E. P. Hooper, Nineteenth Tennessee. Among those mortally wounded was Cadet William H. Porter, of the regular army of the Confederate States, on staff duty with Bell's brigade. This young and gallant officer had his own horse killed under him, when, instantly mounting the horse from which his comrade, Capt. John Bell, had just fallen, in another moment he received a shot, from which he died in forty-eight hours. No official reports of this battle were made by division, brigade or regimental commanders, hence justice cannot be done to many noble men. General Forrest, in an address to his command dated June 28th, referred to Tishomingo Creek as "the crowning glory of your great deeds. Victory was never more glorious, disaster never more crushing and signal."

Another expedition was organized to "whip Forrest," and prevent him from moving on Sherman's communications. Maj.-Gen. Andrew J. Smith, who commanded it, left LaGrange, Tenn., on the 5th of July, 1864, with the First division, Sixteenth army corps, Brigadier-General Mower; Third division, Sixteenth army corps, Colonel Moore; Grierson's cavalry division, Brigadier-General Grierson; First brigade United States colored troops, Colonel Bouton, and 24 pieces of artillery; the aggregate of which, as reported by General Smith, was 14,000 men. Maj.-Gen. Stephen D. Lee, commanding the Confederate cavalry, Forrest second in command, gave battle at Harrisburg, Miss., on the Mobile & Ohio railroad, near Tupelo, on the 14th of July, with 9,100 men and 20 field-pieces. Deducting every fourth man as a horse-holder, and small detachments not present, there were not 8,000 Confederates in action. Chalmers' division consisted of McCulloch's and Rucker's brigades; Buford's division, of Bell's Tennessee brigade, Lyon's Kentucky brigade, commanded by Col. Ed. Crossland, and Mabry's Mississippi brigade; Roddey's division, of the brigades of Colonels Patterson and Johnson. Colonel Lyon was detached from his own brigade and placed in command of Col. J. J. Neely's Tennessee brigade, Gholson's Mississippi brigade, and Beltzhoover's battalion.

On the 12th, Lyon skirmished with the enemy near Pontotoc, and Barteau, with the Second Tennessee, hung upon his rear. Colonel Duff, with part of Rucker's brigade, forced the Federal advance back upon the main body. McCulloch, too, assailed the advance near Houston and drove it back. The Federal general seemed doubtful as to his movements until the 13th, when he boldly turned toward Tupelo as his objective point. Forrest in person, now in the rear, attacked and skirmished with the Federal rear-guard, while General Lee moved forward with Buford's and Chalmers' divisions on the right.

When within six miles of Tupelo, Chalmers, under orders from General Lee, fiercely assailed Smith's column with Rucker's brigade. "We took him by surprise, and got possession of his train at first, and killed the mules, so that he was forced to abandon and burn seven wagons, one caisson and two ambulances; but his infantry rallied, and by superior numbers forced us to retire." Late in the afternoon of the 13th, General Buford, under the orders of General Lee, with Bell's brigade and a section of Morton's battery, attacked the enemy on his right flank during the march. "At no time," Buford reported, "had I found the enemy unprepared. He marched with his column well closed up, his wagon train well protected, and his flanks covered in an admirable manner, evincing at all times a readiness to resent an attack and showing careful generalship. After fighting him about an hour, suffering considerable loss, I was compelled to withdraw the brigade from action. The enemy formed his line at Harrisburg, where he had a strong natural position, and during the night threw up a line of fortifications and awaited an attack from us."

At 7 a. m. of the 14th, General Lee ordered his forces forward to the attack. General Forrest reported the position "almost impregnable," and when General Buford received his order to advance, he "modestly expressed the opinion that the attack should not be a direct one, that a direct charge was what the enemy most desired, and for which he was strongly posted, both by nature and art." Victory was scarcely possible, as the troops fought by fragments, so that brigades were worsted or sadly cut to pieces in detail.

In the battle of the 14th, Roddey's division was placed on the right, Mabry's brigade on the left, Crossland's in the center, supported by Bell; Chalmers' and Lyon's divisions were held in reserve. According to Forrest's report, General Lee gave the order to advance and directed him to swing the right around upon the enemy's left. Repairing to the right and reaching the front, he found that Crossland's brigade had been rashly precipitated forward and was retiring under a "murderous fire." At this point the Federals were strong in numbers, "in an impregnable position." A new line was formed and occupied by Roddey and Crossland, and the battle was closed so far as they were concerned. Meantime Bell, Rucker and Mabry were steadily advancing, driving in the Federal skirmishers; but when these troops gained a position within sixty yards of the main line of defense, they were in turn driven back with considerable slaughter. McCulloch moved up and covered their retreat, but the object of the expedition led by General Smith had been accomplished. He had won a victory, compelling the Confederates to fall back to a strong position where they could repulse an attack.

The Federal general withdrew from his line of fortifications about noon of the 15th and commenced his return, the unconquered Forrest following. At Old Town creek he found Chalmers and Buford hotly engaged. The position of the Federal rear guard was forced by Bell and

Crossland's brigades, but in the outset Forrest was painfully wounded, and he relinquished the command to General Chalmers. Chalmers reported that on assuming command he "found our men falling back and the enemy pressing up to the position on which I had left my brigade." He continued the pursuit for two days, but without result.

Forrest's regiment, commanded by Col. D. C. Kelley, was conspicuous in the combat at Old Town creek. The prestige of the regiment given to it by its original commander, General Forrest, was maintained under Kelley on every field. The church gave Colonel Kelley to the regiment, and after four years of splendid service as a soldier, he returned to the work of his earlier years, where his great talents and noble character have acquired for him an unbounded influence for good.

The Federal losses at Harrisburg amounted to 77 killed, 529 wounded. Chalmers' division lost 57 killed, 255 wounded; Buford's division, 996 killed, wounded and captured; the killed, 153, and the wounded, 794, being equally divided between Bell's, Mabry's and Crossland's brigades. The Seventh Tennessee mourned the loss of Captains Statler and Charlie Claiborne; the Second, of Capt. J. M. Eastes, Lieuts. J. E. Dunning, A. H. French and A.W. Lipscomb. The Fifteenth lost Capt. J. M. Fields and Lieut. T. Hawkins; the Sixteenth, Lieut. S. C. Kennedy and Ensign Thomas Paine; the Nineteenth, Capt. W. D. Stratton, Lieuts. W. T. Hallis and J. P. Meeks. In Morton's battery, Lieut. Joseph H. Mayson, Sergt. John H. Dunlap and Corporal Bellanfant were wounded, and within a few minutes five of the seven cannoneers of Sergeant Brown's piece were seriously wounded. Other gallant men should be mentioned, but official reports of casualties are meager.

The Federal garrison at Memphis was attacked by General Forrest at 4 a. m. of the 21st of August, 1864, and by his quick and bold assault he captured 400 prisoners and 300 horses and mules. Major-General Washburn, the Federal department commander, escaped in his night clothes. To make this daring raid, Forrest left the immediate front of Maj.-Gen. A. J. Smith at Oxford, Miss., who had with him a force of 4,800 cavalry and a large body of infantry and artillery. The troops accompanying Forrest were the company commanded by Capt. W. H. Forrest; Col. J. J. Neely's Tennessee regiment; the Second Missouri; the Fourteenth Tennessee, Colonel White; the Eighteenth Mississippi; the Twelfth and Fifteenth Tennessee, Lieutenant-Colonel Logwood and Lieut.-Col. Jesse Forrest; Bell's Tennessee brigade, with a section of Morton's battery, Lieutenant Sale in reserve, and not engaged in the city proper. This considerable force was withdrawn from the front of Smith without arousing a suspicion on the part of the Federal commander, for the purpose of diverting Smith's column from an advance south of Oxford, the Confederate commander being sensible of the inability of his small command to give battle successfully.

General Washburn, in his official report, remarks that the fact "that Forrest should have left our immediate front at Oxford and made this move on Memphis without its being discovered by our large cavalry force in his immediate vicinity, is somewhat strange." After this censure of his subordinate, he was careful to report that "the impression generally prevailing that Memphis is a fortified city is far from correct;" but he now ordered the immediate construction of earthworks for defense against future attacks. All parts of the city were taken and occupied by the Confederates to the confusion and dismay especially of Major-General Washburn. Lieut.-Col. W. H. Thurston, inspector-general, Sixteenth corps, reported that General Forrest entered Memphis with 400 men under Lieutenant-Colonel Logwood and Lieut.-Col. Jesse Forrest. When Washburn was notified of the taking of the city, "he left his residence as early as possible and made his way to Fort Pickering, without having given any command as to what should be done by our troops." Fear of Forrest and his troopers was dominant with Washburn and his forces. Colonel Thurston added that two days later "the whole town was stampeded at about 10 a. m. by a report that Forrest had returned in force and was again in town. It was the most disgraceful affair I have ever seen." At that date Forrest was 100 miles distant. General Washburn had under his command at Memphis over 5,000 troops, besides the garrison at Fort Pickering. He admitted a loss of 15 killed, 65 wounded, 112 captured. The Confederates sustained a loss of 70 killed and wounded.

Smarting under criticism of his own mismanagement, and reiterating his censure of Gen. A. J. Smith in a dispatch to General Sherman, Washburn communicated the fact that he had ordered General Smith back to Memphis and his division to Georgia. Forrest never failed to destroy the military reputation of the Federal commanders encountered by him, and he now had his revenge on Washburn and Smith for the disaster at Harrisburg.

In a few days Forrest entered upon a campaign through north Alabama and middle Tennessee, the incidents of which show great celerity of movement and how resourceful he was in the face of an enemy greatly superior in numbers and strongly fortified at all points.

With the purpose of operating in north Alabama and Tennessee, Forrest crossed the Tennessee river on the 21st of September, with Bell's and Lyon's brigades of Buford's division, Rucker's brigade, commanded by Col. D. C. Kelley, and Roddey's troops, commanded by Col. W. A. Johnson. On the 20th, the Fourth Tennessee, Col. W. S. McLemore, and Col. Geo. H. Nixon's regiment, Col. J. B. Biffle, Nineteenth Tennessee, commanding brigade, were ordered to report to General Forrest. About 400 men were dismounted.

During the night of the 23d the command reached the town of Athens, Ala., and completely invested it, and at 7 o'clock the next morning an assault was ordered. Hudson's battery, commanded by Lieut. E. S. Walton; a section of Morton's battery, Lieut. Jo. M. Mayson commanding; the other section of Morton's battery, Lieut. Tully Brown commanding, all under the command of Capt. J. W. Morton, opened fire on the Federal position. The troops commenced to advance, when Forrest gave the order to cease firing and to halt, and demanded the surrender of the fort and garrison. Col. Wallace Campbell, One Hundred and Tenth United States infantry, commanding, reported that Forrest's artillery had planted almost every shell inside the works, and satisfied that he could not make a successful resistance to a largely superior force, he yielded to the demand of the Confederate general, capitulating with detachments from the One Hundred and Sixth United States colored infantry, One Hundred and Tenth colored infantry, One Hundred and Eleventh colored infantry, and Third regiment Tennessee Federal cavalry, numbering 571 officers and men.

Pending the negotiations for the surrender, firing was heard in the direction of Decatur, which proved to be a combat between reinforcements approaching Athens and the Fifteenth Tennessee, Col. Thos. H. Logwood commanding. The Federals took refuge behind piles of cordwood and made a stubborn fight. Logwood charged them and forced them out, when they renewed their efforts to gain the fort and fought with great gallantry, but found that the Twenty-first Tennessee, Col. Jesse Forrest, had cut them off. Colonel Nixon and Colonel Carter joined the Twenty-first with 300 men, and in a few minutes the reinforcements, 350 strong, surrendered just in time to see the garrison of the fort march out and stack arms. In this combat Col. Jesse Forrest fell severely wounded.

The garrison of a blockhouse surrendered on demand, but another one refused with defiance. The artillery at once opened on it and the second shot penetrated the walls, killing several of the garrison, which caused its surrender. Two pieces of artillery, a large number of small-arms, 38 wagons, 300 horses, with ammunition and other stores, were captured. The blockhouse and a train of cars were burned and the fort dismantled. The Confederates moved forward at once, and four miles north of Athens another blockhouse with a garrison of 30 men was captured, and the railroad trestle and blockhouse burned.

On the following morning Sulphur Springs trestle was invested, the defenses consisting of a fort and two blockhouses, garrisoned by about 1,000 men. Morton placed his guns in a position commanding the redoubt and opened fire, and Buford's division, Kelley's and Johnson's brigades, dismounted, assaulted the fort. The guns of the forts were silenced and resistance ceased, and after a parley following a demand for surrender, Lieutenant-Colonel Minnis, the Federal commander, yielded. Colonel Lathrop, first in command, was killed, and there were many dead in the redoubt from the effect of Morton's shot and shell. The fruits of the victory besides the prisoners were 700 stand of small-arms, 2 pieces of artillery, 16 wagons, 300 horses, and stores of every description. The trestle and blockhouses were burned and the prisoners sent to the rear. With the horses captured, the dismounted men were provided.

The blockhouse at Elk river was next burned, and the one at Richland creek, with a garrison of 50 men, was captured. Near Pulaski, Forrest encountered the enemy in the open field, and after a combat, almost a battle, in which his entire command was engaged, the enemy was driven with loss to his fortifications. A careful reconnoissance was made, and it was decided that the position could not be taken without too great a sacrifice of life; hence at nightfall the Confederates were withdrawn and were moved through Fayetteville toward Tullahoma, where Forrest learned that troops were being withdrawn from Chattanooga and points in Georgia, and concentrated in large numbers to intercept and capture his command. His artillery ammunition was greatly reduced, and after dispatching Nixon and Logwood to the rear with the prisoners, his command was not strong enough to meet the large force gathering about him. He turned toward the Tennessee & Alabama railroad.

Twelve miles from Columbia, four blockhouses with 120 prisoners were captured. The commanding officer of the garrison of one blockhouse refused to surrender, and the artillery being with Buford on another road, at night ten volunteers from Bell's brigade were selected to burn the bridge, out of hundreds who offered their services. These gallant fellows went forward in the face of a hot fire from the Federals, applied the torch, and destroyed the bridge. "The night was dark," said General Forrest, "but my command marched until 10 o'clock by the light of the burning ruins, which illuminated the country for miles."

On the 2d of October a demonstration was made on Columbia. The next day the Confederates moved toward Florence, Ala., which was reached without incident on the 5th. The river (forded two weeks earlier) was swollen by recent rains, and the enemy, 15,000 strong, was pressing their rear. The ferryboats were ordered to the mouth of Cypress creek and many troops ferried over, but delay could not be considered. At this emergency, General Forrest ordered all troops north of the river, except the Sixteenth Tennessee, under Col. Andrew N. Wilson, to mount and swim across a slough 70 yards wide to an island, from which they could be ferried at leisure.

Unbounded trust was placed in the gallant Wilson and his splendid regiment, and it was not misplaced. Almost surrounded by 15,000 of the enemy for three days, the marvel is that he was not swallowed up. But he stung the Federal flanks, contested their advance, and when pursued, retired to the hills, gaining his subsistence from the enemy. He continued in this perilous position until the entire command crossed the river and the enemy began to retire, when he crossed with the faithful Sixteenth. Wilson lost but 2 men killed and 4 captured, and killed and wounded 75 of the enemy.

Suspecting that the enemy would cross the Tennessee river, Col. D. C. Kelley's brigade, with a section of Hudson's battery under Lieutenant Walton, was moved to Eastport. On the 10th the enemy moved up the river with two gunboats and three transports loaded with troops. Kelley masked his forces until the enemy landed a brigade of infantry and three pieces of artillery, when Walton opened upon them with his guns. Two shots penetrated one gunboat, and a shell was exploded in one of the transports, which was soon enveloped in flames. The troops were stampeded and the boats pushed off, but in the effort to gain the boats many were drowned, 12 men were killed on the bank of the river, and a large number killed and wounded on the boats. Thirty prisoners, 4 field guns, 20 horses and 60 stand of small-arms were captured.

The forces under Col. Geo. B. Hoge, commanding the expedition so gallantly thwarted by Colonel Kelley, consisted of his own regiment, the One Hundred and Thirteenth Illinois, the One Hundred and Twentieth Illinois, Sixty-first United States colored infantry, and Company G, Second Missouri light artillery, with a company of the Twelfth Missouri cavalry. In his official report he stated that "on nearing Eastport the gunboat Key West went above the landing and seemed to be satisfied that there was no enemy near; at least, in a few moments Captain King motioned me to land my troops. Lieutenants Lytle and Boals, of my staff, started out to reconnoiter, and 500 yards from the landing they encountered and exchanged shots with the (Confederate) enemy's pickets. In ten minutes after, a battery of six rifled guns, masked on the hill, opened on the transports, and another battery of three guns opened on us. Every shot was doing more or less execution. One of the gunboats, the Undine, was disabled, and was dropping down the river, the Key West following. I ordered the troops to return to the transports. Just at this time a shell from the enemy struck a caisson on board the Kenton (transport), exploding it and setting fire to the boat. Another caisson on the Aurora (transport) was exploded, setting fire to her. Her steam-pipe was also cut. A scene of confusion then began. The boats backed out, leaving two-thirds of the men on shore, and the men ran down the river bank. After extinguishing the fires I landed and got all on board except the badly wounded and captured." Hoge reported the loss of 4 field guns and 74 men.

This affair was a brilliant one for Colonel Kelley and his Tennesseeans. No artillery officer with two guns ever rendered more effective service than Lieutenant Walton. Every shot was a successful one, and it is not surprising that the discomfited Hoge magnified his two pieces into nine "rifled guns." Hoge's orders were to proceed from Eastport to Iuka, Miss., and destroy the railroad and bridges, but the evening of the 11th found him down the river with a demoralized command, 100 or more miles distant, at Johnsonville, doubtless listening to the echo of Walton's guns.

The fruits of the expedition to north Alabama and Tennessee were 3,360 of the enemy, white and black, killed and captured—one to each man of Forrest's command—7 field guns, 800 horses, 50 wagons loaded with medical and other stores, the destruction of the railroad from Decatur to Spring Hill, the withdrawal of reinforcements from the army in the field, the destruction of numerous posts, and the relief of our people from the presence and oppression of the petty commanders of the captured garrisons.

On the 16th of October, Forrest's command moved into west Tennessee, and in a few days Buford instituted a blockade of the Tennessee river.

Fort Heiman and Paris landing were objective points which now had Forrest's attention. On October 29th, with Chalmers' division, he reached Paris landing, where Buford's division and Lyon's brigade were already on the ground. As usual, his force was magnified by the frightened enemy, and every post commander anticipated an attack. Gen. S. Meredith, commanding Federal forces at Paducah, under date of November 1st, said, "All reports concur that he is to attack me soon." Meredith called for 1,500 more men to insure the safety of Columbus, and 2,000 more for Paducah. Later, on the same day, he reported: "The gunboat Undine captured and sunk at Paris landing. Lyon in command at that point with 4,000 men and seven pieces of artillery. Forrest at Heiman with 8,000 men, five 12-pounders and eighteen siege guns." He reported also the capture of the transport Venus, with troops and supplies. His fears multiplied Forrest's forces by four, and easily converted field into siege guns.

General Forrest reported that on the 29th the steamer Mazeppa with two barges in tow made her appearance. Morton's battery and two Parrott guns opened on the boats and they were disabled and abandoned. A large lot of needed stores was captured and distributed to the Confederates. The next day the steamer Anna succeeded in passing the battery, but was so disabled that she sank before reaching the mouth of the river. The Venus was followed by the Cheeseman, both convoyed by the gunboat Undine. The entire fleet was disabled and captured. Lieutenant-Colonel Kelley, with two companies of his regiment, was thrown across the river, and soon returned with the abandoned boats.

Forrest ordered Captain Morton to take command of the Undine. The latter replied, "General, I can handle your guns on land, but I am not familiar with naval fighting. I have, however, temporarily attached to my artillery, Capt. Frank P. Gracy of Tennessee, a most efficient artillerist and an experienced steamboatman." Captain Gracy was sent for, and the gunboat was inspected and found to be in excellent condition, except that two guns were dismounted, which was easily remedied. A complement of ordnance for a stubborn fight was provided and Captain Gracy was placed in command, with the gunboat for his flagship. A gallant crew selected from the famous battery manned the boat, and she moved majestically out, with Forrest's escort flag nailed to the masthead, with orders to proceed to Johnsonville, where Captain Gracy expected the co-operation of the land batteries.

Some miles below Johnsonville, however, four gunboats from above moved down on his craft, and after a spirited engagement Captain Gracy finally retired down stream, when, to his surprise, seven hostile gunboats appeared from below. Instantly they poured forth a terrible storm of bursting shells, filling the air, the water, and Gracy's boat. His gallant crew replied with volley after volley of deadly missiles, Captain Gracy the while standing on deck giving orders as coolly as though they were at target practice. Several of his guns were dismounted, his boat perforated and shattered, and a few of his men wounded. He saw that in a few minutes it meant capture or a sunken boat, hence he had mattresses ripped open and piled in the magazine; a parting salute was fired at the enemy, and the crew was ordered to jump overboard and make for the shore. The last man to leave the boat, Captain Gracy applied the torch to the magazine, and making his way to the deck sprang into the water. Hardly had he reached shore before there was a terrific explosion, and his gunboat went up in smoke and flame, the hulk sinking to the bottom of the river. (R. F. Hoke, in Nashville Banner.)

On the 1st of November the forces under Forrest moved up the river, arriving on the 3d at Johnsonville. This was a depot of supplies for the Federal armies in the field, and according to Federal accounts the garrison consisted of 1,200 men, with two Parrott guns in position.

Thrall's battery of howitzers was placed in front, above Johnsonville, and Morton's and Hudson's batteries opposite and below the town, all under Captain Morton, acting chief of artillery. The batteries opened at a signal from Lieutenant Brown's section of Morton's battery, and the gunboats and field guns responded vigorously, but in fifteen minutes gunboats, transports, barges, stores and government warehouses were in flames. Everything was consumed by fire. Forrest's three 4-gun batteries were magnified by the Federal Captain Howland into thirty-six pieces of artillery, "twenty of them 20-pounder Parrotts."

The work of the expedition was completed, and the Confederates marched six miles after night, guided by the light of the fire at Johnsonville. In a campaign of two weeks the forces of Forrest had captured and destroyed 4 gunboats, 14 transports, 20 barges, 26 pieces of artillery, and millions of dollars worth of property, with 150 prisoners captured. Captain Howland (Federal) reported that one million dollars would cover the loss of property at Johnsonville.

On the 10th, Forrest's cavalry reached Corinth, Miss., and under orders the commanding general put himself in communication with General Hood, who was preparing to enter upon his disastrous campaign to Franklin and Nashville.

On the 27th of January, 1865, Gen. Richard Taylor, commanding department, assigned General Forrest to the command of the district of Mississippi and Louisiana. On the 13th of the following month Brig.-Gen. W. H. Jackson was assigned to the command of all of the Tennesseeans in the district. Bell's and Rucker's brigades, the Ninth, Tenth, Eleventh, Nixon's and Carter's regiments, and the Twelfth Confederate were consolidated into six regiments, to constitute two brigades, one commanded by Col. T. H. Bell, soon made brigadier-general; and in a few weeks Brig.-Gen. Alexander W. Campbell, just returned from prison and promoted, was assigned to the Second brigade.

On the 22d of March, Major-General Wilson of the Federal army, with three divisions of cavalry, 10,000 strong, left Chickasaw, Ala. On the 30th he reached Elyton, whence Croxton's command was sent to Tuscaloosa. Jackson's Tennessee division forced Croxton to cross to the north side of the Warrior river, and after a forced march of thirty-five miles, guided by negroes through the fields and byways, the Federals entered the undefended town of Tuscaloosa, and with malignant triumph burned the university buildings, the factory, the foundry, the bridge over the Warrior, and the two large warehouses in Tuscaloosa and Northport, on the opposite bank of the Warrior. Captain Hardcastle, commanding the post, reported that Croxton captured an important scout twelve miles away and came into possession of important information through which success was easily attained.

Forrest undertook to concentrate his scattered forces at Selma, Ala. Jackson encountered Croxton's brigade north of Scottsville and punished it severely, capturing prisoners, several stand of colors and several hundred horses. Forrest undertook the defense of Selma with an insignificant force in numbers, Jackson, Chalmers and Buford, with their divisions, not being present, and a gallant fight was made, but the field was lost and Selma was evacuated by the Confederates. At Marion, Forrest was joined by the Tennesseeans under Jackson, and a week was spent gathering together his forces. On the 15th he established his headquarters at Gainesville. Soon rumors of the surrender of the army of Northern Virginia were circulated, though not credited, and a few days later the army of Tennessee was surrendered, followed by the surrender of the troops in the department commanded by General Taylor. On the 9th of May, General Forrest issued an address of farewell to his command, in which he said,

"You have been good soldiers, you can be good citizens." Gen. Richard Taylor said of Forrest, "Like Lord Clive, nature made him a great soldier. His tactics deserve the closest study of military men. He employed the tactics of Frederick at Leuthen and Zorndorf, though he had never heard these names."

The State of Tennessee contributed 115,000 soldiers to the Confederate army, many counties furnishing more men than they had voters. Two hundred and ninety-six battles, combats and skirmishes were fought upon her soil, many of them unimportant and without result, but at all of them brave men were killed or wounded. For four years war was the occupation of her people.

The old men and the women dedicated themselves to the service of husbands, sons and brothers, and through trusted agents, often through faithful slaves, clothing was sent to them. The soldiers were never too distant to escape their careful attention. Federal invasion and occupation of the State brought poverty and distress to every household. The tramp of the hostile soldier was the too familiar sound. Robbers in uniform were ready at all times to sweep away crops and household effects, but there was no diminution of patriotic zeal on the part of either sex. Oppression stimulated their efforts. No man was so old or infirm, and no lady so delicate, as to relax the determination to serve the soldiers in the field; and when the hour for surrender came, the fathers, mothers and sisters of Tennessee endured the poverty that it brought with the same patriotic resolution that sustained them through four years of war.

CHAPTER XIII.

TENNESSEE AND THE NAVY.

THE State of Tennessee furnished 31,000 white men to the Federal government during the war between the States. Among them were David G. Farragut and Samuel Carter.

Admiral Farragut commanded the largest and most powerful force that had ever been controlled by any American naval officer, and the results of the operations of that force in the waters of the Mississippi were more fatal to the Confederacy than any of the military campaigns. The achievements of his fleet enabled General Grant to cross the Mississippi with safety, and to get in the rear of Vicksburg. The fall of that essential position was thus assured, and the Confederacy cut in twain. At the date of it, Texas had become the chief source of supply for cattle, horses and other essentials. The control of the Mississippi river by the Federal naval forces was a fatal blow to the Confederacy, and reduced the war from the position of a contest having many probabilities of success to a purely defensive struggle for safety. (Capt. James D. Bulloch.)

Rear-Admiral Carter, then a lieutenant-commander, U. S. N., was withdrawn from the navy early in 1861, and commissioned as a brigadier-general of volunteers, charged with the organization of the men of Tennessee who were loyal to the Federal union into regiments, and prepare them for the field. His heart, like Farragut's, was in the work. He brought to it professional training, good character, high social standing, and large family influence. He gave respectability to the cause he espoused at the beginning of the war, and very soon perfected organizations which commanded the sympathy and support of the great body of the people of east Tennessee, and secured that division of the State (in the heart of the Confederate States) to the Federal government. Farragut and Carter, both natives of east Tennessee, were important factors in making Confederate success impossible.

Tennesseeans in the United States navy who resigned to accept service in the Confederate States navy were: George W. Gift, J. W. Dunnington, Jesse Taylor, W. P. A. Campbell, Thomas Kennedy Porter, A. D. Wharton, George A. Howard and W. W. Carnes.

Lieutenant Gift is famous for having commanded, with Lieutenant Grimball, the 8-inch columbiads on the Confederate ram Arkansas. The Arkansas was built by Capt. John T. Shirley at Memphis, Tenn. At the fall of New Orleans she was towed up the Yazoo.

On the 15th of July, 1862, the ram started out from Haynes' Bluff, under the command of Capt. I. W. Brown, with a crew of 200 officers and men, for Mobile bay, with orders to raise the blockade of that port. Lieutenant Gift, in his history of the exploits of the Arkansas, states that "Sunrise found us in the Yazoo river with more than twenty ships barring our way, and in for one of the most desperate fights any one ship ever sustained since ships were first made." Lieutenant Gift fought the port gun, with John Wilson, of Baltimore, as his lieutenant. Grimball fought the starboard gun, and had for his lieutenant Midshipman Dabney M. Scales, now a prominent lawyer and ex-State senator from Memphis. Lieut. A. D. Wharton came next on the starboard side, each lieutenant with two guns. Soon three Federal gunboats were seen steaming toward the Arkansas, the ironclad Carondelet, of twelve guns, the Tyler, and the Queen of the West. The Arkansas was steered direct for the Tyler, and Gift fired the first shot with an 8-inch shell, which struck her fair and square, killing a pilot and bursting in the engine-room. The Tyler reported 17 killed and 14 wounded. The Queen of the West coming up, Scales gave her a shell, followed quickly by another from Wharton, and she was just able to retire from the conflict. In a short time the Tyler, badly crippled, took flight and joined her disabled consort. The Carondelet was struck four times by Gift. Lieutenant Reed gave her two shots from the stern guns, when she hauled down her colors; at the same time Wharton opened on the starboard broadside, which brought out white flags at her ports. The Carondelet sank. But the Arkansas had no time to secure a prize, and pursued the fleeing vessels, now in the Mississippi river.

Immediately Farragut and Davis prepared to receive the Arkansas with more than a dozen war vessels. No more gallant action on land or sea was ever witnessed than that of Captain Brown. In addition to Farragut's fleet, batteries of field artillery were in position, and several thousand soldiers prepared to fire into the ports of his vessel. The Arkansas was an untried and an unfinished vessel, with engines that proved to be totally unreliable. The first attack was made by the Federal gunboat No. 6. She fired her 11-inch pivot gun loaded with grape. Gift returned the fire with a shell that went through and through the No. 6, and then a port broadside took her disabled out of the action. The Arkansas now became the target for a hundred guns. Generals Breckinridge and Van Dorn, and thousands of Confederate soldiers, stood as silent witnesses of the uneven contest, unable to render the slightest assistance.

It was a brave fight; nothing comparable to it at Manila or Santiago de Cuba. Gift fired a five-second shell at the Lancaster, as that vessel moved across the path of the Arkansas, which struck the mud-drum, emptying the hot steam and water into the engine-room, and killing a large number of the crew and sharpshooters. But there was no rest for the Arkansas; the shot struck upon her sides as fast as sledge-hammer blows. Captain Brown was twice knocked down and wounded in the head, but he heroically resumed his place. Some one called out that the colors had been shot away, and in an instant, said Gift, Midshipman Dabney M. Scales, a glorious fellow, scrambled up the ladder and, fearlessly treading the terrible path of death, swept by a hurricane of shot and shell, raised the colors again. A shell penetrated the Arkansas and exploded with terrible effect, and when the smoke cleared away, it was found that but one man out of seventeen of Gift's bow-gun crew had escaped death or wounds. In another instant an 11-inch shot crushed through above the port, bringing with it a shower of iron and wooden splinters, which struck down every man at Gift's broadside gun, smashed his own arm, and passing across the deck, killed 8 and wounded 7 of Scales' men. The Arkansas reached Vicksburg, disabled and weakened by heavy losses. The detachment of the land forces serving temporarily on the Arkansas joined its proper command.

At night Farragut's sea-going fleet and Davis' ironclads passed down the river. They came by singly, and each was punished as they crossed the line of fire of the Arkansas. An 11-inch shot from Farragut's flagship penetrated her side just above the water line, killing 2 and wounding 6 others.

On the morning of the 22d of July, the ironclad Essex appeared, followed by the Queen of the West, and undertook to run into the Arkansas, both trying to ram her, but were driven off and disabled, and a mortar boat blown up. The crew of the Arkansas was now reduced to seventeen. With this small force, the repulse of these two vessels will always be considered her best achievement.

When General Breckinridge entered upon his campaign against Baton Rouge, the co-operation of the Arkansas was expected, but her engines gave way in full view of the point of attack, and becoming unmanageable on account of a break in a vital part of her machinery, to avoid capture she was destroyed by fire. Captain Brown was made a commodore, and Stevens, the executive officer, Reed, Gift, Wharton and Scales won great distinction.

The battle of Mobile Bay was fought August 5, 1864. The enemy's fleet, under Admiral Farragut, consisted of 14 steamers and 4 monitors, carrying 199 guns and 2,700 men. The Confederate naval commander, Admiral Franklin Buchanan, had the wooden gunboats Morgan and Gaines, each carrying 6 guns, the Selma of 4 guns, and the ram Tennessee of 6 guns, in all 22 guns and 470 men. In this unequal contest, there could be no question as to the result. The engagement lasted an hour, and serious injury was inflicted on many vessels of the Federal fleet. Frequently during the contest the Tennessee was surrounded by the enemy, and all her guns were in action at the same moment. The noble Confederate admiral was wounded and carried below, and soon the Tennessee was surrendered. The other ships were well fought, and surrendered after they were disabled and overpowered. The Gaines, in a sinking condition, was run on shore near Fort Morgan. The gallant Lieut. A. D. Wharton, of Tennessee, was with Admiral Buchanan on the ram Tennessee, and rendered valuable and conspicuous service.

When Fort Pillow was evacuated by the Confederate forces, the gunboat Pontchartrain, commanded by Lieut. John W. Dunnington, which constituted a part of the fleet commanded by Capt. Geo. N. Hollins, provided for the defense of the Mississippi river, was run up White river. At an earlier date, Lieutenant Dunnington had participated in the operations against Pope's army at Point Pleasant, Mo., and was active in resisting the crossing of the river. At the surrender of the Confederate forces near Tiptonville, the Ponchartrain was ordered to Fort Pillow. On the 16th of June, 1862, Lieutenant Dunnington arrived at St. Charles on White river, with the men necessary to work the 32-pounder cannon, which he had previously placed in battery. He was hardly in position before the approach of the Federal gunboats was announced. After dark, Capt. Joseph Fry, commanding the naval forces, undertook to blockade the river against the enemy's advance, and with his own crew, he sunk the gunboat Maurepas in the main current, remaining on deck until the gundeck was submerged. At 8:30 the next morning the Federal fleet advanced up the river. When abreast of Captain Fry's rifled guns, the gunboats opened with all of their guns, but failed to silence Fry's battery. They then moved up the river until they were in point blank range of one of Dunnington's guns. The boat in advance, the Mound City, moved up for position and placed herself between his two guns. At 10:30, Dunnington's upper gun fired a shot at the Mound City, passing through the boilers, steam chest or pipes, filling the vessel with steam, and causing all that were not killed to jump into the river. More than 50 were killed and as many disabled. The vessel drifted across the stream into the bank. The rifled guns opened on the lower gunboat and sent it disabled down the river.

The naval contingent had no support, and after the Mound City was disabled, and the retreat of the gunboats St. Louis, Conestoga and Lexington, Colonel Fitch, with the Twenty-sixth Indiana infantry, took the batteries in rear and forced the Confederates to retreat. This was conducted in safety by Lieutenant Dunnington. Captain Fry was seriously wounded and captured. He survived wounds and a cruel imprisonment, and was captured in Cuban waters on the 1st of November, 1873, by a Spanish man-of-war, the Toreador, and on the 7th, after a mock trial, in company with fifty-three other American citizens, was murdered in the plaza of Santiago de Cuba. When captured, Captain Fry was in command of the steamer Virginius, with an alleged filibustering expedition.

Dunnington, one of the noblest of men, survived the war for more than ten years.

Wharton has dedicated his life to public education, and is one of the foremost in that field.

Lieut. Jesse Taylor became captain of heavy artillery; his splendid service at Fort Henry has been already chronicled.

Lieut. W. P. A. Campbell was constantly employed on the coast and harbor defenses, and was an efficient and gallant officer. About the year 1870 he was made a major of engineers in the army of Ismail Pasha, the Khedive of Egypt. He was a useful officer, constantly employed, and trusted by those in authority. He was finally sent to the Soudan, with a detachment of troops, and there died a victim of malarial fever.

Geo. A. Howard resigned from the naval academy just before graduation; was made adjutant of the Seventh Tennessee infantry, and was distinguished in the principal battles fought by the army of Northern Virginia. More than once he commanded the regiment in action. He has filled conspicuous places of honor and trust at home and at the Federal capital, and is a leading citizen of Tennessee.

W. W. Carnes resigned from the naval academy before graduation; became captain of artillery in Cheatham's division, and was conspicuous wherever that famous command was engaged. He is now a prominent citizen of Memphis, and is the incumbent of an important civil office, to which he was chosen by the people.

Lieut. Thomas Kennedy Porter resigned from the United States navy in 1861, and was appointed to the same rank in the Confederate navy, but accepted the command of a company of field artillery tendered him by the governor of Tennessee. He commanded Porter's battery at the battle of Fort Donelson, and was severely wounded and disabled for a year. Returning to the army, he was promoted, and commanded the artillery of Buckner's corps at Chickamauga. He then resigned from the army, took service in the navy, and was for several months executive officer of the ironclad North Carolina, a steamer provided for coast and harbor defense. He was then ordered to Bermuda, where he joined the cruiser Florida as her executive officer. The Florida continued her career as a commerce destroyer until the 4th of October, 1864, when she arrived at Bahia, Brazil, to procure coal and provisions, and for repairs, after a cruise of 61 days. At 3:00 a. m. of the 7th of October, the United States man-of-war Wachusett, Captain Collins, ran into the Florida, intending to sink her, and very serious injury was inflicted upon the ship. At the same time the Wachusett fired about 200 shots from her small-arms, and two from her great guns, and then demanded her surrender. At the request of the Brazilian naval commander, the Florida had anchored inshore of his squadron, steam had gone down and fires were hauled. Commander Morris, with several officers and 70 of the crew of the Florida, was on shore on liberty. In this condition of affairs the cruiser was surrendered. The officers were paroled and with two-thirds of the men transferred to the Wachusett. The men were outraged by being put in double irons. One poor fellow, Henry Norman, was ironed to a stanchion with his hands behind him for having a key to a pair of the Florida's irons in his pocket. Another was put in a sweat-box for eighteen nights, because, said Captain Collins, "He was seen talking, and when his master-at-arms came up, he stopped." Eighteen of the crew were put ashore penniless, on the Island of St. Thomas, after Collins had promised to restore their money which had been taken from them. No restoration was made.

On the arrival of the Wachusett at Fortress Monroe, the officers and men were sent to Point Lookout prison, whence the officers were sent to the Old Capitol prison at Washington, and a few days later joined the men at Fort Warren, Boston. At Fortress Monroe, Lieutenant Porter, hearing that the money-chest of the Florida had been opened, called on Collins to restore several hundred dollars, private funds, belonging to the ward-room mess. This was refused.

At Fortress Monroe an offer was made to the men, through Lieutenant Beardsley, U. S. N., to release them from prison, upon condition that they would subscribe to an oath of allegiance. Only one man out of 53 deserted his flag, and that desertion occurred the day of the capture.

At Fort Warren the men were all put in one room, and the eleven officers in another with 32 other prisoners. The rooms were casemates, 50 feet long and 18 feet wide. At 8:00 a. m. the prisoners were marched around to the cook-house and given a loaf of bread each. After 12 they were marched around again and received their dinner, consisting of 8 ounces of cooked meat with a half pint of thin soup, three days of the week, and two potatoes, some beans or hominy the other days.

On the 24th of December, the officers of the Florida were locked up in a casemate and kept in close confinement day and night, upon the report of a prison spy that a plan for capturing the fort was under discussion. This continued until the 19th of January, when the prisoners were relieved from close confinement, and notified that they would be released on condition that they would sign a parole to leave the United States in ten days. Lieutenant Porter informed the secretary of the navy that they would give the parole, but asked for the return of the $13,000 taken from the Florida, saying that it was necessary to have that, unless the United States would send the officers and men to Europe. No attention was paid to this request, and finding that the Federal authorities would do nothing, an arrangement was made with an English passenger ship for their transportation to Europe by giving a draft to be paid at Liverpool. (Report of Lieutenant Porter.)

Upon the demand of Brazil, the act of Collins, commander of the Wachusett, was disavowed, and on the 20th of December, Mr. Seward informed the minister of Brazil that the prisoners would be set at liberty. He said the act "was an unauthorized, unlawful and indefensible exercise of the naval force of the United States within a foreign country." Professor Soley, of the United States navy, discussing the conduct of Collins, has said: "The capture of the Florida was as gross and deliberate a violation of the rights of neutrals as was ever committed in any age or country. It is idle to attempt to apologize for it or to explain it; the circumstances were such that the question does not admit of discussion." ("The Blockade and the Cruisers," Soley, p. 189.)

If it had been within his province, he could have added that in the judgment of contemporaneous history, Collins' act was a cowardly one, and his treatment of the prisoners was brutal, not more so, however, than that by the authorities at Fort Warren and Washington.

H. M. Doak, Esq., of Nashville, in an interview with a reporter of a city paper in 1896, said: "I knew Capt. T. K. Porter at Wilmington, N. C., where he was executive officer of the gunboat North Carolina, a heavy ironclad. He was a graduate of the naval academy, and had resigned to cast his fortunes with his native State and his people. He had served as captain of a battery of artillery in the army of the West, where his battery was known as 'Porter's battery.' I saw it in action, and heard it thunder at Fort Donelson. His fame as a skillful artillery officer and brave commander will never be forgotten by the soldiers of the West. His battery had such fame as attached to the Washington artillery, or to Cheatham's or Hardee's commands in infantry. Physically, he was one of the noblest-looking of men. As an officer, everything about his ship was in perfect order, its discipline superb, and yet his command as gentle as it was firm and rigid. Affable and kind, the soul of lofty honor, calm, true and fearless, he was loved and respected by all. He left Wilmington to report as executive officer of Maffitt's ship, the Florida. Shortly after he came to the Florida, that famous cruiser was captured in one of the South American ports by a flagrant violation of the neutrality laws. He was confined in Fort Warren, Mass., and lost his life after the war, while in command of a merchant steamer on the Pacific. I have never known a more superb gentleman, never a man who seemed to me so entirely to discharge a gentleman's duty—to be a gentleman at all times and under all circumstances. I say this to you for print, for the memory of such men should be continually recalled, and many an old soldier will remember 'Porter's battery' and remember its true and noble commander, and be better for thinking once more of his old comrade, whom to have known intimately, as I did, was to have loved him, and to have been the better for such acquaintance."

H. M. Doak and John F. Wheless joined the Confederate navy, the first after Shiloh. Doak was for a long time on the ironclad Wilmington, where his services were as conspicuous as they had been as adjutant of the famous Nineteenth Tennessee infantry at Fishing creek and Shiloh. Since 1865 he has been a leader and director of public opinion in Tennessee; for years the leading journalist of the State, and is now in possession of an honorable office connected with the courts of the country. Captain Wheless served for a year as captain of the First Tennessee, and then on the staff of Lieutenant-General Polk; after Chickamauga he was made a paymaster in the Confederate navy. After 1865 he entered upon a successful business career, and died in late years, too soon for his friends and for the State.

CHAPTER XIV.

TENNESSEE AND THE MEDICAL DEPARTMENT.

THERE was no difficulty in finding qualified medical officers in Tennessee. Medical education had attained a high standard, and surgeons were supplied as soon as regimental organizations were made.

Dr. B. W. Avent, a man of ripe experience, great skill and administrative ability, was made surgeon-general of the provisional army of the State. So perfect was his system that the department was adopted by the Confederate authorities without material change. The subsequent efficiency of this branch of the service is largely due to the foresight and skill of this eminent man.

As soon as the troops were mustered, the demand for the establishment of hospitals was created. The men from the rural districts were the victims of measles to such an extent that camps of instruction were converted into hospitals. Dr. S. H. Stout, surgeon of the Third Tennessee infantry, states that this regiment was sent to Camp Cheatham, near Nashville, in May, 1861, 1,100 strong, and within two months 650 men were treated for this disease alone. This was about the percentage prevailing in all of the regiments.

This condition demanded an immediate hospital service, and Nashville became the chief post of the Southwest. Troops from other States were being concentrated at Bowling Green, Ky., Fort Donelson, and other accessible points; and before the battle at the point last named, there were in the hospitals established at Nashville nearly 13,000 sick men under treatment, provision having been made for them by the State of Tennessee out of her own abundant resources.

On the fall of Fort Donelson and the abandonment of Nashville, provision for the sick was the greatest care and responsibility. To the medical officers alone can be accorded commendation for their removal. Hospitals with capacity for the care of the large number of sick had been provided at Nashville, with all needed appliances. Intelligent medical officers, aided by the noble women of that city, had made them not only inviting, but a positive luxury to the sick. But they were hastily broken up and the sick transferred to other points.

When Gen. A. S. Johnston assumed command of the department, his medical director, Dr. D. W. Yandell of Kentucky, a Tennesseean by birth and education, a very able and accomplished man, assumed direction of the hospital service of the State and controlled it with great success. On the fall of General Johnston and the assignment of General Bragg to the command of the army, Dr. A. J. Foard, medical director on his staff, became the supreme authority.

When General Johnston retired from Nashville he gave orders to Dr. Samuel H. Stout, already detailed to hospital duty at Nashville, to proceed to Chattanooga to take charge of the small hospital at that point and to organize others as the exigencies of the service required. General Johnston had his attention directed to Dr. Stout after an inspection of his regimental hospital at Bowling Green, and of the general hospital at Nashville. Soon the sick and wounded accumulated so rapidly at Chattanooga that new and more complete buildings were provided and ample provision made for the care of all.

In July, 1862, General Bragg (then about to inaugurate his Kentucky campaign), in company with Medical Director Foard, made a thorough personal inspection of the hospitals at Chattanooga—the buildings, the beds, the laundries, the cook rooms. Soon after this, Dr. Stout was summoned to the medical headquarters of the army, where he was informed by Dr. Foard that

General Bragg had directed him to be assured that he was satisfied and pleased with his management of his hospitals. Three days after this, General Bragg issued orders placing the general hospitals of the army and department under Dr. Stout, as superintendent, with power to locate them and to assign medical officers to duty. As often as military reasons demanded the evacuation of our territory, the medical department was so managed that hospitals could be removed, with their organizations preserved. An illustration is found in the "Academy hospital" at Chattanooga. Upon the evacuation of that place it was removed to Marietta, Ga., then to Atlanta, to Forsyth, to Auburn, Ala., to Corinth, Miss., and finally returned to Auburn.

After the battle of Murfreesboro, Dr. Avent was left in charge of about 500 Confederates, too badly wounded for removal. He so impressed General Rosecrans that orders were given to honor any requisition made for supplies for his wounded. On his return to the South, at his own request, he was assigned to hospital duty.

General Bragg was keenly alive to the importance of a complete hospital service, and gave the subject his personal attention. In a communication addressed to Dr. Stout under date of January, 1864, he said: "The operations of the hospital department of our army of Tennessee, especially since systematized by you, I have always claimed as perfect so far as means allowed, and I have every reason to believe it is considered by our government as superior to any in the country. I hope you will find it agreeable to continue your service, so important to the sick and wounded, and so beneficial to the army."

Dr. Stout is a native of Nashville, an alumnus of her university, which, in gratitude for his eminent services, conferred upon him the degree of LL. D., supplementing those of A. B. and A. M. He is a graduate of the medical department of the University of Pennsylvania, and is now a citizen of the State of Texas, where he enjoys the highest personal and professional consideration.

When Dr. Stout was called upon to name the Tennesseeans who in his opinion were most distinguished for their services to the general and field hospitals, he named Doctors B. W. Avent, Frank Rice, J. R. Buist, R. W. Mitchell, W. L. Nichol, J. B. Murfree, Clayton, John Patterson, Compton, R. C. Foster, G. W. and John H. Currey, J. M. Kellar, J. B. Cowan, G. B. Thornton, C. C. Abernathy, J. F. Grant, and Bell, killed at Island No. 10. A notice of this service is incomplete unless mention is made of the services of Dr. J. H. Bryson, a clergyman of Tennessee, appointed by General Bragg to look after the religious interests of the sick and wounded in the general hospitals. This devoted man gave every moment of his time to this service, and won the love and gratitude of all with whom he came in contact. His task was a herculean one, but he met it with the same courage characteristic of the men whose spiritual welfare he was seeking to promote.

No body of men in the service were more patriotic, more courageous and more self-sacrificing than the medical officers of Tennessee. They were on the battlefield, in the hospitals, often surrounded by contagious disease, but no one of them failed to discharge his full duty.

CHAPTER XV.

TENNESSEE AND THE CHURCH, BY REV. M. B. DEWITT, CHAPLAIN OF THE EIGHTH TENNESSEE.

TO one who had an active part in the great struggle of the war between the States, the religious element must ever be an important factor. Indeed, to the thoughtful general reader and to the historian it must have great significance. The reason is simple and ample. It may be unhesitatingly said that no people ever entered into a mighty conflict of arms with a clearer apprehension and deeper appreciation of their constitutional, natural and religious rights and obligations than did the citizens of those States which withdrew from the American Union and formed the Confederate States of America. They inherited from their forefathers those great qualities and views of life which combine to constitute the finest character of an intelligent, courageous, patriotic and God-fearing people. They drank the essence of freedom and faith from their mothers' breasts, and their noble aspirations and invincible honor were kindled from the teachings and examples of their fathers.

It is not too much to say here, that doubtless no part of the world was ever more thoroughly permeated by the spirit and power of the doctrines of the Bible than that part of the United States which has been long distinctly and historically designated as "the South." The brave people of this broad region believed in God and in His written word, and the foundations of their commonwealths were laid in faith in the Author of their lives and liberties. The Christian religion was as substantially a reality to them as the delights and comforts of home, and the blessings of free government under wise laws. The Church in its various branches had its organizations and services in every portion of the territory, and the homogeneity of population, by reason of but small influx of foreign irreligious elements, assured the transmission of the dear old beliefs from sire to son without serious admixture of diluting skepticism. The power of religion among the Southern people was never greater than at the very period when came the awful crisis of internecine war.

Keeping these leading facts in mind, it is scarcely to be wondered at that, when the actual call to arms was made, the universal sentiment of the South was a solemn appeal to heaven for the rectitude of its purposes and devout prayer to God for His abiding presence and blessings in the mighty struggle. The very initiation of preparations, enlistments of men, organizations of companies and regiments, contributions of clothing, supplies of food, and every step taken for war, witnessed religious services in churches all over the land, besides innumerable smaller gatherings for prayer, with special reference to the departure of the beloved husbands, fathers, sons, brothers, friends and neighbors to join the army. A profound sense of dependence on the divine providence was a common feeling throughout the Confederate States. It is to be admitted that while this is true, it is also true that a large number of the young men of the South were at first almost swept off their feet by the intense excitement created by open hostilities. Many went wild with the sentiment of resistance to the combined attempts of the United States government and the various Northern States to force the South into submission to Federal authority, and the natural exuberance of youth was released from the common wholesome restraints of home and ordinary social life by separation from them, and by the formation of military camps where thousands of volunteers were assembled for preparation to enter active service. It did not require a long time to bring very general seriousness of mind when burdens began to be laid upon the young shoulders and when much sickness prostrated large numbers, and many deaths occurred before a blow had been struck for the cause. The older heads and the preponderating Christian sentiment felt the responsibility of the hour from the beginning, and in this record we shall see that the very leaders of the great movement were men who had found God and sought His favor both privately and publicly.

A very grave mistake was made by great numbers of people in supposing, at first, that the war would be ended in a short time. This mistake added to the excitement in youthful minds so that they were in a hurry to enlist and do some fighting, for fear that the contest would be but "a breakfast spell" and they get no part in it. A gradual real and powerful change came by reaction, and volunteers became experienced veterans enlisted for the war; laying everything upon the altar of country and facing the stern future without fear. A conviction forced itself into the common consciousness that a long, desperate and bitter struggle was before the people of the South. The wise, the rich, the rulers and the people, the small and the great, became deeply engaged in solving the problem of national life, and of the rights and freedom of States and men. The extreme gravity of the situation impressed the entire population, so that from the date of the election of Abraham Lincoln to the presidency of the United States in 1860, to the end of the war in 1865, a great volume of prayer ascended to the God of our fathers.

The national recognition of the superintending providence of God was made so early in the strife that Jefferson Davis issued a call for a day of fasting and prayer, to be observed on June 13, 1861, only a few weeks after the opening of hostilities. This call by the President of the Confederate States was honored by the churches throughout the Southern States, and it created a deep sense of the needs of the country. Such proclamations were made from time to time by our Christian President until the close of the strife. A characteristic order of General Lee was one for the careful observance of the Sabbath day, as far as it was possible. The second section of this "General Order, No. 15" is in these words: "He [the general commanding] directs that none but duties strictly necessary shall be required to be performed on Sunday, and that all labor, both of men and animals, which it is practicable to anticipate or postpone, or the immediate performance of which is not essential to the safety, health, or comfort of the army, shall be suspended on that day." He followed this with orders to all officers commanding to "give their attention to the maintenance of order and quiet around the place of worship, and prohibit anything that may tend to disturb or interrupt religious exercises."

Of all the great leaders in the Confederate armies, it is doubtless true that many persons, North and South, held the opinion that Gen. N. B. Forrest was the most reckless and wicked. The famous cavalier issued a general order from Tupelo, Miss., May 14, 1864, in which he said: "The major-general commanding, devoutly grateful to the providence of Almighty God, so signally vouchsafed to his command during the recent campaign in west Tennessee, and deeply penetrated with a sense of dependence on the mercy of God in the present crisis of our beloved country, requests that military duties be so far suspended that divine service may be attended at 10 o'clock a. m. to-morrow by the whole command. Divine service will be held at these headquarters, at which all soldiers who are disposed to do so are kindly invited to attend. Come one, come all. Chaplains, in the ministrations of the gospel, are requested to remember our personal preservation with thanksgiving, and especially to beseech a throne of grace for aid in this, our country's hour of need."

A very brown clipping lies before the writer, which is an article from the "Army and Navy Herald," published during the war, headed "Forrest and Providence," in which the above "General Order, No. 4" is printed, and the editor says: "The general is far from being a Christian, it is true, in many of his moments of excitement, but no man is more truly a believer in the God of the Bible and Providence, or more ready to acknowledge his wrongs and his faith." Let it be written here that that belief, which was theoretical in his head during the war, became, after its close, experimental and practical by his public profession of it, in uniting with the church in Memphis, of which his devout wife was a member.

What has been recorded above is given simply as examples of the spirit and course of the great body of the leaders in both civil and military circles of the Confederate States, and it is scarcely necessary to say how positive, consistent and constant was the religious life of Stonewall Jackson, Leonidas Polk, Joseph E. Johnston, D. H. Hill, J. E. B. Stuart, A. P. Stewart, and others in all the fearful days of conflict. The President of the Confederacy and all in authority under him, the governors of all the States, and the people with them, promoted every enterprise by financial and personal aid and by giving whatsoever of opportunity and liberty may have been practicable in war, in order to secure the direct religious welfare of soldiers and citizens.

This survey of the general spirit of the government and all under it on this great subject, prepares us for considering more specific, united and individual efforts toward the same important end—the religious interests of the people. It way be truly stated that it is impossible to set forth a faithful and full view of the religion of the Confederate army. The present writer honestly believes that history presents no accurate or ample parallel. The stern piety and invincible principles of Cromwell and his forces in war with Charles I of England are freely admitted and much admired, but they had no such happy influence on men and communities as the tender and refining power of the faith of the Confederate soldiers had on them and this country. The religious devotion of Havelock, John and Henry Lawrence, "Chinese" Gordon, and other great English heroes, was circumscribed too greatly by conditions to produce anything like a national result in India and elsewhere. Even our own revolutionary fathers, while led by the wisdom, the patience, the faith and constancy of George Washington, to whom the world is indebted for American freedom and institutions, left us no such general record of religious fervor and faith in God as had their grand illustration in the armies of the Confederate States. From the inception of the war between the States of the Union, chaplains were provided for by civil authority and by the action of regiments, brigades and other portions of troops, and were enlisted with the men in all sections of the Confederacy. Missionaries to the soldiers were commissioned by all the great Christian denominations, among whom were many of the ablest and most consecrated preachers in the South. It would simply be invidious to mention names, because of the number and influence of the men who were representative of the pulpit and people of all the churches. Many of these men worked right through the war from first to last, and while some dropped out, others died, and some were recalled, the vacancies were rapidly filled, additions were made from time to time, and the ministry of the gospel in one way or another was effectively continued until the surrender. The fact is, that the army was permeated with the power of the Christian religion by preaching, by distribution of Bibles and religious literature, by systematic evangelization, by special services of all kinds, by correspondence of friends at home, and in other ways not essential to mention. Great and general earnestness among the people was exhibited to promote and maintain religious life and moral conduct among the soldiers. Regular Bible societies were organized for the publication, sale and gift of Bibles, with a special reference to dissemination in the army. Religious newspapers were established in many places, and many thousands of copies were regularly circulated, week by week and month after month, so as to provide fresh and attractive reading matter of good character for the noble boys who were deprived by war of all the privileges enjoyed in life at home. Tract societies printed and published tens of thousands of pages of religious reading, so that by one agency alone, 84,000 such pages were distributed and readily received and read in one month; millions were thus given out and used, and there is no possible estimate to be made of the sum total of the amount eventually provided, or of the good done by this Christian service.

Striking facts, like the following, occurred: The American Bible Society, with headquarters in New York, made a number of donations of Bibles, 20,000 at one time, for our Southern soldiers, and the British and Foreign Bible Society of London donated through a Confederate agent, at one time, 10,000 Bibles, 15,000 New Testaments, and 250,000 parts of scriptures, and it is safe to say that there was no difficulty in finding readers for as many copies as could be brought to the armies. To give further impression of the work done, and to record a word of credit due, I quote from Rev. W. W. Bennett's book, "The Great Revival in the Southern Armies," who says that the General Association of Baptist churches in Virginia was the first organized body to plan for religious literature to be distributed to the men in camps, and that in May, 1861, the second month of the war, it directed its Sunday school and publication board to proceed at once to provide and disperse through trained colporteurs the results of its efforts in that direction, so that Dr. Dickinson, the superintendent, reported at the end of one year: "We have collected $24,000, with which forty tracts have been published, 6,187,000 pages of which have been distributed, besides 6,095 Testaments, 13,845 copies of the little volume called 'Camp Hymns,' and a large number of religious books." Giving report in 1863, the superintendent said: "Modern history presents no example of armies so nearly converted into churches as the armies of Southern defense. On the crest of this flood of war which threatens to engulf our freedom rides a pure Christianity; the gospel of the grace of God shines through smoke of battle with the light that leads to heaven, and the camp becomes a school of Christ." It was but a short time, after what the Baptists thus started, until Episcopalians, Methodists, Presbyterians, Cumberland Presbyterians and other denominations were vigorously pursuing the same pious work, and many Union organizations and individuals did likewise. One earnest North Carolina preacher published and gave away, by the help of friends, more than 2,500,000 pages of tracts in less than a year, besides selling at cost about the same number. This kind of beneficent service greatly aided the systematic labors of the ministry of the gospel in all parts of the Confederacy, and as the mighty conflict of war deepened, most powerful and practical results followed in the conversion of many thousand soldiers to Christ as their Savior, among whom were hundreds of officers, from the rank of general down to that of corporal of the guard.

Let it here be recorded that an institution was established in accord with all these religious movements, which seems to have been a sort of culmination of the grand denominational and other enterprises for the promotion of morals, intelligence, good order and Christianity in the Confederacy. That was the organization or covenant known among all the army ministers as "The Army Church." In brief, it was agreed by men of different denominations that administration of sacraments and reception of men into the fellowship of the church would be recognized by all ministers as authoritative and acceptable. This had a fine effect, and promoted union and earnestness in the cause of religion.

In illustration of what is meant, on one occasion the Rev. W. Burr of Tennessee, a Methodist minister, held services and men were converted whom he received in communion of the churches, and afterward reported his work, part of which was to the writer of these lines, who, as a Cumberland Presbyterian minister, accepted the names given to him as if they came from a pastor of his own denomination. This course was pursued in a great many instances, and besides the benefit derived from influence exerted on the new converts, many other happy effects resulted from the work of the Army Church, among which may be mentioned that of the wide extension of the spirit of Christian charity and co-operation ever since the war. Many a brave soul lived to get home after the surrender, to report for duty in the warfare with sin and all wrong, having been equipped for it by his enlistment during the war in the South in the army of the King of Kings.

The following creed was adopted by one section of the Army Church, and it presents an excellent view of the existing conditions in spirit and comprehensive thought. It is copied from "The Army and Navy Herald," February 15, 1864:

Articles of Faith and Constitution of the Church of the Army, Trans-Mississippi:

The Christian men in the army, believing that the habitation of God by His spirit constitutes the Church, agree, for their edification and for the conversion of their fellowmen, to organize the Church of the Army, with the following articles of faith and constitution:

I. We believe the scriptures of the Old and New Testament to be the word of God, the only rule of faith and obedience.

II. We believe in one God: the Father, the Son, and the Holy Ghost, the same in substance, equal in power and glory.

III. We believe in the fall in Adam, the redemption by Christ, and the renewing of the Holy Spirit.

IV. We believe in justification by faith alone, and therefore receive and rest upon Christ as our only hope.

V. We believe in the communion of saints and the doctrine of eternal rewards and punishments.

The Christian men who have been baptized, adopting these articles of faith and constitution in each regiment, shall choose ten officers to take the spiritual oversight of the same. Of the officers so elected, the chaplain, or one chosen by themselves for that purpose, shall act as moderator. The officers will meet once a month and oftener, if necessary, and in the exercise of discipline will be guided by the directions of Christ. They will keep a record of the names of all the members and the manner in which their ecclesiastical connection with this Church is dissolved.

Some features of the religious state in the army were full of interest. Sunday-schools and Young Men's Christian Associations were organized and carried on with marked results in many regiments. The men took deep interest in the study of the Bible, and not only did chaplains and missionaries conduct the meetings, but many officers and privates acted as officers and teachers in the classes and services. Discussions of scripture truth became thoroughly interesting and full of instruction. This gave subjects of conversation for the camp, the bivouac, and the march, and without doubt suggested thought and comfort in the hour of pain and weakness as the result of battle. Sympathetic services of prayer were held in regiments, company by company, besides the regular public worship on Sundays for the whole regiment. Separate Bible classes of congenial spirits were formed and conducted. At least one instance is noted of an anti-swearing association formed, that in the Third battalion of Virginia reserves. The prevailing influence led to a large cessation of profanity, gambling, and even of card playing. It is not surprising that schools were held in which soldiers learned to read and write, but it is astonishing that men actually studied for the ministry of the gospel amid such scenes as the soldier's life daily presented. This occurred both in camp and in prison. It was a grand thing to witness the lives of such men as Lieut.-Gen. A. P. Stewart of Tennessee, and Brigadier-General Lowrey of Mississippi, whose religion was so practical that they not only lived worthily, but the former, as an elder in his church, assisted the ministers in conducting communion services, distributing the sacramental elements, leading in prayer, addressing the men in exhortation, etc., and the latter, as a minister himself, preached to his men, instructed inquirers, baptized believers, and gave all practicable aid to his chaplains and their work. These are only examples of the conduct of leaders.

It was always an important occasion when the army went into winter quarters, for then there was every opportunity for much religious work. Those of us who participated in it can never forget the excellent spirit which prompted the general and regimental officers to make details of men to fell, saw up, hew and adapt trees, rive boards, prepare timbers as needed, and build churches and chapels for regimental and brigade worship. Large shelters on posts and beams, open all around, were provided in places for brigade services, where in good weather great audiences gathered, and where series of meetings were held in which thousands were converted to Christ. In the summer of 1863, while the army of Tennessee under General Bragg was resting and recruiting along the base of Missionary ridge near Chattanooga, Wright's brigade of Tennesseeans made a large brush arbor, where the three chaplains in that command, Rev. W. H. Browning, Tilman Page and the present writer, held a series of meetings for five weeks, in which we estimated that 225 men became Christians, and we quit the work to enter upon the famous campaign which culminated in the great battle of Chickamauga. There is no doubt that scores of those converts fell in that awful conflict, heroically illustrating two grand principles—patriotism and piety. Similar Christian service was done throughout the army, and the effect of it was most powerful, both in the support it gave to fidelity to the flag of their country in all the perils of war to its close, and the courage it imparted to their tried souls in the stern, dark days which followed the final surrender of our arms, and through which Confederate soldiers, as citizens of the United States, having returned to peaceful pursuits of life at home, exemplified the power of Christian principle and the honor of exalted manhood. Looking backward over the thirty-three years of post-bellum history, there is no reason to be ashamed of the patriotism and piety of the Confederate soldier-citizen.

As the present history emphasizes the part which Tennessee bore in the great scenes of the civil war, it is important to give some definite view of the service rendered to her 115,000 soldiers by the churches of Christ through their ministry. All the best enterprises carried forward for the army's good were promotive of the welfare of Tennesseeans in common with others; but the specific work of preaching and holding many and manifold services was done by Tennessee chaplains and missionaries with earnestness and constancy to the day of surrender. The following list of names is given in the alphabetical order of churches as far as is known to the writer. Earnest efforts to procure a fuller list have failed of signal results. Sincere thanks are extended to Rev. J. H. McNeilly, D. D., and Rev. S. M. Cherry, of Nashville, for special favors. There may be errors in initials and church relations in the appended list, and it is not supposed to represent all, or nearly all, the religious influence exerted on the soldiers of the army of the Confederate States from Tennessee, but the names given are those of men who gave themselves fully to the cause of Christ for our men in the awful conflict. Some names are added which represent great religious benefits to the soldiers because of the character of the men who bore them in the military service of the Confederacy, although they were ministers. Of course, it is impracticable to estimate the value of Christian men in the army who were not preachers, because of its general effects, as there were many of those good men, officers and privates. Would that a complete roster of our chaplains and missionaries could be had.

CHAPLAINS AND MISSIONARIES.

Baptist—W. T. Bennett, Twelfth Tennessee; C. S. Hearn, Fifth Tennessee; L. H. Milliken, Thirteenth Tennessee, chaplains. R. W. Horton, Nineteenth Tennessee; W. H. Whitsett, Fourth Tennessee cavalry, now one of the most eminent men in the church.

Cumberland Presbyterian—B. W. McDonald, missionary, army of Tennessee; Aaron Burrow, Forrest's old regiment cavalry; J. W. Poindexter, Sixteenth Tennessee; E. B. Crisman, Seventeenth Tennessee; David Tucker, Eighth Tennessee; M. B. DeWitt, Eighth Tennessee; G. L. Winchester, L. Dickey, W. W. Hendrix (commands not known); B. M. Taylor, Twenty-third Tennessee.

Methodist Episcopal South—J. B. McFerrin, missionary, army of Tennessee; S. M. Cherry, chaplain and missionary, army of Tennessee; A. Tribble, Fourth Tennessee; F. E. Pitts, Eleventh Tennessee; J. A. Ellis, Twentieth Tennessee; R. P. Ransom, Sixteenth Tennessee, W. Burr, Twenty-eighth Tennessee; T. Page, Fifty-first Tennessee; W. H. Browning, Carter's brigade; A. W. Smith, Twenty-fifth Tennessee; J. Cross, W. Mooney, J. P. McFerrin, J. W. Johnson, R. A. Wilson, F. A. Kimball, F. S. Petway, M. L. Whitten, P. G. Jamison, J. G. Bolton, J. W. Cullom (commands not known).

Presbyterian—J. H. Bryson, missionary, army of Tennessee; W. Eagleton, R. McCoy and R. Lapsley, chaplains to hospitals; J. B. Chapman, Thirty-second Tennessee; J. H. McNeilly, Forty-ninth Tennessee; J. B. Mack, Fifty-fifth Tennessee; H. B. Bonde, captain and chaplain.

Protestant Episcopal—C. T. Quintard, First Tennessee, and missionary, army of Tennessee, and Rev. Mr. Schrevar (command not known).

MINISTERS AS OFFICERS.

(Very imperfect list.) Col. D. C. Kelley, Methodist; Col. W. M. Reed, Cumberland Presbyterian; Lieut.-Col. J. W. Bachman, Presbyterian; Maj. J. D. Kirkpatrick, Cumberland Presbyterian; Adjt. W. L. Rosser, Presbyterian; Capt. W. A. Haynes, Cumberland Presbyterian. There was, it is thought, a Colonel Miller, Baptist, and many others not now remembered. These may be taken as examples.

BIOGRAPHICAL.

BIOGRAPHICAL.

Brigadier-General John Adams, a gallant soldier was born at Nashville, July 1, 1825. His father afterward located at Pulaski, and it was from that place that young Adams entered West Point as a cadet, where he was graduated in June, 1846. On his graduation he was commissioned second lieutenant of the First Dragoons, then serving under Gen. Philip Kearny. At Santa Cruz de Rosales, Mexico, March 16, 1848, he was brevetted first lieutenant for gallantry, and on October 9, 1851, he was commissioned first lieutenant. In 1853 he acted as aide to the governor of Minnesota with the rank of lieutenant-colonel of State forces, this position, however, not affecting his rank in the regular service. He was promoted in his regiment to the rank of captain, November, 1856. May 27, 1861, on the secession of his State, he resigned his commission in the United States army and tendered his services to the Southern Confederacy. He was first made captain of cavalry and placed in command of the post at Memphis, whence he was ordered to western Kentucky and thence to Jackson, Miss. In 1862 he was commissioned colonel, and on December 29th was promoted to brigadier-general. On the death of Brig.-Gen. Lloyd Tilghman, May 16, 1863, Adams was placed by General Johnston in command of that officer's brigade, comprising the Sixth, Fourteenth, Fifteenth, Twentieth, Twenty-third and Forty-third Mississippi regiments of infantry. He was in Gen. J. E. Johnston's campaign for the relief of Vicksburg, in the fighting around Jackson, Miss., and afterward served under Polk in that State and marched with that general from Meridian, Miss., to Demopolis, Ala., thence to Rome, Ga., and forward to Resaca, where he joined the army of Tennessee. He served with distinction in the various battles of the campaign from Dalton to Atlanta, he and his gallant brigade winning fresh laurels in the fierce battles around the "Gate City." After the fall of Atlanta, when Hood set out from Palmetto for his march into north Georgia in the gallant effort to force Sherman to return northward, Adams' brigade was much of the time in advance, doing splendid service, and at Dalton capturing many prisoners. It was the fate of General Adams, as it was of his friend and classmate at West Point, Gen. Geo. E. Pickett, to reach the height of his fame leading his men in a brilliant and desperate, but unsuccessful, charge. But he did not come off so well as Pickett; for in the terrific assault at Franklin, Adams lost his life. Though wounded severely in his right arm near the shoulder early in the fight and urged to leave the field, he said: "No; I am going to see my men through." He fell on the enemy's works, pierced with nine bullets His brigade lost on that day over 450 in killed and wounded, among them many field and line officers. Lieut.-Col. Edward Adams Baker, of the Sixty-fifth Indiana infantry, who witnessed the death of General Adams at Franklin, obtained the address of Mrs. Adams many years after the war and wrote to her from Webb City, Mo. This letter appeared in the Confederate Veteran of June, 1897, an excellent magazine of information on Confederate affairs, and is here quoted: "General Adams rode up to our works and, cheering his men, made an attempt to leap his horse over them. The horse fell upon the top of the embankment and the general was caught under him, pierced with bullets. As soon as the charge was repulsed, our men sprang over the works and lifted the horse, while others dragged the general from under him. He was perfectly conscious and knew his fate. He asked for water, as all dying men do in battle as the life-blood drips from the body. One of my men gave him a canteen of water, while another brought an armful of cotton from an old gin near by and made him a pillow. The general gallantly thanked them, and in answer to our expressions of sorrow at his sad fate, he said, 'It is the fate of a soldier to die for his country,' and expired." The wife of General Adams was Miss Georgia McDougal, daughter of a distinguished surgeon of the United States army. She was in every way worthy to be the wife of so gallant a man. Though left a widow with four sons and two daughters, she reared them, under all the severe trials of that sad period, to be useful men and women.

Brigadier-General Samuel R. Anderson, of Nashville, when Tennessee began to make ready for war, was made major-general in the army of the State, May 9, 1861, and upon the transfer of the troops to the Confederate government he accepted the position of brigadier-general in the provisional army of the Confederate States, being commissioned July 9, 1861. He commanded a splendid brigade, consisting of the First, Seventh and Fourteenth Tennessee infantry and one company of Tennessee cavalry. This brigade was assigned to the division of General Loring in West Virginia during the summer and fall of 1861. One of his colonels, George Maney of the First Tennessee, after serving with distinction in Virginia was transferred to the western field of operations, and as brigadier-general did valiant work in the army of Tennessee, from Shiloh to the close of the Atlanta campaign. Another colonel, Robert Hatton of the Seventh Tennessee, also became a brigadier-general, succeeding Anderson in brigade command, and was killed at the battle of Seven Pines. General Anderson commanded his brigade during the movements in western Virginia from August to November, 1861; and from December, 1861, to March, 1862, under the renowned Stonewall Jackson. In August, 1861, Gen. Robert E. Lee was sent to command in West Virginia. He went to work with great vigor to get his army ready for an offensive campaign. But heavy rains set in, which in that mountainous region soon rendered roads impassable. All sorts of camp diseases, such as measles, typhoid and intermittent fever, broke out and prostrated at least one-third of the soldiers. Camp and picket duty bore heavily on those who were well. But the Federal army was enduring the same hardships and had no advantage over the Confederates in that respect. So Lee ordered Loring's troops from Huntersville and Henry R. Jackson's brigade from Greenbrier river to assail the Federal garrison on Cheat mountain. The battle, however, did not come off, on account of the failure of Colonel Rust to open the fight at the time intended. The fall passed away in the routine duties of guard and picket service, marching and countermarching. In the winter, Anderson was called upon to join the forces of Stonewall Jackson near Winchester, and he participated in the campaign to Hancock, Bath and Romney. Subsequently he commanded the brigade on the Peninsula under General Magruder, until in March he withdrew from active service and soon afterward resigned his commission, but continued to labor in other capacities for the success of the cause. His brigade gained fame under the leadership of General Archer. On November 4, 1864, he was recommissioned brigadier-general.

Brigadier-General Frank C. Armstrong, in 1854, accompanied his stepfather, Gen. Persifer Smith, upon an expedition of United States troops into New Mexico. He was then a handsome youth of twenty years, six feet tall, straight as an arrow, and the ideal of a daring young cavalryman. As the party were nearing Eagle Spring a detachment was made under John G. Walker to punish some Indian marauders, and Armstrong was so distinguished in the fight which resulted that he was reported to the war department, and got a lieutenancy of cavalry without the ordinary four years of preparation at West Point. With-

Brig.-Gen. GEO. G. DIBRELL. Brig.-Gen. WM. H. CARROLL.
Brig.-Gen. TYREE H. BELL. Brig.-Gen. JOHN W. FRAZER. Brig.-Gen. SAM'L R. ANDERSON.
Brig.-Gen. FRANK C. ARMSTRONG. Brig -Gen. JOHN ADAMS. Brig.-Gen. A. E. JACKSON.
Maj.-Gen. JOHN CALVIN BROWN. Maj.-Gen. WM. B. BATE.

drawing from the United States service in 1861, he accompanied Col. James McIntosh in the march of his force from Arkansas into the Indian country, and participated in the battle of Chustenahlah, in the Cherokee nation, December 26, 1861, in which the power of the Union chief Hopoeithleyohola was broken, serving as a volunteer aide on the staff of Colonel McIntosh. He next, with the rank of lieutenant, became assistant adjutant-general on the staff of Gen. Ben McCulloch, his friend, Col. D. H. Maury, being adjutant-general on the staff of General Van Dorn, commanding. In the famous battle of Elkhorn Tavern, he was with McCulloch until the latter was killed, and afterward, with Lomax and Bradfute and other fellow staff officers, went to the assistance of General Van Dorn, who warmly commended their services in his official report. On March 17th, Van Dorn, in a communication to the war department, strongly urged the promotion of these experienced officers, declaring that if he could have substituted some of them for some of his highest commanders, he could have put the enemy to utter rout. After serving a time as adjutant-general of Steen's Missouri brigade, Armstrong was elected colonel of the Third Louisiana infantry. Van Dorn renewed his recommendation that he be promoted to brigadier-general, and after the army had crossed to the east of the Mississippi, Gen. Sterling Price, having the same appreciation of the ability of the gallant young officer, appointed Armstrong to the command of all the cavalry of the army of the West, giving him, with the consent of General Bragg, the rank of acting brigadier-general. His energy and ability were soon manifest in the organization and increased efficiency of his command. On July 17th, Bragg, about to move to Chattanooga from Tupelo, ordered General Armstrong to advance toward Decatur, Ala., to cover the transfer of the army. With portions of the squadrons and companies of Webb, Barteau, McCulloch, Hill, Sanders, Roddey and Newsom he attacked the enemy at Courtland, Ala., July 25th, and won a brilliant victory, taking 133 prisoners and gaining possession of the fertile Tennessee valley from Decatur to Tuscumbia. His continued successes brought him the warm congratulations of General Bragg. In August, 1862, he was sent with about 2,000 cavalry to make a demonstration in west Tennessee in co-operation with Bragg, and preparatory to Price's advance. He crossed the Hatchie river, passed between Jackson and Bolivar, destroyed bridges and trestles on the Memphis & Charleston railroad, drove the Federals into Bolivar, August 30th, and on his return defeated their infantry, cavalry and artillery at Britton's lane, near Denmark, capturing 213 prisoners and two pieces of artillery. Said General Price: "The highest praise should be awarded to General Armstrong for the prudence, discretion and good sense with which he conducted this expedition." His cavalry force, the regiments of Wirt Adams and Slemons, did gallant service during the fighting of Price's army at Iuka in September, and on October 3d, 4th and 5th at Corinth and the crossing of the Hatchie, covering the retreat as well as providing a bridge for the transportation of the army. General Maury writes that to Armstrong more than any other officer, Price's army owed its safe retreat from Iuka, and at Corinth, Armstrong found a safe retreat for Van Dorn's broken command. He was promoted to brigadier-general January 30, 1863. Under Van Dorn he was one of the brigade commanders in western Tennessee in March, 1863, and had a conspicuous part in the victory at Thompson's Station on March 25th. His brigade, under his command, captured the Federal garrison at Brentwood after a spirited fight. On April 10th he was in battle at Franklin, and on June 4th again attacked the Federal garrison there. In the organization of the cavalry corps of the army of Tennessee, following the Kentucky campaign, he commanded a brigade of Forrest's division, consisting of the Third Arkansas, Second Kentucky, First Tennessee,

McDonald's battalion and Brady's escort company. Upon the organization of a corps under Forrest, he was put in command of a cavalry division including his brigade and Dibrell's. He rendered important service after the evacuation of Chattanooga, attached to Polk's corps, and on September 20th participated in the battle of Chickamauga in command of his division fighting dismounted. "The charges made by Armstrong's brigade while fighting on foot," said General Forrest, "would be creditable to the best drilled infantry." In command of a division including the brigades of W. Y. C. Humes and C. H. Tyler, he was in the East Tennessee campaign with Longstreet during the winter of 1863-64, in frequent battle, and was commended for gallantry by Gens. Joseph Wheeler and W. T. Martin. Early in February, 1864, he obtained leave of absence from this field with authority to ask for transfer to the command of Gen. S. D. Lee. On March 5th he was ordered to report to Lieutenant-General Polk at Demopolis, Ala., and was soon under the orders of Lee, who named him as deserving of promotion to major-general and becoming his own successor in division command. On April 4th he was assigned to the Mississippi brigade of W. H. Jackson's division, consisting of the cavalry regiments of Pinson, Dillon, Starke and Ballentine, which was his command, with some temporary additions, until the close of the war. He accompanied Polk's army to Georgia and served with credit in the campaign from Resaca to Atlanta and Jonesboro (part of the time in command of Jackson's division), Hood's north Georgia campaign, the advance into Tennessee, the campaign against Murfreesboro, and was one of the leaders of the heroic rear guard under Forrest after the disaster at Nashville. During the early months of 1865 he continued in command of his brigade, and was ordered to Selma, Ala., March 23d, where he and his men participated in the gallant defense against the overwhelming forces of Gen. James H. Wilson, on April 2, 1865. At the last he was in command of the Mississippi division of cavalry, with headquarters at Macon.

Major-General William Brimage Bate was born near Castalian Springs, Tenn., in the year 1830. Early in his youth he manifested a bold and adventurous spirit that characterized his career as a Confederate soldier. Leaving school to become a clerk on a steamboat plying between Nashville and New Orleans, he subsequently enlisted for the Mexican war and served as a private in a Louisiana and a Tennessee regiment. On his return to Tennessee he was elected to the legislature by his admiring friends in his native county, and after this he began the study of law in the famous school at Lebanon. He was graduated professionally in 1852, and then made his home at Gallatin, the scene of his earlier efforts in the profession which has been honored by his intellectual ability and manly worth. In 1854 he was elected attorney-general of the Nashville district for a term of six years. That calm, masterful and judicious leadership for which his life has been distinguished was already manifested in the political field, and having declined congressional honors, his name was put upon the Breckinridge electoral ticket. In May, 1861, Tennessee began the official negotiations which promptly resulted in her league with the other Southern States for defense against the war being waged upon them, and Bate entered the military forces as a private. He was speedily promoted captain and then colonel of the Second Tennessee regiment, and during the early months of the conflict served at Columbus, Ky., and elsewhere, in the command of General Polk. His first great battle was at Shiloh, where he shared the work of Cleburne's brigade of Hardee's corps. Bravely leading his regiment in the second charge, through a murderous cross-fire, he fell severely wounded, a minie ball breaking his leg and disabling him for field service for several months. This participation in battle, though brief, was marked with such gallantry that he was mentioned with praise in the reports of Cleburne and Hardee, and on October 3, 1862, he was promoted brigadier-general. About this time, though still unable to return to the field, he was on garrison duty at Huntsville, Ala., and was given temporary command of the district of Tennessee. In February, 1863, he was again in the field, assigned to command of Rains' brigade in Polk's army, and in June, commanding the Ninth Alabama, Thirty-seventh Georgia, Fifteenth and Thirty-seventh and Twentieth Tennessee and Caswell's battalion, in the division of A. P. Stewart, he took part in the Tullahoma campaign with much credit, fighting the battle of Hoover's Gap on the 24th, driving the enemy back, and holding at bay the Federal advance. In this action he was in command of the Confederate forces, Stewart not arriving on the field until nightfall. According to Rosecrans' report, Bate delayed his army at this point thirty-six hours, preventing the Federals from getting possession of Bragg's communications and forcing him to disastrous battle. General Bate and his men took a prominent part in the fighting at Chickamauga. They fired the first gun in this historic struggle on "the river of death," driving the Federal guard from Thedford's ford, in preparation for the Confederate advance. Crossing the stream next morning, they went into action only a third armed, but drove the enemy back toward the position subsequently held with such heroism by Virginian George H. Thomas, the "Rock of Chickamauga." As a result of this first day's fight, the brigade was fully armed with Enfield rifles. About 11 o'clock Sunday morning, Stewart threw his division again upon the enemy, the brigade of Brown, "followed by the gallant Clayton and indomitable Bate," pressing on beyond the Chattanooga road and driving the enemy within his line of intrenchments. "During this charge, which was truly heroic," Stewart reported, "General Bate and several of his staff had their horses killed—the second lost by General Bate that morning." In the evening he again led his brigade in an action near Kelly's house, in an action of the division, routing the enemy and capturing many prisoners; and finally the Eufaula artillery, attached to his brigade, fired the last gun of the battle. At Missionary Ridge, commanding Breckinridge's division, he was first on duty in the trenches at the base of the ridge, and later held a position on the crest near the headquarters of General Bragg. Fighting in a position where the whole magnificent panorama of the overwhelming army advancing upon them was visible, his troops bravely held their ground until both their left and right were turned, and then with the personal aid of General Bragg, a second line was formed, which checked the headlong advance of the victorious Federals. General Bragg reported General Bate among those distinguished for coolness, gallantry and successful conduct through the engagements and in the rear guard on the retreat. He continued in division command, after this battle, of his own brigade, Lewis' Kentuckians and Finley's Floridians, and was commissioned major-general February 23, 1864. Throughout the Georgia campaign he commanded a division of Hardee's corps, so often and so bravely in action; at Resaca handsomely repulsed the enemy from his front; at Dallas vigorously assailed Logan's intrenched Fifteenth Federal corps with his single division; on July 22d led the flank movement under Hardee which brought on the famous "battle of Atlanta." In the ill-fated campaign under General Hood, which brought General Bate and his men back to their native State, but with circumstances of suffering and disaster, he led his division, now including Jackson's brigade, from Florence, Ala., November 21st; marched with Cheatham's corps to Spring Hill, where he was in readiness for orders to attack; fought heroically at Franklin, in the desperate assault many of his men gaining the interior works and remaining there until the Federal retreat; and after attacking Murfreesboro in co-operation with Forrest, marched his men, a fourth of them barefooted, over the icy roads to Nashville, where upon arrival he encountered stragglers already in rapid retreat, indicating the disaster that was impending. Even under such circumstances his troops bravely took position, intrenched as best they could in such weather, and made a gallant fight against the Federal assault. After the supporting troops were driven back, he rode along his advanced line, urging the men to hold fast, though under fire from three directions. His Tennesseeans at the "angle" were almost annihilated; two Georgia regiments fought until surrounded; all three brigade commanders were captured. The military service of General Bate was closed in the spring of 1865, with the capitulation of the army of Tennessee. During the four years he had been three times severely wounded, and had demonstrated in a remarkably brilliant way the ability of the American volunteer to rise to important command and win renown there as well as in the ranks. He resumed his legal practice, making Nashville his home. As he has eloquently said of the Confederate soldier in general, "He returned home from the fields of disaster, vanquished but not destroyed; sorrowful, but not without hope; . . . the irrepressible pride and indomitable pluck of Southern manhood were still with him," and General Bate speedily gained a lucrative practice and honorable fame in his profession, and a prominent place in political councils. In 1868 he was a delegate to the Democratic national convention; for twelve years he served on the State executive committee of his party; was presidential elector-at-large in 1876; and in 1882 and 1884 was elected governor of Tennessee. At the expiration of this service, which is remembered as capable and dignified, he was elected United States senator. To this position, in which he was one of the most able representatives of the South, he was re-elected in 1893. At the dedication of the Chickamauga and Chattanooga National

Park he was selected by the secretary of war to speak for the Confederates, and his words on that occasion are monumental in their strength and calmness, presenting in unassailable force the rectitude of the Confederate cause; while he pointed out that the "record of the heroic past, which, though written in the blood of civil war, yet was essentially American in all the glorious attributes of American citizenship," is to be cherished by a united people.

Brigadier-General Tyree H. Bell, one of the many gallant officers given by the Volunteer State to the Southern Confederacy, entered the service as captain in the Twelfth Tennessee infantry, June 4, 1861, and was elected lieutenant-colonel. His military duties during 1861 were with the army under Maj.-Gen. Leonidas Polk at Columbus, Ky. He commanded the regiment at the battle of Belmont, November 7, 1861, the colonel being that day in command of a brigade. At Shiloh he was again in command of his regiment, Col. R. M. Russell having charge of the First brigade, First division, army of Mississippi. Colonel Russell in his report of the operations of his brigade at Shiloh says: "Lieutenant-Colonel Bell and Maj. R. P. Caldwell were distinguished by their courage and energy. The former had two horses shot under him." In July, 1862, Bell was promoted to colonel of the Twelfth Tennessee and led it in the Kentucky campaign, participating in the battle of Richmond, Ky. Colonel Bell after this had a cavalry command operating in Tennessee and Kentucky. He was raiding in rear of the Union army during the Murfreesboro campaign, and at the time of the battle of Chickamauga, and afterward, was busy upon the flank and rear of the Federal troops. On the 25th of January, 1864, Major-General Forrest, who had assumed command of all the cavalry operating in north Mississippi, west Tennessee and Kentucky, placed Colonel Bell in command of a brigade in his division, consisting of the regiments of Russell, Greer, Newsom, Barteau and Wilson. General Forrest in his account of the battle of Fort Pillow says: "I cannot compliment too highly the conduct of Colonels Bell and McCulloch and the officers and men of their brigades which composed the forces of Brigadier-General Chalmers. They fought with courage and intrepidity, and without bayonets assaulted and carried one of the strongest fortifications in the country." In his report of the brilliant victory at Tishomingo creek, Forrest declares that General Buford "had abundant reason to be proud of his brigade commanders, Colonels Lyon and Bell, who displayed great gallantry during the day." Forrest again speaks in a complimentary manner of Bell at the battle of Harrisburg, in the Tupelo campaign, a battle in which, though repulsed, Forrest gained the substantial fruits of victory by breaking up the strongest of all the Federal expeditions into north Mississippi during 1864. Still later, Forrest made an expedition along the Tennessee river in October and November, 1864, in which he destroyed 4 gunboats, 14 transports, 20 barges, and over $6,700,000 of Federal property, besides capturing 26 pieces of artillery; and in this brilliant expedition Colonel Bell again won the praise of Forrest. He was soon afterward commissioned brigadier-general, and he continued to act with Forrest's command until the close of the war.

Major-General John Calvin Brown was born in Giles county, January 6, 1827. When nineteen years of age he was graduated at Jackson college, Tenn., and two years later was admitted to the bar at Pulaski. From that time (1848) until May, 1861, he practiced law successfully. He then entered the Third infantry regiment of the provisional army of Tennessee as captain, and on the 16th of May was commissioned colonel of that regiment, which, with the other soldiers of Tennessee, became a part of the provisional army of the Confederate States upon the accession of Tennessee to the Southern Confederacy. At the battle of Fort Donelson (February 14-16, 1862) we find Colonel Brown commanding the Third brigade of General Buckner's division, and acting a conspicuous part in the charge which opened the way for the retreat of the Confederate army to Nashville. The fact that the opportunity was not improved detracts nothing from the gallant achievement of the men who made that brilliant charge. When, on the 16th, the fort was surrendered, Colonel Brown became a prisoner of war and remained in the enemy's hands for six months. Shortly after his exchange he was commissioned as brigadier-general (August 30, 1862). He participated in the Kentucky campaign, and was wounded at the battle of Perryville, October 8, 1862; with his usual gallantry fought at Chickamauga, where he was again wounded, and recovered in time to act an heroic part at Missionary Ridge. In all the movements of the Dalton-Atlanta campaign he was distinguished, and on the 4th of August, 1864, he was commissioned major-general. In Hood's gallant but disastrous effort to retrieve the waning fortunes of the Confederacy by his Tennessee campaign, General Brown was again among the foremost, commanding Cheatham's division. In the fierce charge at Franklin, in which so many of the choicest spirits of the army of Tennessee laid down their lives, he was severely wounded. At the close of the war he resumed the practice of law at Pulaski, Tenn. He was a member of the constitutional convention which met at Nashville in 1870, and was elected president of that body. The next year he was elected governor of the State, being the first Democrat chosen to that position after the war. He was the second member of his family to be thus honored, his brother, Neil S. Brown, having been governor from 1847 to 1849. One of the leading issues of Governor Brown's administration was the State debt, which at the beginning of his term amounted to $43,000,000 bonded, besides a large floating debt. At the close of his administration in 1875 (he having served two terms), the bonded debt had been reduced to $20,000,000, the large floating debt had been paid, and the credit of the State had been fully re-established. After retiring from the executive office he engaged in various railroad enterprises, exhibiting marked ability in every position which he held. In 1864 he married Miss Bettie Childress, one of the most beautiful and cultured women of the South. Their elegant home was in Nashville. The death of General Brown occurred at Red Boiling Springs, Tenn., August 17, 1889.

Brigadier-General Alexander W. Campbell entered the Confederate army in 1861 as colonel of the Thirty-third Tennessee infantry, and served in the army of General Polk at Columbus, Ky., during the campaign of that year. There was one battle in his district, at Belmont, Mo., in which General Grant attacked the Confederates and was at first successful; but upon the arrival of Confederate reinforcements and the renewal of the battle, was defeated and with difficulty made his escape. In this battle Colonel Campbell and his regiment were not engaged, being in observation on the Kentucky side of the river. When the armies were being concentrated for the attack upon Grant at Shiloh, Colonel Campbell's regiment was part of the army that marched from central Kentucky, to Corinth, Miss. Colonel Campbell led his regiment at the battle of Shiloh, and at one time during the fight the Fifth Tennessee, Col. C. D. Venable, was also under his orders. Gen. Leonidas Polk, in his report of this battle, mentions as one of several other instances of "brilliant courage," the conduct of these two regiments. The report says: "Shortly after they were first brought forward as a supporting force, they found themselves ordered to support two regiments of the line before them, which were lying down, engaging the enemy irregularly. On advancing, they drew the enemy's fire over the heads of the regiments in their front. It was of so fierce a character that they must either advance or fall back. Campbell called to the regiments before him to charge. This they declined to do. He then gave orders to his own regiment to charge, and led them in gallant style over the heads of the regiments lying in advance of him, sweeping the enemy before him and putting them completely to rout." In this battle Colonel Campbell received a wound which incapacitated him for active service for several months. Just before the battle of Murfreesboro he was appointed adjutant and inspector-general on the staff of Gen. Leonidas Polk. This position he held during 1862 and 1863. On the 15th of March, 1864, he was commissioned brigadier-general, and in this rank he commanded a cavalry force during the remainder of the war.

Brigadier-General William H. Carroll was born in the year 1820. When Tennessee decided to cast her fortunes with the Confederate States, he was appointed a brigadier-general in the provisional army of the State of Tennessee. He assisted in the organization of the splendid bodies of troops which Tennessee turned over to the authorities at Richmond. On the 21st of October, 1861, he was commissioned a brigadier-general in the army of the Confederate States. His brigade was assigned to the army under Albert Sidney Johnston, and was for a time on duty at Memphis. General Johnston, becoming apprehensive about affairs in east Tennessee, ordered Carroll to that section of the State. The Unionists had risen in scattered bands and threatened to give much trouble, but on the approach of armed men under Carroll these bands dispersed. On December 11, 1861, he issued the following proclamation: "The exigencies of the times requiring, as is believed, the adoption of the sternest measures of military policy, the commanding general feels called upon to suspend for a time the functions of the civil tribunals. Now, therefore, be it known that I, William H. Carroll, brigadier-general in the Confederate army and commander of the post at Knoxville, do hereby proclaim martial law to exist in the city of Knoxville and the surrounding country to the distance of one mile from the corporate limits of said city." General Carroll showed great vigor in arresting all parties that were openly disaffected to the Confederate States. As soon as he felt assured that he could safely do so, he revoked the proclamation of martial law and restored the civil authority. His brigade was part of the force with which General Crittenden made an attack on General Thomas not far from Mill Spring, Ky., January, 1862, and in the report of the affair by Crittenden, General Carroll was commended for "his dispositions and conduct during the engagement," his "military skill and personal valor." Carroll's brigade brought up the rear on the retreat and retired from the field in order. On February 1, 1863, General Carroll resigned his commission in the Confederate army.

Brigadier-General John C. Carter entered the Confederate service in 1861 as a captain in the Thirty-eighth Tennessee infantry. He was still a captain at the battle of Shiloh, where he won the praise of Col. R. F. Looney, commander of his regiment, who declared that "Captain Carter deserved the highest praise for his great coolness and high courage displayed throughout the entire engagement. At one time he took the flag, and urging his men forward, rendered me great assistance in advancing the entire regiment." His promotion was rapid through the grades of major and lieutenant-colonel to that of colonel of the regiment. He had reached this latter position when, at the battle of Perryville, he commanded his regiment in one of the hottest fights of the war. Here he won fresh plaudits for his gallant bearing in the presence of the enemy. His brigade was led in this battle by Col. John H. Savage, and the division by Brig.-Gen. Daniel S. Donelson, of the right wing under Major-General Cheatham. At the battle of Murfreesboro, Donelson's brigade still formed a part of Cheatham's division, which took an active part in the grand charge which drove the Federal right a distance of between three and four miles, capturing many prisoners, cannon, small-arms, wagons and other spoils of victory. In this brilliant attack Colonel Carter again led his regiment with his accustomed skill and courage. At Chickamauga, Colonel Carter commanded his regiment in Wright's brigade. At the time of the battle of Missionary Ridge he was with his regiment at Charleston, Tenn. He succeeded Gen. Marcus J. Wright in command of his Tennessee brigade, and after leading it for some time as colonel in the Atlanta campaign, he was promoted to brigadier-general with temporary rank, July 7, 1864. At Jonesboro, September 1st, he was in temporary command of Cheatham's division. He led his brigade in Brown's division at Franklin, November 30, 1864, up to the enemy's works, but fell mortally wounded in the charge, and gave up his life for the cause so dear to his heart.

General Benjamin Franklin Cheatham.—There was no name in the army of Tennessee more familiar to the soldiers than that of Cheatham, and no officer of the Confederate army possessed to a higher degree than he the affectionate regard of his men. He was born in the city of Nashville, October 20, 1820. He was captain of volunteers in the Mexican war, and was distinguished in its severest battles. On the outbreak of the war between the States he espoused heartily the cause of the South and was appointed major-general in the provisional army of Tennessee, May 9, 1861. On July 9th of the same year he was made a brigadier-general in the provisional army of the Confederate States. From the very first, General Cheatham gained the reputation of being a brilliant fighter. He understood well the art of managing men. He was careful in looking after their comfort, and when it was proper to do so, carefully guarded their safety. But when duty required it, he was ready to face any peril and set before his soldiers an example of valor which they followed with alacrity and zeal. It is praise enough for his command to say that it was the equal of that led by the renowned Pat Cleburne. He was in many fierce battles and always bore a conspicuous part. In the battle of Belmont he led three regiments of Pillow's force, and it was his movement to the enemy's rear that won the day. He was commissioned major-general March 10, 1862, and we find him on the field of Shiloh commanding the second division of the first corps under Leonidas Polk. At Perryville, Ky., it was Cheatham's division that opened the fight, and throughout that hotly-contested battle pressed steadily forward. Again at Murfreesboro Cheatham's was one of the four divisions which drove the Federals back a distance of between three and four miles, doubling them back upon their center until their line was at right angles to its original position. At Chickamauga we find Cheatham's division attached to the right wing under Leonidas Polk, sustaining the reputation gained on so many former occasions. At the battle of Missionary Ridge, when the Confederate left center had been broken, Hardee threw a part of Cheatham's division directly across the path of the advancing Federals and held the ground until darkness closed the fight. In all the movements of the army of Tennessee in 1864, Cheatham and his men had their full share of peril and of honor. At the battle of Kenesaw Mountain (June 27th), Cheatham's and Cleburne's divisions probably inflicted upon the Federals a heavier loss than they suffered on any other part of the field. In the battles around Atlanta, Cheatham had command of a corps, and in the battle of July 22d, his men captured five cannon and five stand of colors. In Hood's final campaign he led his corps into the thickest of every fight. At the close of the war, Cheatham returned to the pursuits of peace, blessed with the society of his neighbors, whose esteem and friendship he always enjoyed, surrounded by a lovely family and cheered by his noble wife. General Cheatham's personal appearance was thus described a few years after the war by the historian, E. A. Pollard: "General Cheatham is squarely and firmly built, and is noted for his extraordinary physical strength. He is slightly round-shouldered, and his weight is about two hundred pounds. His height is about five feet eight inches; his eyes are light blue, clear and expressive; his hair, light brown; his complexion, fair; and his moustache—he wears no other beard—very heavy. His forehead is broad and his face expressive of that imperturbable good humor which characterizes him not more in social life than on the battle-field." General Grant, who was a personal friend of his, offered him an appointment in the civil service, but he declined. He served four years as superintendent of the State prison. In 1885 he became postmaster at Nashville, a position he retained until his death, September 4, 1886. The love and esteem in which he was held were evidenced by the vast attendance upon his funeral, which was declared at the time to be the most imposing ever held in Nashville.

Brigadier-General Henry B. Davidson, a true son of the Volunteer State, received his appointment at the United States military academy as a reward for gallant services as a sergeant of Tennessee volunteers at the battle of Monterey, Mexico, September 21 to 23, 1846. He was graduated at West Point in 1853, and promoted to brevet second lieutenant of dragoons. He served at the cavalry school for practice, in garrison duty at Jefferson barracks, Mo.; on scouting duty at Fort Union and Albuquerque; was engaged with Apache Indians in a skirmish on Penasco river, New Mexico, January 18, 1855, and again with hostile Indians in Oregon, March 27, 1856; in the combat of the Four Lakes on September

Brig.-Gen. J. E. Rains.
Brig.-Gen. George Maney.
Maj.-Gen. Bushrod R. Johnson.

Maj.-Gen. J. P. McCown.
Brig.-Gen. R. C. Tyler.
Brig.-Gen. W. McComb.

Brig.-Gen. T. B. Smith.
Brig.-Gen. Wm. A. Quarles.
Brig.-Gen. A. J. Vaughan.

1st; on the Spokane plains, September 5th, and on Spokane river, September 8, 1858. He was quartermaster of First dragoons from December 5, 1858, to May 13, 1861. Being on leave of absence when the Confederate war began, he resigned his commission as captain in the United States army and entered the service of the Confederate States, actuated by a sense of duty to his native State, whose command he felt bound to obey. Reporting to the Richmond government, he was assigned in 1862 to the command of the post at Staunton, Va., with the rank of colonel. In August, 1863, he was commissioned brigadier-general, and early in 1864 he was at Rome, Ga., in command of a cavalry brigade belonging to Wheeler's corps. On the 17th of May, as the enemy was approaching Rome, Ector's brigade of French's division, supported by the cavalry of Ross, Morgan and Davidson, had quite a spirited affair, in which Davidson attacked the enemy on the right, driving in their skirmishers. General Davidson did not long remain in Georgia, but was sent back to Virginia and assigned to the command of a brigade of cavalry attached to the division of General Lomax, operating in the valley under General Early. This brigade consisted of the First Maryland and the Nineteenth, Twentieth, Forty-sixth and Forty-seventh Virginia battalions of cavalry. After the war, General Davidson moved to the city of New Orleans, of which he was deputy sheriff, 1866 and 1867. From 1878 to 1886 he was inspector of United States public works at San Pedro, Cal. In 1887 he was appointed deputy secretary of state of California.

Brigadier-General George Gibbs Dibrell was born in White county, Tenn., April 12, 1822. After receiving a common school education, which was supplemented by one year at the East Tennessee university, he engaged for a while in farming and then in mercantile pursuits. In 1861 he was elected to the Tennessee convention as a

Union delegate. But when his native State at last decided on secession, like most of those who held similar views, he obeyed the voice of the majority and was among the first to enlist under the banner of the new Confederacy. He entered the service as a private, but was elected lieutenant-colonel of his regiment, receiving his commission as such, August 10, 1861. In September of the same year he was commissioned colonel of partisan rangers. In the reports of the movements of Forrest's command, we find Colonel Dibrell's name favorably mentioned on many occasions. In one of many brilliant affairs in which Dibrell's regiment participated, Col. R. G. Ingersoll is mentioned as one of the captives. In March, 1863, General Bragg requested Forrest to send a force to defend the manufacturing establishments at Tuscumbia and Florence, Ala., against Federal raiders. Colonel Dibrell's command was detached for this purpose, and on March 25th, near Florence, he defeated two Union gunboats and a body of raiders. During the summer campaign of 1863, when Rosecrans was trying to maneuver Bragg out of Tennessee, Forrest sent Dibrell to reinforce Wheeler. Near Sparta, Tenn., they had a fierce fight with the enemy, which, after varied fortune, was finally decided in favor of the Confederates, who chased their opponents for several miles and then returned to camp. They found to their delight that the ladies of Sparta had cooked and sent to the camp a fine breakfast for the entire command. On the 26th of July, 1864, Colonel Dibrell received well-merited promotion and was commissioned brigadier-general of cavalry. He continued to sustain his high reputation in the campaigns of Forrest and afterward of Wheeler. Toward the close of the war he served in North Carolina. After the fall of Richmond and the surrender of Lee's army he had charge for a while of the Confederate archives. After the long agony of war had ended he returned to his native State. In 1870 he served in the Tennessee constitutional convention. He was twice elected to Congress, and served from 1875 to 1879. At Sparta, Tenn., in September, 1883, General Dibrell's old cavalry command organized a brotherhood, officered with members of his old regiment, the Eighth Tennessee. At their second meeting, held at Gainesboro in 1884, the following commands were added to the organization: The Eighth, Sixteenth, Seventeenth, Twenty-fifth, Twenty-eighth and Thirty-fifth Tennessee infantry and Colms' battalion, Hamilton's, Bledsoe's and Bennett's battalions of cavalry. General Dibrell commanded this "reunion brigade" up to his death in 1886, and never failed to attend its meetings.

Major-General Daniel S. Donelson was born in Tennessee in 1802. He entered the United States military academy in 1821, and four years later was graduated and promoted to second lieutenant of the Third artillery. He resigned January 22, 1826. From 1827 to 1829 he was brigade major of the Tennessee militia, and brigadier-general from 1829 to 1834. From 1841 to 1843 he was a member of the house of representatives of the State of Tennessee, and again from 1855 to 1861, being speaker of the house. He was a planter in Sumter county, 1826 to 1834, and in Florida Territory, 1834 to 1836, then returning to Tennessee and continuing planting until 1861. When Tennessee resolved to secede from the Union he offered his services, and in May, 1861, was made a brigadier-general of the State forces. On July 9th he was commissioned in the same rank in the army of the Confederate States. He commanded a brigade in West Virginia under General Loring in 1861, and at the beginning of 1862 was sent to Charleston, S. C. He was ordered to the western army under Bragg, at Tupelo, and there had command of the First brigade of the Second division of the First army corps. At the battle of Murfreesboro he commanded the First brigade of Cheatham's division and was in the celebrated charge which broke to pieces the whole right wing of the Federal army. On January 17, 1863, he was assigned to command of the department of East Tennessee, and was succeeded in brigade command by Gen. M. J. Wright. In the important region of which he was given charge as the successor of Gen. E. Kirby Smith, he had under his orders the brigades of General Gracie, Colonel Palmer, Gen. A. E. Jackson, Gen. John Pegram, Gen. Humphrey Marshall, and scattered organizations. General Donelson was promoted to major-general while in command of this department, but soon afterward he died at Knoxville, April 17, 1863. In general orders, April 24th, General Bragg said: "The general commanding announces to the army the death of Brig.-Gen. D. S. Donelson. He died in the department of East Tennessee, which he had commanded. The regret with which his death is announced will be felt by the army and his country. He was an educated soldier, of great purity of character, singleness of purpose, and goodness of heart. Conspicuous for gallantry on the field, after the excitement had passed he was foremost in providing for the wants of his command, and devoted to the sick and wounded. His comrades in this army, and those who served under his orders, will long remember his deeds and virtues."

Brigadier-General John W. Frazer was a native of Tennessee, and was appointed to the United States military academy from Mississippi. At his graduation in 1849 he was promoted to brevet second lieutenant. He served in garrison at Fort Columbus, N. Y.; on frontier duty at San Miguel, Cal., and at Bernicia and Camp Far West in the same State; in garrison at Fort Monroe, Va., and on recruiting service until 1857; and then as captain, Ninth infantry, at Fort Simcoe and Fort Colville, Washington. He resigned his commission March 15, 1861, and entered the Confederate service with the rank in the regular army of captain of infantry. When the Eighth

Alabama was organized, Captain Frazer was appointed by the war department, lieutenant-colonel. After serving with this regiment a while, he resigned to take the position of colonel of the Twenty-eighth Alabama. This regiment reached Corinth, Miss., after the battle of Shiloh; was first under fire in a skirmish at Corinth; was with Bragg in the Kentucky campaign, and under the command of Colonel Frazer was slightly engaged at Munfordville, Ky. Subsequently he resigned, and on May 19, 1863, was commissioned brigadier-general and sent into east Tennessee, where his command consisted of the Fifty-fifth Georgia, Sixty-second and Sixty-fourth North Carolina, and Rains' battery. He had charge of Cumberland Gap in September, when the Union army under Burnside approached that post. General Frazer, finding that Knoxville had been occupied by the Union forces and that General Buckner had been obliged to retreat toward Chattanooga, knowing that the force of the enemy was greatly superior, surrendered to General Burnside on September 9, 1863. He was at first somewhat censured, but when all the facts were made known was exonerated. After the war he became a merchant and planter in Memphis.

Brigadier-General George W. Gordon, one of the youngest of the Confederate general officers, was born in Giles county, Tenn. He was graduated at the Western military institute at Nashville in 1859. At the outbreak of the civil war he entered the service of his native State as drill-master for the Eleventh Tennessee infantry, which with other troops was soon after turned over to the Confederate authorities. He was successively made captain, then lieutenant-colonel, and finally colonel of this regiment (December, 1862). While serving in east Tennessee in the summer of 1862 he was captured at Tazewell, but being soon exchanged he participated in the Kentucky campaign. Just after receiving his commission as colonel he led his men in the fierce battle of Murfreesboro. In this engagement he was again captured, but was back with his command at the battles of Chickamauga and Missionary Ridge, winning fresh laurels on these famous fields. In Cheatham's division during the arduous Dalton-Atlanta campaign, he and his men sustained their reputation for valor and efficiency, and on August 15, 1864, he was commissioned brigadier-general, succeeding A. J. Vaughan. He commanded his brigade at Jonesboro, and in the fearful battle at Franklin on the afternoon of November 30, 1864, in which fell the flower of the army of Tennessee, Gordon led his brigade in an impetuous charge upon the Federal works, he and his men being the first to reach the parapet and pierce the enemy's lines. But such masses of Federals were poured upon them at this point that they were forced back over the parapet, Gordon and some of his men having held on so stoutly as to be captured by the enemy within their lines. He remained a prisoner of war until August, 1865, and was then released on parole. Returning home, General Gordon took up the practice of law. In 1883 he was appointed one of the railroad commissioners of Tennessee. In 1885 he was appointed to a position in the interior department of the United States government, and served four years among the western Indians. In 1892 he became superintendent of the public schools of the city of Memphis.

Brigadier-General Robert Hatton.—The civil war developed the fact that many men who have never known any but peaceful pursuits are fitted, when occasion demands, to become leaders of men, and to show upon the battlefield those talents which belong to the trained soldier. Some of the most prominent and successful soldiers developed by the war were civilians who, until the outbreak of that tremendous struggle, never had dreamed of their own talent for military affairs. One of these citizen-soldiers was Robert Hatton of Tennessee, who was born in Sumter county in 1827. He received his education at Harvard, then studied law, and was admitted to the bar in 1849. A gentleman of high culture and social standing, his success in his profession was steady and rapid. He was elected a member of the Tennessee house of representatives in 1856, and two years later was elected to the Congress of the United States. When the long sectional quarrel flamed out at last into civil war, he ranged himself with his native State on the side of the South. He joined the Confederate army and was made colonel of the Seventh Tennessee. In July, 1861, his regiment was ordered with other commands to Staunton, Va., where we find him on the 28th of that month. It was just after the great victory of the First Manassas, when the whole South was wild with joy over its wonderful triumph, and the ambition of every Southern soldier was to join the victorious army led by Joe Johnston and Beauregard and move at once upon Washington. But affairs had not gone well in West Virginia, and an effort was to be made to recover what had been lost in that region. Hatton's regiment was assigned to S. R. Anderson's brigade and placed under Loring's command in West Virginia. There they participated in the Cheat Mountain campaign, prolific in marches and hardships, making a splendid training school for new soldiers. Though the scheme for bringing on a great and decisive battle at Cheat mountain miscarried, there was just enough of danger connected with operations in that quarter to give the men a taste of soldier life. When toward the last of December, Loring's command, marching back across the mountains and through the Shenandoah valley, joined Stonewall Jackson at Winchester, they had additional lessons in the duties of a soldier. The winter campaign of Jackson to Bath, Hancock and Romney, in January, involved as much genuine hardship as any of the whole war, and but for the interference of the war department, Jackson always claimed, would have been productive of permanent good to the Confederacy. The Seventh regiment was next ordered to the army under Gen. Joseph E. Johnston. On May 21, 1862, Colonel Hatton was commissioned brigadier-general. Ten days later, on the field of Seven Pines, in command of the First, Seventh and Fourteenth Tennessee, afterward Archer's brigade, he met a soldier's death while leading his brigade into the spirited fight by the forces under Gen. G. W. Smith, in which Gen. J. J. Pettigrew was wounded and captured, and Wade Hampton seriously wounded. General Smith said in his report: "The personal bearing and conduct of the lamented General Hatton upon the field were gallant, noble and true to his high social and official character. He fell while bravely and skillfully leading his brigade in the extreme front of the battle."

Brigadier-General Benjamin J. Hill was commissioned colonel of the Thirty-fifth Tennessee upon its organization in September, 1861. During the first four months this regiment had very little hard service, but with the spring of 1862 came the stern realities of war with all its horrors. The regiment, now known as the Fifth Tennessee, was in Gen. Pat Cleburne's brigade at the battle of Shiloh, and when Cleburne was in the presence of the enemy there was sure to be sharp work. In this battle, Hill commanded for a time the left of Cleburne's brigade and several other regiments, and was highly commended for his gallantry. During the Kentucky campaign of 1862 Cleburne commanded a division, and at the battle of Richmond, Ky., Colonel Hill commanded Cleburne's brigade to the complete satisfaction of that officer, which is praise enough. This was the first brigade to strike the enemy at Richmond, and from the first volley until the close of that victorious day its progress was onward. At Murfreesboro, Colonel Hill, again in command of his regiment, Lucius Polk commanding the brigade, was with Cleburne's division in the very hottest part of the battle. At Chickamauga the gallant colonel won from Lieut.-Gen. D. H. Hill the following tribute: "The extraordinary merit of Colonel Hill of the Thirty-fifth Tennessee came under my personal observation. This noble officer has been distinguished on many a hard-fought field, and has been content with a subordinate position, provided he can serve his country." At Missionary Ridge, Cleburne's division not only held its ground, but charged the enemy and captured prisoners and colors. In this battle, Colonel Hill commanded the Thirty-fifth and Forty-eighth Tennessee regiments. During part of 1863 and 1864 he was general provost-marshal of the army of Tennessee. In the Atlanta campaign he was part of the time provost-marshal, and then again at the head of the Thirty-fifth Tennessee, which shared in the hard marching, watching and fighting of the Atlanta campaign, and toward the last was assigned to Granbury's brigade. During the Tennessee campaign of General Hood, Colonel Hill commanded a cavalry force and co-operated with Forrest in the siege of Murfreesboro. In the latter part of the year he was promoted to brigadier-general, his commission being dated November 30, 1864. At Decatur, Ala., on April 23, 1865, he was in battle with a portion of Wilson's command. General Hill died at McMinnville, Tenn., on January 5, 1880.

Major-General W. Y. C. Humes.—It is interesting to note how many men during the protracted struggle which began in April, 1861, and ended in April, 1865, rose from the lower grades to be general officers. It is difficult for those who have never passed through such scenes to realize the indifference to danger which many men exhibited. Nearly the whole population of the South capable of bearing arms were from first to last brought into the field, and men learned to look upon danger and death as matters that could not be helped. Just as men strive to win their way in business by diligent application to duty, so men strove to win their way to promotion by proving themselves efficient and bold in battle. Maj.-Gen. W. Y. C. Humes of Tennessee entered the Confederate army as a lieutenant of artillery, and in June, 1861, was commissioned captain of that branch of the service in the army of the Confederate States. General McCown, in one of his reports from New Madrid Bend, bears this testimony to his worth: "Captain Humes, commanding artillery on the island, deserves commendation for his energy and proper bearing." He was with the force that was captured at Island No. 10. After being exchanged, he entered the cavalry service and rose rapidly until we find him a brigadier-general, November 16, 1863, commanding a brigade of cavalry in Wheeler's corps. During the Atlanta campaign he commanded a division of cavalry, one of the best. Throughout the whole campaign from Dalton to Atlanta the cavalry were kept busy, sometimes guarding the flank of the army, at times making raids to the rear of the enemy, and at other times meeting Federal raiders and defeating them. No army ever had a more splendid body of cavalry than that of the army of Tennessee in 1864. When Hood marched into Tennessee, Wheeler's splendid cavalry corps accompanied him until he crossed the Tennessee. Then Forrest with his corps of cavalry took Wheeler's place, and the latter returned into Georgia with his troops to harass and impede the march of Sherman as much as possible. Twice these brave horsemen saved Augusta from the fate of Atlanta and Columbia; once by repelling the Federal cavalry near Waynesboro, and afterward by a decisive defeat of Kilpatrick at Aiken, S. C. Humes with his division formed a part of Wheeler's force during this period also. He was again with the army of Tennessee in the Carolinas, and participated in the last battle fought by that army at Bentonville. In March,

1865, he was commissioned major-general. He had commanded a division for more than a year. After the return of peace, General Humes settled in Huntsville, Ala., where he died September 12, 1883.

Brigadier-General Alfred E. Jackson, in 1861, was quartermaster of Zollicoffer's brigade, and very active in collecting supplies for the soldiers and whatever things needed for their full equipment, in which duty he was very efficient. During 1862 he served in the department of East Tennessee under Gen. E. Kirby Smith, and proved himself so capable that he was commissioned brigadier-general, and on February 9, 1863, was assigned to the military department of East Tennessee, then commanded by General Donelson. In this region he had command of a brigade under Donelson and Maury, and was kept on the alert against raiding parties of the enemy. On the 7th of September, 1863, when all the available Confederate forces had been ordered to Bragg at Chattanooga, and after Burnside with his army corps had occupied Knoxville, about 500 Federal infantry advanced as far as Telford's depot in Washington county. A small force of Confederates under Gen. Alfred E. Jackson was in the upper corner of northeast Tennessee. Col. Henry L. Giltner, of the Fourth Kentucky cavalry, with a small body of troops occupied the department of southwestern Virginia. When Jackson and Giltner heard of this advance of the detachment from Burnside's army, they united their forces and under Jackson's command marched to attack the Federals. They encountered the Union troops with about equal numbers on the 8th of September at Telford's depot. After a short but sharp engagement, in which they lost 60 killed and wounded, while 100 succeeded in making their escape, the remaining 350 Federals finding retreat cut off, surrendered. On the theater of Jackson's operations there was a good deal of this sort of detachment work in which there was plenty of marching and fighting, but very little chance for renown, because the great battles so obscured the small affairs that in many parts of the country they were never even heard of. In October, under Gen. John S. Williams, he took a gallant part in the victory at Greeneville, east Tennessee. His command was included in Ransom's division during Longstreet's operations in east Tennessee. On November 23, 1864, being unfit for active service in the field, he was ordered to report temporarily to General Breckinridge. After the war had ended, General Jackson, like the thousands of other citizen-soldiers, returned quietly to the pursuits of peace. On October 30, 1889, he died at Jonesboro, Tenn.

Brigadier-General William H. Jackson, one of the most prominent living soldiers of Tennessee, was born at Paris, Tenn., October 7, 1835. At twenty-one years he was graduated at the United States military academy (1856), and assigned as brevet second lieutenant to the mounted riflemen. In December of the same year he was commissioned second lieutenant while serving at the cavalry school for practice at Carlisle, Pa. He was on frontier duty at Fort Bliss, Tex., 1857, and in December of that year was engaged in a skirmish against the Kiowa Indians near Fort Craig, N. M. In 1859 he was engaged in scouting in the Navajo country, and took part in the Comanche and Kiowa expedition of 1860. On May 16, 1861, in obedience to the command of his State, he resigned his commission in the United States army and entered the service of the Confederate States as captain of artillery. In the battle of Belmont, November 7, 1861, he acted as aide on the staff of General Pillow, and was seriously wounded while executing that officer's orders. His name is flatteringly mentioned in the reports of Generals Polk and Pillow and of Col. S. F. Marks, who, at the request of Colonel Barrow, tendered the thanks of the Eleventh Louisiana regiment to Capt. Wm. H. Jackson for valuable and gallant service rendered them. This gallant young officer was in the field again early in 1862 as colonel of the First Tennessee cavalry, winning compliments from his superior officers in every affair in which he was engaged. His name is mentioned in all the reports, and by his merit as chief of cavalry in Pemberton's department he richly earned the commission of brigadier-general, which was bestowed upon him December 29, 1862. He had acted as chief of cavalry for Van Dorn and Price in the campaign which culminated in the battle of Corinth. On the retreat from that disastrous field he had well protected the rear of the Confederate army. He increased his already high reputation throughout the Vicksburg campaign, and after its disastrous close he was indefatigable in his labors and rendered invaluable assistance to Gen. Joseph E. Johnston. In the Meridian campaign of February, 1864, Jackson commanded the cavalry of Polk's army, hanging upon the flanks of the enemy and compelling his foragers to keep close to the main line. During the Atlanta campaign, Jackson commanded the cavalry corps of the army of the Mississippi, which participated in all the arduous labors and many brilliant successes of the cavalry arm of the Confederate service. When, after the brilliant cavalry victory at Newnan, Wheeler moved into the rear of Sherman's army, Jackson's cavalry shared in the movements that defeated Kilpatrick's raid against the Macon road. He led his division of cavalry through the Nashville and Murfreesboro campaign, and then retiring to Mississippi, was there, in February, 1865, assigned to command of all Tennessee cavalry in Forrest's department, with other brigades, to form Jackson's division, one of the two provided for in Forrest's reorganization. His last military service was the cutting off of Croxton's brigade from the main body of Wilson's expedition, April, 1865. Since the close of the war General Jackson has engaged in stock raising, and is proprietor of the celebrated Belle Meade stock farm near Nashville, Tenn.

Major-General Bushrod R. Johnson, a distinguished Confederate officer and citizen of Tennessee, was born in Ohio in 1817. He was a cadet at the United States military academy from 1836 to 1840, when he was appointed second lieutenant in the Third infantry. He served in the Florida war, and was on frontier duty at Fort Leavenworth, Kan., when he was promoted to first lieutenant, February, 1844. He participated in the Mexican war, and was engaged in the battles of Palo Alto, Resaca de la Palma and Monterey, and the siege of Vera Cruz. After the fall of that city he remained there on commissary duty until October. In that month he resigned and returned to the United States. He was professor in the Western military institute of Kentucky from 1848 to 1851, when he became its superintendent. Four years later he became superintendent of the military college of the university of Nashville, Tenn., which place he held at the outbreak of the Confederate war. He was also at that time colonel of Tennessee militia. During his stay in Kentucky he had been lieutenant-colonel of militia. He was appointed colonel of engineers in the provisional army of Tennessee, June 28, 1861, and when the Tennessee troops were turned over to the Confederate States, he was assigned to the army acting in Tennessee and Kentucky under the command of Gen. Albert Sidney Johnston. He commanded with great ability a brigade at Fort Donelson, having been commissioned brigadier-general January 24, 1862. Though captured on the fall of that important post, he was exchanged in time to bear a conspicuous part in the battle of Shiloh, where he was severely wounded April 6, 1862. On his recovery he went into the Kentucky campaign, and at the battle of Perryville, his and Cleburne's brigades, charging together, captured three batteries and many prisoners. General Johnson also led his brigade in Hardee's brilliant and successful charge in the battle of Murfreesboro. At Chickamauga, in the second day's battle, he was the first to detect and enter the gap in the Federal lines. Of this, Gen. D. H. Hill says: "With the coolness and judgment for which he was always distinguished, he took in the situation at a glance, and began a flank movement to the right. Longstreet adopted the plan of his lieutenant and made his other troops conform to Johnson's movement," thus sweeping away one wing of the Federal army and with it the commanding general himself. General Johnson also served under Longstreet in the unfortunate campaign into east Tennessee, commanding Buckner's division, brigades of Gracie, Johnson and Reynolds; shared in the disastrous assault on Fort Sanders (Knoxville), and fought the battle of Bean's Station. When the campaign of 1864 opened in Virginia, General Johnson, with his division, was near Petersburg, where he assisted in the defense against Butler's attack upon the Richmond & Petersburg railroad. His services were also eminent in the battle of Drewry's Bluff, where Beauregard "bottled up" Butler. A few days after this battle Johnson was commissioned major-general (May 21, 1864). At the battle of the Crater, before Petersburg, he commanded the troops who repulsed the Federal assault. He continued to serve with distinguished ability until the end came and the banners of the Confederacy were furled forever. At the evacuation of Richmond he commanded the division of Anderson's corps, comprising the brigades of Wallace, Moody, Ransom and Wise, South Carolina, Alabama, North Carolina and Virginia troops; was engaged in severe fighting preceding and during the retreat, and after the battle of Sailor's Creek was ordered by General Lee to collect all the scattered forces of Anderson's and Ewell's commands. In 1866 he resumed his favorite occupation, that of a teacher, and served as professor of engineering, mechanics and natural philosophy in the Western military institute at Georgetown, Ky., until 1880. On December 7th of that year he died at Brighton, Ill., at the age of sixty-three years.

Brigadier-General William McComb, a gallant Tennessee soldier, was a native of Pennsylvania. About 1856 he went to Montgomery county, Tenn., where he engaged in superintending the erection of a large flouring mill at Price's landing, on the Cumberland river. In that section of the State he was living at the beginning of the civil war. Since his sympathies were with the South, he enlisted as a private in one of the companies of the Fourteenth Tennessee regiment. He was promoted to lieutenant soon afterward, and made adjutant of the regiment by Col. W. A. Forbes. This regiment was part of the brigade of Gen. S. R. Anderson in the Cheat Mountain campaign in northwest Virginia, and next, with the rest of Loring's division, shared in the hardships of Stonewall Jackson's winter campaign to Bath, Hancock and Romney. At the reorganization of the regiment at Yorktown, Va., in the winter of 1862, William McComb was elected major. As such he took part in the battle of Seven Pines, where the brigade commander, General Hatton, was killed. Gen. James Archer was now placed in command of this brigade. At the battle of Cedar Run Lieut.-Col. George Harrell was mortally wounded and was succeeded by McComb. In the second battle of Manassas Colonel Forbes was killed, and now McComb became colonel of the Fourteenth Tennessee, September 2, 1862. At the battle of Chancellorsville, Colonel McComb was wounded, and did not recover in time to take part in the battle of Gettysburg. He was repeatedly wounded in battle, but always returned to duty as soon as he was able. On the death of General Archer, his and Gen. Bushrod Johnson's old brigades were consolidated, and Colonel McComb was placed in command of the consolidated brigades, receiving his commission as brigadier-general on the 20th of January, 1865. In the final battles around Petersburg, McComb and his men did their duty with their accustomed zeal and alacrity. This gallant brigade and its commander were faithful to the last, and when the end came returned to their homes with the consciousness of duty well performed.

Major-General John Porter McCown was born in Tennessee in 1815, and graduated at West Point in 1840, with commission as second lieutenant of Fourth artillery. He served in the removal of the Indians to the West in 1840, and on the frontier during the Canada border disturbances, 1840-41; in the military occupation of Texas, 1845-46, and in the Mexican war, 1846-47, being engaged in the battles of Palo Alto, Resaca de la Palma, Monterey, Vera Cruz, Cerro Gordo, and in the assault and capture of the City of Mexico. He was brevetted captain for gallant and meritorious conduct at Cerro Gordo. After the Mexican war he served in various capacities, part of the time on frontier duty on the Rio Grande, being engaged in several skirmishes. On the 9th of January, 1851, he was commissioned captain of the Fourth artillery. He also served in Florida against the Seminole Indians, 1856-57. When Tennessee seceded and cast her lot with the Confederacy, he resigned his commission and was made lieutenant-colonel of artillery in the Confederate army. His promotion was rapid; to colonel in May, 1861, brigadier-general, October, 1861, and major-general, March, 1862. At the time of the battle of Belmont, General McCown was sent up the east bank of the Mississippi with a force of infantry and artillery. He found no enemy threatening Polk's position, and the information thus obtained enabled Polk to send men enough across the river to insure victory at Belmont. He commanded at New Madrid in March, 1862, but was assigned to duty elsewhere before the investment of that post by General Pope. June 20, 1862, he was assigned to command of the army of the West, Van Dorn taking department command. He was sent to take command at Chattanooga just before the advance of Bragg to that point in 1862. He had command of a division in the army of

Kentucky under Kirby Smith, and for a while in the fall of 1862 had charge of the department of East Tennessee. At Murfreesboro he and Cleburne formed the right of Hardee's corps, which fell upon McCook with such impetuosity as to sweep completely that part of the field, driving the Union left a distance of four miles, capturing cannon, small-arms, and thousands of prisoners. McCown's infantry and Wheeler's cavalry are spoken of in the reports as killing, wounding or capturing half the force in their front. Throughout the war McCown performed to the satisfaction of his superiors whatever duties fell to his lot. At the close of hostilities he settled near Knoxville and engaged in school-teaching. He afterward settled at Little Rock, Ark., where he died January 22, 1879.

Brigadier-General George Maney was one of the most gallant officers of Tennessee. Before Tennessee had decided the question of secession, he was ready to serve her in the field if his services should be required. Espousing the cause of the South with all his heart, he was appointed colonel of the First Tennessee infantry on May 8, 1861. In July he was sent to Staunton, Va., and in the brigade of Gen. S. R. Anderson was ordered to report to General Loring in northwest Virginia. He served in the Cheat Mountain campaign, and was sent with General Anderson's command to join Gen. Stonewall Jackson at Winchester, Va., in December, 1861. His regiment was part of the force with which Jackson marched against Bath, Hancock and Romney in January, 1862. In February, 1862, after the fall of Forts Henry and Donelson, he made an earnest appeal to the Richmond government to send himself and regiment to assist in the defense of Tennessee. This request was granted, and he was placed in command of the Second brigade, Cheatham's division of Polk's corps of the army of the Mississippi. He led this command at the battle of Shiloh with such ability that on the 16th of April, 1862, he was commissioned a brigadier-general. In this, his first battle in command of brigade, General Cheatham reported that he led a charge in person with dashing gallantry, "one of the most brilliant, as it was certainly one of the most decisive, movements of the day." His brigade consisted at first of the First, Fourth, Sixth, Ninth and Twenty-seventh Tennessee regiments of infantry, Major Maney's battalion of Tennessee infantry, and Capt. Melancthon Smith's battery of light artillery. The Forty-first and Fiftieth Tennessee regiments of infantry were afterward added to this brigade. At the battle of Perryville the Forty-first Georgia was also in his command. General Maney was in the hottest of the fight at Perryville, also at Murfreesboro, Chickamauga and Missionary Ridge. Through the marching, digging and fighting of the long death-grapple known as the Atlanta campaign, Maney's brigade was still conspicuous, and among the most trusted of the soldiers of Johnston and Hood. Throughout the war there was no more faithful soldier of the Confederate States than Gen. George Maney. Attentive to every detail, a good disciplinarian, careful of the wants of his men, skillful and courageous in battle, implicitly relied upon by his division and corps commanders, he ranked among the best of the many excellent brigadier-generals of the army of Tennessee, a body of men that needed only a Lee or a Jackson to make it the equal in fortune as in valor of the noble army of Northern Virginia. General Maney is one of the few officers of the army of Tennessee who had the distinction of serving at any time under Gen. Stonewall Jackson. It was in the Bath expedition that Jackson directed Loring to send a regiment to advance from the Confederate left along the mountain which commanded the town. Jackson in his report says: "He [Loring] directed Colonel Maney to execute the order, and it was undertaken with a patriotic enthusiasm which entitles the First

Tennessee regiment and its commander to special praise." General Maney is still living in Nashville, Tenn. (1898).

Brigadier-General Joseph B. Palmer, at the beginning of the war, was a prominent lawyer of Murfreesboro, Tenn. He opposed secession, and insisted that the South should make her fight in the Union. But like the vast majority of Southern Union men, he believed that his first allegiance was due to his State. So when Tennessee resolved upon secession, he obeyed her voice and raised a company for the defense of the South. Of this company he was elected captain, and when it, with nine other companies, was formed into the Eighteenth Tennessee regiment of infantry, Captain Palmer was unanimously elected colonel. This regiment was assigned to the army commanded by Gen. Albert Sidney Johnston. It formed a part of the army at Fort Donelson, sharing in the glories and disasters of that fierce conflict. When the fort was surrendered, February 16, 1862, Colonel Palmer and his men found themselves prisoners of war. He was kept in prison at Fort Warren until his exchange in August, 1862, then joined his regiment, which had also been just exchanged at Vicksburg. Shortly afterward the regiment was reorganized at Jackson, Miss., and re-elected Palmer as its colonel. In Breckinridge's brilliant, though unsuccessful charge at Murfreesboro on the 2d day of January, 1863, Palmer's regiment suffered heavily, and Palmer was himself badly wounded in three places. These wounds incapacitated him for service for about four months, but he returned to his regiment in time for the battle of Chickamauga, where, while leading his command in one of the headlong charges of that hotly-contested field, he received another dangerous wound in the shoulder, which bled so profusely as to threaten death before help could come. It was not until the army reached Atlanta that he was in condition to resume his duties. Here he was appointed to the command of his brigade, and commissioned brigadier-general November 15, 1864. His brigade, formerly commanded by John C. Brown, comprised the Third, Eighteenth, Thirty-second and Forty-fifth Tennessee regiments. In the campaign of Hood into Tennessee, this brigade was detached from the army at Nashville and sent to co-operate with Bate and Forrest in a movement against Murfreesboro. On the retreat of the army, Palmer's brigade formed part of the force under Walthall and Forrest which brought up the rear, and did its duty so bravely as to win the applause of even the enemy. During the North Carolina campaign of 1865, all the decimated infantry regiments of Tennessee then serving under Johnston were consolidated into four regiments and placed in a brigade commanded by General Palmer. Mr. G. N. Baskette, of Nashville, Tenn. (Confederate Veteran, November, 1897), relates a remarkable exploit of Palmer's brigade at the battle of Bentonville, the last one fought by the gallant army of Tennessee. On this occasion, "part of Palmer's brigade charged through the enemy's line and kept on to the rear of the Federal army, capturing a number of prisoners, and by a detour, after a long and painful march of about a week, rejoined the brigade." The same writer, summing up the character of General Palmer, says: "He was ever courteous to his subordinate officers and the men in the line, and while maintaining proper discipline had always a warm sympathy for the boys in the trenches or on the march. On the battlefield he was cool and collected, bearing himself always as a leader who felt the weight of his responsibility, and yet was ever ready to brave any danger which promised to benefit the cause to which he was devoted." At the close of the war General Palmer proved himself as good a citizen as he had been a soldier. He died on the 4th of November, 1890, mourned by his many friends and regretted by his countrymen.

Brigadier-General Gideon Johnson Pillow was born in

Williamson county, Tenn., June 8, 1806. In 1827 he was graduated at the university of Nashville, after which he commenced the practice of law at Columbia and rapidly rose to prominence. He was a delegate to the National Democratic convention of 1844, and aided largely in securing the nomination of his neighbor, James K. Polk, for the presidency. In July, 1846, he abandoned peaceful pursuits to accept a commission as brigadier-general of Tennessee volunteers in the Mexican war. At first he served with Taylor in northern Mexico, but was transferred to Scott's command at the beginning of the siege of Vera Cruz. In this siege he took an active part, and was appointed one of the American commissioners to receive the surrender of the city. At Cerro Gordo he commanded the right wing, and in the impetuous charge received a severe wound. On April 30, 1847, he was commissioned major-general. He fought with great gallantry at Churubusco, Molino del Rey and Chapultepec, in which last affair he was a second time wounded. A sharp difference between General Scott and himself led to a court-martial, requested by himself. By the decision of this court he was fully acquitted of the charge of insubordination which Scott had brought against him. After the close of the Mexican war he resumed the practice of law, and also engaged in planting. In the great Southern convention held in Nashville in 1850, he took a conservative course and opposed extreme measures. At the beginning of the war for Southern independence he was appointed, by Governor Harris, major-general in the provisional army of Tennessee, in which capacity he aided largely in the organization of the State forces. On July 9, 1861, he was commissioned brigadier-general of the provisional army of the Confederate States. Being assigned to General Polk's department as second in command to that officer, he fought the battle of Belmont successfully against General Grant. At Fort Donelson he was second in command to Brigadier-General Floyd, and handled his troops with skill and ability. The gallant fighting of the Confederates was all in vain, for they found themselves hemmed in by superior numbers and had to surrender. Floyd and Pillow turned over the command to Buckner, who surrendered the fort and garrison to General Grant. Before the surrender, Floyd embarked his Virginia troops upon steamers and carried them off. General Pillow and a portion of his staff crossed to the opposite side of the Cumberland and made their way to Clarksville. At Decatur, Ala., General Pillow was relieved from duty. He subsequently led a detachment of cavalry in the Southwest under Beauregard, and still later was made chief of conscripts in the Western department. At the close of the war he found himself ruined in fortune and left, in advanced age, without other means of support than the earnings of his professional labors. During the war he had ordered the seizure of the coal of a Pittsburg company. The coal had been sold and the proceeds turned over to the State, and everything else received for the property of the company had been applied to military purposes. The general was sued by the Pittsburg company for $125,000 damages, which resulted in a judgment against him for $38,500. Although a new trial was granted, the general's claims as a belligerent were not allowed. His State could not come to his relief. He was compelled to go into bankruptcy. General Pillow said that the loss of his property gave him "less anguish than the humiliation of bankruptcy." He attempted the cultivation of his farm in Maury county and of his plantation in Arkansas, but labored under many discouraging circumstances. He died in Lee county, Ark., October 6, 1878.

Brigadier-General William A. Quarles, when the Forty-second Tennessee was organized in 1861, was elected and commissioned its colonel. The regiment was placed in the army of Gen. Albert Sidney Johnston, and in February, 1862, was quartered at Clarksville, Tenn. On the 12th of February they received orders from Brigadier-General Pillow to go to Fort Donelson. The order was immediately obeyed, and going on board a transport they arrived next morning under a heavy fire. The companies were formed on the transport and marched off in regular order. In passing through the village of Dover, three men were wounded, one mortally, by the Federal shells. Then, assigned to Colonel Heiman's brigade, the regiment was thrown into the trenches. This was the introduction of these gallant men to the stern realities of war. On the 13th, 14th and 15th of February occurred the severest fighting at Donelson. Both superiors and subordinates bore testimony to the gallantry of Colonel Quarles in the trying ordeal of this first battle. "In this attack," says Gen. Bushrod Johnson, speaking of the first assaults of the enemy, "Captain Maney's company of artillery and Colonels Abernathy's and Quarles' regiments principally suffered and deserve more particular notice." During the three days' fighting the conduct of Colonel Quarles was such that Lieut. T. McGinnis, acting adjutant of the Forty-second Tennessee, said in a note to General Buckner: "Before closing my report, I will call your attention to the cool and gallant conduct of Colonel Quarles. He was always at the head of his regiment, and set a gallant example for his officers and men." After being exchanged, Colonel Quarles was put in command of the Forty-second, Forty-sixth, Forty-eighth and Fifty-third Tennessee regiments, consolidated, and the Ninth Tennessee battalion, and assigned to Maxey's brigade, which with other troops was under command of Gen. Frank Gardner at Port Hudson. Maxey's brigade was transferred, at the beginning of the siege of Vicksburg, from Port Hudson to the command of Gen. Joseph E. Johnston at Jackson, Miss. On August 25, 1863, Colonel Quarles was promoted to brigadier-general, at that time being under the orders of Gen. Dabney H.

Brig.-Gen. J. C. Vaughn.	Brig.-Gen. Preston Smith.	Maj.-Gen. C. M. Wilcox.
Brig.-Gen. L. M. Walker.	Brig.-Gen. O. F. Strahl.	Brig.-Gen. Jos. B. Palmer.
Brig.-Gen. Gideon J. Pillow.	Brig.-Gen. Felix K. Zollicoffer.	Brig.-Gen. M. J. Wright.

Maury. Quarles' brigade was sent to Bragg in anticipation of the battle of Missionary Ridge, but did not reach him in time to share in that engagement. He was ordered back to Mississippi after it seemed certain that Bragg would not be attacked again at Dalton, but was returned to Georgia on the opening of the Atlanta campaign. During the long continued conflict from Dalton to Atlanta this brigade exhibited a steady bearing. At Pickett's mill, General Cleburne expressed to General Quarles and his brigade his thanks for timely assistance rendered. At the battle of Franklin, General Walthall reported: "Brigadier-General Quarles was severely wounded at the head of his brigade, within a short distance of the enemy's inner line, and all of his staff officers with him on the field were killed; and so heavy were the losses in his command that when the battle ended its officer highest in rank was a captain." After the war General Quarles made his home in Clarksville, Tenn., where he died December 28, 1893.

Brigadier-General James Edward Rains, one of the many civilians who rose to high military command during the great war between the States, was born in Nashville, Tenn., in April, 1833. He was graduated at Yale in 1854, and then studied law. He became city attorney at Nashville in 1858, and attorney-general for his judicial district in 1860. In politics he was a Whig, and was for some time editor of the Daily Republican Banner. When the summons to war came, he enlisted in the Confederate army as a private, but was elected colonel of the Eleventh Tennessee infantry and commissioned May 10, 1861. The greater part of his service was in east Tennessee. During the winter of 1861-62 he commanded the garrison at Cumberland Gap. This position he held as long as it was possible to do so, repulsing several attempts of the enemy upon his lines. It was not until the 18th of June, 1862, that the Federals turned his position and rendered it untenable. Had this occurred earlier, east Tennessee would have been completely lost to the Confederates in 1862. But the forces which Kirby Smith was now gathering about Knoxville, in addition to those in the neighborhood of Cumberland Gap, made the Union occupation of that post almost a barren victory. When, in August, Smith advanced into Kentucky, he left Gen. Carter L. Stevenson with a strong division to operate against the Union general, Morgan, who was holding the gap with about 9,000 men. Colonel Rains commanded a brigade in Stevenson's division, and so efficient was his work that his name frequently appeared in both the Confederate and Union reports. Kirby Smith's success in Kentucky, and the steady pressure brought to bear upon Morgan by the Confederates, at last forced the Union commander to abandon Cumberland Gap and retreat through eastern Kentucky to the Ohio river. The efficient service rendered by Colonel Rains in all these movements was rewarded by a brigadier-general's commission, November 4, 1862. When Bragg was concentrating his army at Murfreesboro (November, 1862), after the return from the Kentucky campaign, the brigade of General Rains, composed of Stovall's and J. T. Smith's Georgia battalions, R. B. Vance's North Carolina regiment and the Eleventh Tennessee under Colonel Gordon, was ordered to that point and assigned to the division of General McCown, serving in Hardee's corps. In the brilliant charges made by this corps in the battle of December 31, 1862, by which the whole Federal right was routed and bent back upon the center, with immense loss in killed, wounded, prisoners and guns, McCown's division bore an illustrious part. But, as in all great battles is to be expected, the division lost many brave men and gallant officers. Among the killed was Brigadier-General Rains, who fell shot through the heart as he was advancing with his men against a Federal battery. He left to his family, to his native State and to the South the precious legacy of a noble name.

Brigadier-General Preston Smith was born in Giles county, December 25, 1823. He received the advantages of a good country school and of Jackson college, Columbia. In this town he studied law and practiced several years. Then he moved to Waynesboro, and subsequently to Memphis. At the outbreak of the civil war he entered the service of the Confederate States, and was made colonel of the One Hundred and Fifty-fourth regiment of Tennessee. From the first his services were effective and brilliant. At Shiloh his regiment was attached to Bushrod Johnson's brigade and Cheatham's division. He was severely wounded in this battle, but was in the field again in time to share in the Kentucky campaign. In the magnificent victory of Richmond, Ky., he commanded a brigade under Cleburne, and upon the wounding of that general, succeeded him in command of the division. In no battle of the war did either side win a more brilliant victory than was gained by the Confederates on this memorable field. On October 27th, Colonel Smith was commissioned brigadier-general, and no promotion was ever more worthily bestowed. General Smith's useful career was brought to a close at Chickamauga, Ga., September 19, 1863, at the close of the first day's fight on this hotly-contested field. At 6 o'clock p. m., General Smith was informed that a night attack had been determined upon, and was ordered to support General Deshler's brigade as soon as it should move to the front. During this advance, in the confusion caused by a night attack, a portion of Deshler's brigade became somewhat disordered and blocked the advance of Smith, who ordered them to move forward. They obeyed, but obliqued too much to the left and uncovered the two right regiments of General Smith's brigade. This being unknown to General

Smith, when he again came upon the troops at a halt in his immediate front, supposing them to be a part of General Deshler's command, he and Capt. Thomas H. King, a volunteer aide, rode forward to ascertain the cause of the delay. Coming up to the line, which proved to be the enemy, and asking who was in command of their troops, the Union soldiers recognized him as a Confederate officer and fired, killing him and Captain King. A. J. Vaughan, Jr., the senior colonel of the brigade, made a similar mistake and was likewise fired upon, but escaped unharmed, though Captain Donelson, acting assistant adjutant-general, who was riding by his side, was killed. By order of Colonel Vaughan, some files of the Twelfth Tennessee now opened fire and the enemy in the front surrendered. Gen. B. F. Cheatham, in his report of the operations of his division in this battle, says: "It was in this night attack that Brig.-Gen. Preston Smith of Tennessee received his mortal wound, from which he died in 50 minutes. At the head of his noble brigade, of which he had been the commander as colonel and brigadier-general for two years and a half, he fell in the performance of what he himself, with his expiring breath, simply said was his duty. Active, energetic and brave, with a rare fitness to command, full of honorable ambition in perfect harmony with the most elevated patriotism, the whole country will mourn his fall and do honor to his memory." General Bragg in his official report also says: "Brig.-Gens. B. H. Helm, Preston Smith and James Deshler died upon the field in the heroic discharge of duty. They were true patriots and gallant soldiers, worthy of the high reputation they enjoyed." Tennessee has good reason to be proud of Preston Smith.

Brigadier-General Thomas Benton Smith, entering the Confederate service in the Twentieth Tennessee, first stood the crucial test at Shiloh, where the colonel of the regiment, J. A. Battle, was captured. When Breckinridge attacked Baton Rouge on August 5, 1862, Smith had been promoted to colonel of the regiment. On this occasion he commanded one of the two brigades of the division of Gen. Charles Clark. The Confederates were at first successful, defeating the enemy in the field, though exposed to the fire of the Federal fleet as well as of the army. General Breckinridge says in his report of the battle: "Colonel Smith, commanding Fourth brigade, composed of the consolidated Tennessee regiments and the Twenty-second Mississippi, was ordered forward, and moved against the enemy in fine style." At the battle of Murfreesboro, Gen. William J. Hardee bears this testimony concerning Colonel Smith: "The Twentieth Tennessee, of Preston's brigade, vainly endeavored near the river to carry a battery, and after a heavy loss, including their gallant commander, Col. T. B. Smith, who was severely wounded, were compelled to fall back under cover." At the battle of Chickamauga, Colonel Smith was again ready for duty. At the opening of the Atlanta campaign in May, 1864, Colonel Smith appears at the head of Tyler's brigade, its gallant commander having been disabled by a wound. On July 29, 1864, he was commissioned brigadier-general. His brigade embraced the Second, Tenth and Twentieth Tennessee, the Thirty-seventh Georgia, the Fiftieth, Thirtieth and Thirty-seventh Tennessee, consolidated, and a Georgia battalion of sharpshooters. Throughout the battles of the Atlanta campaign, from Dalton to Jonesboro, General Smith led the old Tyler brigade and won new fame for himself and his command. He accompanied the army in the same capacity in the Tennessee campaign, participated in the battle of Franklin and the siege of Murfreesboro; and at Nashville on the fateful 16th of December he was with his gallant men fighting against overwhelming disaster until captured. Two others of General Bate's brigade commanders, Major Lash and Gen. H. R. Jackson, shared his fate as a prisoner of war. General Bate, in his report, said of Smith that he bore himself with heroic courage, both through good and evil fortune, always executing orders with zeal and alacrity, and bearing himself in the face of the enemy as became a reputation theretofore bravely won.

General Otho French Strahl, one of the choicest spirits that embraced the cause of the South, and finally offered all upon her altar, was a native of Ohio, who had settled in Tennessee and was practicing law at Dyersburg when the great war of States began. Although of Northern birth, both of his grandmothers were Southern women, and perhaps had much to do with moulding the sentiments which made him such an ardent sympathizer with the South. When Tennessee was making ready to cast in her lot with the Southern Confederacy, the young lawyer entered the Fourth Tennessee regiment as a captain (May, 1861). Early in 1862 he became lieutenant-colonel of the regiment. As such he shared in the hardships and glories of the campaigns of Shiloh, Bentonville and Murfreesboro, in which he so conducted himself as to be promoted colonel early in 1863, and then to the rank of brigadier-general, July 28, 1863. In the hundred days' campaign from Dalton to Atlanta in 1864, he and his men added to their already magnificent record. Mr. S. A. Cunningham, who was a boy soldier in his brigade at Franklin, November 30, 1864, has given in his magazine a graphic account of the conduct and death of his commander on that fateful day. Mr. Cunningham being that day right guide to the brigade, was near Strahl in the fatal advance, and was pained at the extreme sadness in his face. He was surprised, too, that his general went into the battle on foot. The account of Mr. Cunningham continues: "I was near General Strahl, who stood in the ditch and handed up guns to those posted to fire them. I had passed to him my short Enfield (noted in the regiment) about the sixth time. The man who had been firing, cocked it and was taking deliberate aim when he was shot, and tumbled down dead into the ditch upon those killed before him. When the men so exposed were shot down, their places were supplied by volunteers until these were exhausted, and it was necessary for General Strahl to call for others. He turned to me, and though I was several feet back from the ditch, I rose up immediately, and walking over the wounded and dead took position, with one foot upon the pile of bodies of my dead fellows and the other upon the embankment, and fired guns which the general himself handed up to me, until he, too, was shot down." The general was not instantly killed, but soon after received a second shot and then a third, which finished for him the fearful work. "General Strahl was a model character, and it was said of him that in all the war he was never known to use language unsuited to the presence of ladies." While the army was camped at Dalton on the 20th of April, 1864, services were held in the Methodist church by Bishop Charles Todd Quintard, of the Episcopal church. On this occasion Bishop Quintard baptized General Strahl and presented him to Bishop Stephen Elliott for confirmation, with three other generals of the Confederate army—Lieutenant-General Hardee and Brigadier-Generals Shoup and Govan.

Brigadier-General Robert C. Tyler, a highly heroic officer, was a native of Maryland, born and reared in the city of Baltimore. Being of a naturally enterprising disposition, and imbued with the idea that American destiny pointed to the control by the United States of all the North American continent, he joined the Nicaraguan expedition of Gen. William Walker in 1859. After the unsuccessful issue of that enterprise he went to Memphis, Tenn., and there the war of 1861 found him. He entered the Confederate service as quartermaster of the Fifteenth

Tennessee; in the autumn of 1861 he was promoted to major on the staff of General Cheatham, in the same department, and in a few months was made lieutenant-colonel of the Fifteenth. He commanded it at the battle of Shiloh, was soon promoted to colonel, and led it with distinction in all the engagements of the Southwest until, on the promotion of General Bate, he was made brigadier-general. At Missionary Ridge he was dangerously wounded and permanently disabled, and was not in the field again until Major-General Wilson, with 10,000 cavalry, was sent to Alabama and Georgia to lay waste and destroy the country. General Tyler, still on crutches, was sojourning near West Point, Ga., when Col. O. H. LaGrange, commanding a brigade of Wilson's cavalry, entered that place on the 16th of April and made an easy capture of a lot of quartermaster and commissary stores. Hearing of the approach of LaGrange, General Tyler organized a lot of convalescents and Georgia militia, and undertook the defense of a little earthwork provided for the protection of a railroad bridge and called that day "Fort Tyler." Colonel LaGrange reported that it was defended by two field pieces and a 32-pounder, and "265 desperate men." There were no trained gunners in the garrison, so no one of the attacking force was injured by the artillery. This fort, said Colonel LaGrange, was "a remarkably strong earthwork, 35 yards square." He assailed it with a brigade composed of the Second and Fourth Indiana, First Wisconsin and Seventh Kentucky regiments, dismounted, and the Eighteenth Indiana battery, and reported that the assault was made "under a scathing fire;" and his chief, Major-General Wilson, in his report to Maj.-Gen. George H. Thomas, said the assault was made "under a withering fire of musketry and grape," but in this large attacking column, Colonel LaGrange stated his loss was only 7 killed and 29 wounded. He reported the loss of the defenders of the fort at "18 killed and 28 seriously wounded, mostly shot through

Brig.-Gen. Wm. H. Jackson. Brig.-Gen. Robert Hatton.
Brig.-Gen. John C. Carter. Brig.-Gen. Alex. W. Campbell. Brig.-Gen. Benj. J. Hill.
Maj.-Gen. Daniel S. Donelson. Brig.-Gen. H. B. Davidson. Maj.-Gen. Benj. F. Cheatham.
Brig.-Gen. G. W. Gordon. Maj.-Gen. W. Y. C. Humes.

the head." General Thomas reported the affair to General Grant on the 1st of June, and stated that the defense was "stubborn" and that LaGrange had captured 300 prisoners. Colonel LaGrange, in a dispatch to General Upton, dated the day of the capture, reports the number of prisoners at 200. On the 17th of April, in a dispatch to General Canby and in one dated the 21st to General Sherman, General Wilson claimed for LaGrange the capture of the same number. No exact information has been obtainable from Confederate sources, but the importance of the unfortunate affair and the strength of the garrison were exaggerated by the Federal commanding general through all grades down to Col. A. S. Bloom, of the Seventh Kentucky, who reported to the brigade commander that "after a fight raging furiously for over two hours, I prepared to charge the fort and helped to carry it," and naively added that he had a second lieutenant and two men slightly wounded. The gallant Tyler, two captains and one lieutenant were killed early by the sharpshooters. It was honorable to the little garrison that in spite of the fall of their leader they displayed no white flag, but maintained the defense of the earthwork until they were overrun and captured by a force ten to fifteen times their own strength. The men around General Tyler were representatives of Tennessee, Georgia and other States, imperfectly armed and organized at a moment's notice; the garrison lost 48 killed and wounded; the shots were received in the head, showing that the men did not take cover; it was the last fight east of the great river; it was a brave one, and a memorial stone should mark the place where Tyler and his heroes fell.

Brigadier-General Alfred J. Vaughan was born in Dinwiddie county, Va., May 10, 1830, and was graduated at the Virginia military institute, July 4, 1851, as senior captain of cadets. He adopted civil engineering as his profession, and going West located at St. Joseph, Mo. Afterward he was deputy United States surveyor for the district of California. Returning east, he settled in Marshall county, Miss. He was very much opposed to the dissolution of the Union, but when his adopted State, Mississippi, and his native State, Virginia, declared for secession, he promptly determined to abide by their decision, and at once raised a company for the Confederate service. Since Mississippi was not yet ready to arm and equip this company, he went with most of his men to Moscow, Tenn., and was mustered into service as captain in the Thirteenth Tennessee. At the reorganization of this regiment in June, 1861, he was elected lieutenant-colonel. From his first affair with the enemy he gained the reputation of a fighting officer, and maintained this renown to the close of his military career. He was engaged in every battle under Polk, Bragg and Joseph E. Johnston, including Belmont, Shiloh, Richmond (Ky.), Perryville, Chickamauga, Missionary Ridge, and all the battles and numberless skirmishes of the Dalton-Atlanta campaign until the affair at Vining Station near Atlanta. At Richmond he ably commanded his brigade. At Chickamauga he was made brigadier-general on the field, and succeeded to the command of the brigade of Preston Smith, who was killed in that battle. When he fell, Colonel Vaughan was near his side and immediately took charge of his brigade, and by skill and courage richly earned the honor bestowed upon him by the President of the Confederacy. From the beginning of his career up to the battle of Chickamauga he had eight horses killed under him. At Vining Station, July 4, 1864, his leg was taken off by an exploding shell, and he was permanently disabled for military duty. After the war he returned to Mississippi and engaged in farming until 1872. The next year he opened a mercantile house in Memphis, Tenn. In 1878 the people of Shelby county elected him clerk of the criminal court by 6,000 majority. He has served officially as major-general, commanding the Tennessee division of United Confederate Veterans, in all the affairs of which he takes a lively interest.

Brigadier-General John C. Vaughn was born in Grayson county, Va., February 24, 1824. His family soon after moved to Tennessee and settled in Monroe county, where his youth and early manhood were passed. As soon as he was old enough to be elected to an office, he was chosen to a position of importance in his county. Although that section of the State has been noted for heated political strife, the people of Monroe county always stood by him. When the United States became involved in war with Mexico, young Vaughn entered the Fifth Tennessee volunteers as a captain and served throughout the war. At its close he returned to his home in east Tennessee and became a merchant in the little village of Sweetwater. He was frequently placed in responsible positions by his fellow citizens. He was in Charleston, S. C., at the commencement of the Confederate war, and participated in the opening of the bloodiest drama of modern times. Returning to east Tennessee, after the capture of Fort Sumter, he raised a company in Monroe county and aided in the organization of a regiment in Knoxville, of which he was elected colonel. It is said that this was really the first Tennessee regiment raised, but that the colonels of two other regiments reached Richmond first and offered their commands to the Confederate government. Thus Colonel Vaughn's regiment was numbered the Third Tennessee. The State of Tennessee having not yet seceded, Colonel Vaughn took his men to Lynchburg, Va., where they were mustered into the Confederate service on the 6th of June, and ordered to report to Gen. Joseph E. Johnston, then at Harper's Ferry. His command was stationed for a time at Romney. With a detachment of his own regiment and two companies of the Thirteenth Virginia, Colonel Vaughn dispersed a body of the enemy at New Creek bridge, on the Baltimore & Ohio railroad, and captured two pieces of artillery, the first taken by the Confederates in the field. The regiment was subsequently attached to Kirby Smith's brigade and participated in the first battle of Manassas. In the spring of 1862 Colonel Vaughn was ordered to east Tennessee. On September 20, 1862, he was commissioned brigadier-general, and in the winter following was sent with his brigade of East Tennesseeans to Vicksburg, where he assisted in repelling Sherman's attack in December. During the long and tedious siege of that important post in 1863, Vaughn was in command of the upper defenses of the city. At last, worn out and decimated, his brigade was surrendered with the rest of Pemberton's army, July 4, 1863. General Vaughn was soon exchanged, and sent with a brigade of mounted men to operate in east Tennessee and southwest Virginia. When General Hunter began his march against Lee's communications in 1864, Vaughn assisted in repelling his advance. In the performance of this duty he was engaged in the battle of Piedmont, and after the death of General Jones assumed command and brought off the shattered forces successfully. He was with Early in his successful campaign against Hunter, and in the last advance in Maryland and the valley of Virginia. Being wounded near Martinsburg, he was furloughed and returned to Bristol, Tenn. After the death of Gen. John H. Morgan, he took command of the forces in east Tennessee. When Lee surrendered, Vaughn's command was at Christianburg confronting Stoneman. On hearing the news he formed his war-worn Confederates in line and told them that the army of Northern Virginia had surrendered, but that if they would follow him, he would join Joe Johnston in North Carolina. The men who had followed their leader through four weary years, once more turned their backs upon their homes, cut down their artillery, destroyed their baggage wagons and marched into North Carolina.

After the surrender of Joe Johnston, General Vaughn's troops formed part of the escort of President Davis in his attempt to make his way to the Trans-Mississippi department, and at Abbeville, S. C., Vaughn was one of the five brigade commanders who took part in the last council of war held by President Davis. At the close of the war General Vaughn went to south Georgia. He afterward returned to Tennessee and was elected to the State senate, of which he was made presiding officer. At the close of his term he returned to south Georgia, where he remained until his death, being engaged either as a merchant at Thomasville or in planting. He died at his residence in Brooks county, Ga., August 10, 1875.

Brigadier-General Lucius M. Walker was born in the State of Tennessee in the year 1829. He entered the United States military academy in 1846, and was graduated in 1850 as brevet second lieutenant of dragoons; served on frontier duty and scouting, and reached the full grade of second lieutenant in 1852. In that year he resigned and became a commission merchant in Tennessee, continuing in mercantile business until the spring of 1861. On the 11th of November of that year he was commissioned colonel of the Fortieth Tennessee, and was appointed commandant at the post of Memphis. On March 11, 1862, he was commissioned brigadier-general and was posted at Madrid Bend. He retreated from that point by order of General McCown, his commanding officer, when it became evident that his whole force would be captured if he remained longer. Sickness prevented his presence with the army at the battle of Shiloh. He was with the army at Corinth before the retreat to Tupelo, and in the affair at Farmington on the 9th of May, 1862, his brigade, under his command, attacked and drove the enemy from their works. He was with the army at Tupelo for a time. On March 23, 1863, he received orders from Richmond to repair to the headquarters of the Trans-Mississippi department and report to Gen. E. Kirby Smith for assignment to duty. He was assigned to the command of the cavalry brigade and participated in the battle of Helena, and in other operations of the cavalry in this department. An unfortunate difference arose between General Walker and Gen. John S. Marmaduke, which led to a duel between these officers. An attempt to prevent the duel was made by General Price, who ordered both generals to remain closely in their quarters. The order did not reach General Walker, but was received by General Marmaduke. By an unfortunate series of mishaps the duel was not prevented, and taking place on the morning of September 6, 1863, General Walker was wounded, and died on the 19th of the same month.

Major-General Cadmus M. Wilcox, a skillful Confederate officer, distinguished in all the campaigns of the army of Northern Virginia, was born in Wayne county, N. C., May 29, 1826. His father carried him to Tennessee when he was two years old, and hence he is accounted a son of the "Volunteer State." He studied for awhile at Cumberland college, in the city of Nashville; in 1842 was appointed to the United States military academy from the Memphis district, and upon graduation in 1846 went at once to the army at Monterey, joining the Fourth United States infantry as brevet second lieutenant. He was appointed aide to Maj.-Gen. John A. Quitman, acting as adjutant at Vera Cruz and Cerro Gordo. For gallant conduct at Chapultepec, Garite de Belen and City of Mexico, young Wilcox was brevetted first lieutenant, and was commissioned as such August 24, 1851. In the autumn of 1852 he was ordered to West Point as assistant instructor of military tactics, and he remained in this position until the summer of 1857, when, on account of failing health, he was sent to Europe on a twelve months' furlough. On his return he published a work on rifles and rifle firing. The war department ordered a thousand copies of this work for distribution to the army, and it was made a text-book at West Point. Wilcox also translated and published a work on infantry evolution as practiced in the Austrian army. He was ordered to New Mexico in 1860, and on December 20th was promoted captain. At this distant post in June, 1861, he learned of the secession of Tennessee. Sending in his resignation, he repaired to Richmond, where he was commissioned colonel of the Ninth Alabama regiment, July 9, 1861. On the 21st of October of the same year he was commissioned brigadier-general and placed in command of the Third Alabama, First Mississippi and First Virginia regiments and a battery. At Williamsburg this brigade bore a prominent part. At Seven Pines, Wilcox commanded two brigades, and at Gaines' Mill three—his own, Featherston's and Pryor's. Some of the hardest and most brilliant fighting of this day was done by this command. At Frayser's Farm other laurels were won. In this fight nearly every regimental officer in Wilcox's command was killed, and Wilcox himself had his clothing pierced by six bullets. The loss in Wilcox's brigade was heavier in the Seven Days' battle than that of any other brigade in Longstreet's division. Wilcox did not happen to have such a difficult part to perform in the other battles of 1862, but at Chancellorsville, in 1863, his opportunities were again great, and he measured fully up to the occasion, adding much to his already splendid reputation. On the field of Gettysburg, the magnificent fighting of Wilcox's men gave new glory to the brigade and its dashing commander. On the 9th of August, 1863, Wilcox was commissioned major-general and assigned to the command of the division in Hill's corps that had been commanded by Pender at Gettysburg. It comprised Lane's North Carolina brigade, five regiments; Thomas' Georgia brigade, four regiments; McGowan's South Carolina brigade, five regiments; and Scales' North Carolina brigade, five regiments. In the campaigns from the

Wilderness to Appomattox, Wilcox's division constantly added to its already great reputation. Notwithstanding the many brilliant victories of the final campaigns in Virginia, superior numbers and resources won at last. In the last fighting around Petersburg two small forts, Battery Gregg and Battery Whitworth (or Alexander), were ordered to be held to the last extremity. Two hundred men, most of them from Harris' Mississippi brigade, at that time of Wilcox's command, were placed in Fort Gregg and the rest of Harris' brigade in Fort Alexander. These two points were all that barred the enemy out of Petersburg, for Longstreet's forces which were to occupy the interval between the right of the Petersburg line and the Appomattox river had not yet had time to arrive. It was the obstinate defense of these works that enabled Lee to hold his interior line until night. When the overwhelming masses of the Federals after many repulses at last carried the two forts, only 30 of the brave defenders of Gregg were unhurt, and nearly 1,000 Federals had been killed or wounded. In the final charge at Appomattox, Wilcox had been ordered to support Gordon in the desperate attempt to force the way to Lynchburg. But the negotiations between Lee and Grant stopped the fighting before his troops became engaged. After the close of the war General Wilcox was offered a command in the Egyptian army, but declined. In 1886 he was appointed chief of railroad division in a government department at Washington, D. C.

Brigadier-General Marcus Joseph Wright was born at Purdy, McNairy county, Tenn., June 5, 1831. His grandfather, John Wright, was a native of Savannah, Ga., and was a captain of the Georgia line in the revolutionary war. His father, Benjamin, was also a native of Savannah, and was an officer of the Thirty-ninth infantry, U. S. A., serving under Gen. Andrew Jackson in the Creek war, and subsequently in the war with Mexico. His brother, Judge John V. Wright, was colonel of the Thirteenth Tennessee infantry, was in the battle of Belmont, Mo., in which he commanded his regiment, and was afterward elected a member of the Confederate Congress, serving two terms. General Wright was educated in the academy at Purdy, receiving a classical education. He studied law and removed to Memphis, where he became clerk of the common law and chancery court of that city. He was lieutenant-colonel of the One Hundred and Fifty-fourth regiment of Tennessee militia, which was armed, uniformed, and otherwise equipped several years prior to the beginning of the civil war. He entered the Confederate service with his regiment early in April, 1861. On the 29th of April, taking a battalion of his regiment and the Steuben artillery, he fortified Randolph on the Mississippi river, above Memphis, which was named Fort Wright. In February, 1862, he was appointed military governor of Columbus, Ky., continuing in this position until its evacuation by the Confederate forces under Gen. Leonidas Polk. He commanded his regiment in the battles of Belmont and Shiloh, being wounded in the last-named battle. As assistant adjutant-general, with the rank of lieutenant-colonel on the staff of Major-General Cheatham, he participated in the Kentucky campaign, and the battles of Munfordville and Perryville. He was promoted to brigadier-general, December 13, 1862, and in January was given command of Hanson's, formerly Breckinridge's Kentucky brigade, which he relinquished to take command of Donelson's Tennessee brigade, which he led at the battles of Chickamauga and Missionary Ridge. He was afterward assigned to the district and post of Atlanta, Ga., and remained in command of the same until its evacuation, when he was assigned to duty at Macon, Ga. His last military duties were performed as commander of the district of North Mississippi and West Tennessee, under Gen. Richard Taylor, by whom he was surrendered at

Grenada, Miss. General Wright was warmly commended for his services at Belmont and Shiloh. At Murfreesboro he commanded the Eighth, Sixteenth, Twenty-eighth, Thirty-eighth, Fifty-first and Fifty-second Tennessee regiments, Murray's battalion and Carnes' battery, a command which was distinguished in the fighting and suffered heavy losses. After the surrender he returned to his home at Memphis, and resumed the practice of law. Since 1878 he has been the agent of the United States war department for the collection of Confederate records for publication by the government, with his office at Washington, D. C. He has been twice married, and has five children living—Marcus J., Jr., of the United States weather bureau; Benjamin, of the United States navy; John Womack, and two daughters.

Brigadier-General Felix K. Zollicoffer, of Tennessee, fell in battle before the war had lasted a year; but at that time there had been no death which inspired more genuine regret. He was born in Maury county, Tenn., May 19, 1812, of Swiss descent. His grandfather was a captain in the war of American independence. His early education was limited, being only such as could be obtained in the common schools of that day, and with but little preparation for the battle of life he was thrown upon his own resources. While yet a boy he was employed in a printing-office, and soon became very proficient. In 1835 he became editor of the Columbia Observer. Afterward he edited the Nashville Banner, with great ability, conducting it in the interest of the Whig party, earning for himself considerable fame as a political leader. In 1841 he was appointed attorney-general of Tennessee, and in the same year was elected by the legislature as comptroller. In 1849 he was chosen a member of the State Senate. He was elected a member of Congress from the Nashville district in 1853. This position he held for three successive terms, and won much distinction as a debater on all the leading issues of the day. He was so skillful in his wielding of figures and statistics that he frequently vanquished more eloquent men by the strong array of facts which he presented. In this way he was regarded as a formidable opponent in debate. To be a Whig at that day was to be for the Union. This sentiment Zollicoffer held in common with his party; but the continual agitation of the slavery question finally drove him, as it did many other devoted Unionists of the South, into the ranks of the State rights men. He was devoted, however, to the Union, and was convinced that its preservation could be secured through the policy advocated by the political followers of Bell and Everett. Therefore he earnestly advocated the election of these two leaders in 1860 on the brief platform, "The Constitution, the Union and the enforcement of the laws," and canvassed the State of New York for that ticket, declaring that the election of Abraham Lincoln on the platform adopted by the Republican party would result in a sectional war. Having, as he thought, done what he could to avert such a calamity, when the issue was squarely made, he did not hesitate to espouse the cause of the South. He had some experience in military affairs, having been first a private soldier, and then a commissioned officer in the Seminole war. He assisted in the organization of the provisional army of Tennessee, and was appointed one of the major-generals of State forces, May 9, 1861. He received his commission as brigadier-general in the provisional army of the Confederate States, July 9, 1861, and was assigned to command in east Tennessee. He was beset by many difficulties, but acted with great justice and moderation. His efforts to overcome the hostility to the Confederate cause which existed in so large a part of his department met with considerable success. He issued conciliatory orders, and declared that no act or word would be tolerated on the part of officers or men, which was calculated to alarm or irritate the people of his district. Finding that Federal forces were gathering in Kentucky in such a position as to menace his department, he led a portion of his men to Barboursville, and without serious difficulty dispersed a Federal camp. Then marching in the direction of Somerset, he caused the retreat of General Schoepf in such disorder that it received the name of the "Wildcat stampede." In January, 1862, he and his force of about 4,000 men, near Mill Spring, Ky., came under command of Major-General Crittenden, who was his superior in rank. Here occurred, January 19th, the disastrous battle in which General Zollicoffer lost his life. The circumstances of his death were as follows: The day was apparently going well for the Confederates, and Zollicoffer was ascending a hill where the enemy had collected his strength. As he rode forward to supposed victory, he came upon a regiment of Kentuckians (Union) commanded by Colonel Fry, concealed in a piece of woods. He did not become aware of his dangerous position until it was too late. Although a rubber overcoat concealed his uniform, a man who recognized his features called out, "There's Zollicoffer! Kill him!" An aide to Zollicoffer instantly fired and killed the man who had recognized the general. Zollicoffer, hoping still to deceive the enemy, rode within a few feet of Fry and said, "You are not going to fight your friends, are you?" pointing to a Mississippi regiment some distance off. The reply was a pistol shot from the colonel and a volley from his men, and General Zollicoffer fell from his horse, dead, pierced through by many balls. General Zollicoffer at the time of his death was between forty-five and fifty years of age. He was a man of unblemished moral character, amiable and modest in deportment, but quick to resent an insult. He was untiring in application to his duties and, had he lived, would probably have won distinction as a division commander. Many public honors were paid to his memory in the South.